5
25

Crosses on the Ballot

Crosses on the Ballot

PATTERNS OF BRITISH VOTER ALIGNMENT SINCE 1885

Kenneth D. Wald

PRINCETON UNIVERSITY PRESS

Published by Princeton University Press, 41 William Street, Princeton,
New Jersey
In the United Kingdom: Princeton University Press, Guildford, Surrey

All Rights Reserved
Library of Congress Cataloging in Publication Data will be found on
the last printed page of this book

Publication of this book has been aided by a grant from the Paul
Mellon Fund of Princeton University Press

This book has been composed in Linotron Baskerville type
Clothbound editions of Princeton University Press books are printed on
acid-free paper, and binding materials are chosen for strength and
durability. Paperbacks, while satisfactory for personal collections, are
not usually suitable for library rebinding.

Printed in the United States of America by Princeton University Press,
Princeton, New Jersey

To my parents—who may finally understand
what I've been doing with my time.

Contents

Tables

Preface

This study began as yet another inquiry into the development of class politics in Great Britain. As the initial research unfolded, it became increasingly clear to me that the rise of class politics could not be understood without first paying attention to a development which made class politics possible—the decline of religion as a political factor. This discovery took me back yet another step, to attempt to understand how religion had become a major source of political division in Britain and to chart the various ways in which denominational conflict impinged on political attitudes and behavior. The title is meant to reflect my interest in the factors which promoted a political system built largely on religious conflicts, the subtitle to indicate a focus on how and why that system decayed.

In the course of research, I was struck by the confidence with which scholars had offered as facts what were really untested assertions about the structure of party coalitions in late Victorian-Edwardian Britain. Much of my time was spent simply trying to collect the kinds of information that might permit a test of these descriptions and hypotheses. The difficulty of finding suitable data brought to mind the complaint of Henry Thomas Buckle, the Victorian writer, that poor record-keeping forced students of past politics to "collect the facts, as well as conduct the generalization."[1]

---

[1] Henry Thomas Buckle, *History of Civilization in England*, cited in Lee Benson, *Toward the Scientific Study of History: Selected Essays* (Philadelphia: J. B. Lippincott, 1972), p. 99.

In presenting the results of my quarrying, I tried to keep in mind the chastening sentence in a Wolverhampton newspaper story about the address of a municipal councillor: "Towards the end of his speech, Councillor Steward ceased to be interesting and became statistical."[2] Mindful of what that implies, I have tried to strike a balance in the narrative between the demands of presenting statistical tabulation and readability.

In researching and writing the book, I have picked up more debts than I can repay or even remember. At Washington University, where it all began, I received sage advice and counsel from Robert Salisbury, John Sprague, and Richard W. Davis. Thanks to the timely intervention of Merle Kling, I also received money and some elegant instruction in motivation. Later on, Memphis State University provided me with additional research funding, computer time, and, in the person of Deborah Brackstone, an invaluable interlibrary loan service—all of which enabled me to complete the dissertation which became the foundation for this book.

The major expansion of the study was supported by the National Science Foundation under grant SES 7805765 and by a research grant from Memphis State University. Though I doubt that these institutions have corporate opinions, least of all about the matters discussed in these pages, I nevertheless must hasten to absolve them of any responsibility for the opinions, findings, conclusions, and recommendations expressed in the publication.

Two British institutions provided hospitality and sustenance. At the London School of Economics, Dr. Tom Nossiter was kind enough to supervise my initial work and comment frankly and repeatedly on the direction of the thesis. A few years later, Professor Richard Rose invited me to spend a year as a visiting fellow in the Centre for the Study of Public Policy at the University of Strathclyde.

[2] *Express and Star* (Wolverhampton), October 29, 1904, p. 4.

I am grateful to Professor Rose for that productive year and to Dr. William Miller for supplying data and encouragement.

For giving me access to restricted materials, I thank officials of the British Library of Political Science, British Museum, Gladstone Library, Bradford Central Library, and the research divisions of the Conservative, Liberal, and Labour parties. Such generosity was not restricted to institutions: Jeffrey Hill, George Jones, Anthony King, Stanley Pierson, and Hugh Stephens shared with me a variety of unpublished material. Some of the material contained herein first appeared in article form in *Political Studies* and the *British Journal of Political Science*; for allowing me to reprint that material, I want to thank the publishers, Oxford University Press and Cambridge University Press. I also appreciate the permission to ransack some material from other scholars who published under the aegis of Routledge and Kegan Paul Ltd. (Table 2.2); University of Toronto Press (Tables 2.2, 2.3); Macmillan, London and Basingstoke (Tables 2.3, 3.1); and St. Martin's Press, Inc. (Table 3.1).

The manuscript would have improved dramatically if I had taken more advice from Peter Clarke, Henry Pelling, Ivor Crewe, Donald Stokes, Hugh Stephens, and the countless thousands who had occasion to comment on the material in its various guises. Though scholarly etiquette requires that they be absolved of responsibility, especially for some of my wilder notions, I do think that guilt by association should still count for something.

On the personal front, I must thank my parents for their support and encouragement; I hope the dedication repays some of that. Robin Lea West assisted me as critic, (paid) research assistant, babysitter, keypuncher, typist, therapist, cheerleader, and wife—I'm immensely grateful for all that and even more thankful that psychologists seldom write books. My daughter Dara probably delayed the book by at least a year, but we both had fun in the interim. I hope the persons mentioned in this paragraph won't begrudge a salute to my cats, who spent many hours on top of the manuscript, guarding it from all manner of dangers.

Persons interested in German-American understanding will doubtless be relieved to learn that I have forgiven the German pilot who made life difficult for me by so thoughtlessly bombing certain sheds at the British Newspaper Library during World War II. I will not forgive so easily if it happens again.

In order, the quotations on page 3 are from Neal Blewett, *The Peers, the Parties and the People: The General Elections of 1910* (London: Macmillan, 1972), p. 346; David Watson Rannie, *The Origin of Party in England* (Edinburgh: David Douglas, 1882), p. 13; Patrick O'Donovan, "Catholicism and Class in England," *Twentieth Century* 173 (Spring 1965), 52; and letter to E. B. White, cited in *Selected Letters of James Thurber*, ed. Helen Thurber and Edward Weeks (Boston: Little, Brown, 1981), p. 7.

Crosses on the Ballot

Take my vote and let it be
Consecrated Lord to thee.
Guide my hand that I may trace
Crosses in the proper place.
—*A Sheffield prayer (1910)*

Nothing in history is more striking than the way in which
motives wholly or even partially religious invade the domain of
other motives, however powerful they may be, and overcome
them. —*David Watson Rannie (1882)*

Ideally religion is a lonely relationship between man and God—
alone with the alone. Or else it is man acting in society in
accord with what he conceives as his God's requirements.
—*Patrick O'Donovan (1965)*

Over here [in England] everybody turns Catholic when
anything is the matter. —*James Thurber (1937)*

CHAPTER 1

The Context of the Study

. . . what sort of divisions can be found in British society which provide the basis for partisan opposition?[1] —*Leslie Lipson*

This study of the pattern of voter alignments in Britain since the late nineteenth century is directed to a pair of topics which have long commanded the attention of political sociologists. First, it explores the relationship between social structure and voting patterns in a mass electorate. The goal is both to specify the various social formations which achieved political relevance after 1885 and to identify the mechanisms which translated social divisions into lines of partisan cleavage. Beyond a static portrayal of mass political behavior, the study has a second aim—to enhance understanding of the dynamic properties of the British party system. It attempts to explain why certain social divisions, once of considerable electoral significance, became less important over time until they were superseded altogether by new patterns of sociopolitical conflict. Despite its concentration upon a single political system, the study thus addresses problems which Lipset and Rokkan regard as "fundamental questions for comparative research."[2]

[1] Leslie Lipson, "The Two-Party System in British Politics," *American Political Science Review* 47 (June 1953), 351.

[2] Seymour M. Lipset and Stein Rokkan, "Cleavage Structures, Party Systems and Voter Alignments: An Introduction," in *Party Systems and Voter Alignments*, p. 6.

RATIONALE

Most of the material for the book has been drawn from an intensive study of electoral patterns between 1885 and 1910, dates which mark the first and last general elections held under the provisions of the Third Reform Act. Though not so neglected as it once was, this stretch of years remains something of a dark age in terms of electoral analysis.[3] The British party configuration of this period has not been subject to the same careful scrutiny as the party system of the middle nineteenth century, which has been studied profitably through analysis of the rich store of data contained in pollbooks, the published records of individual votes at general elections.[4] Nor has the party system between 1885 and 1910 received anything like the attention devoted to the era which followed it, a period for which the full resources of modern electoral analysis have been deployed.[5] The relative neglect of the late Victorian-Edwardian party system is unfortunate because it was during this period that British mass politics first assumed a recognizably "modern" format.

During the period of the Third Reform Act, elections acquired their decisive modern function as the major mechanism linking the actions of the rulers with the wishes of the ruled.[6] The fate of a Government, which had depended primarily on its ability to survive confidence votes in the House of Commons, came instead to depend upon the support it could command in the cities and counties at a general election. As the concept of the popular mandate

[3] Note the assessments in G.S.R. Kitson Clark, *An Expanding Society: Britain, 1830–1920* (London: Cambridge University Press, 1967), pp. 55–56, and Alan J. Lee, "Conservatism, Traditionalism and the British Working Class, 1880–1918," in *Ideology and the Labour Movement*, ed. David E. Martin and David Rubinstein (London: Croom Helm, 1979), p. 86.

[4] D. C. Moore, *The Politics of Deference* (Hassocks, Sussex: Harvester Press, 1976); T. J. Nossiter, *Influence, Opinion and Political Idioms in Reformed England* (Hassocks, Sussex: Harvester Press, 1975); J. R. Vincent, *Pollbooks: How Victorians Voted* (London: Cambridge University Press, 1967).

[5] William L. Miller, *Electoral Dynamics in Britain Since 1918*.

[6] John P. Mackintosh, *The British Cabinet*, 2nd ed. (London: Stevens and Sons, 1968), pp. 173–209.

gained legitimacy, elections were treated as referenda upon current issues, and the distribution of the vote was taken as a measure of public reaction to party policy. To a greater degree than ever before, the major issues of the day—Irish government, imperialism, free trade, the role of the Lords, the status of the Church—were debated with reference to electoral considerations. This development had its parallel outside Westminster as constituency life, formerly dominated by the peculiar features of the local community, responded more fully to national influences.[7] These influences were channeled through political parties which increasingly functioned as agents of mass electoral mobilization. For leaders and followers alike, in other words, the votes counted.

The institutional structure for counting votes, the electoral system, also appeared in modern guise during the period.[8] The scope and influence of electoral corruption and "influence" were lessened appreciably by the adoption of the secret ballot (1872) and the passage of corrupt practices legislation (1883). The old constituencies, based on a series of medieval communities which had long since ceased to correspond to social reality, were replaced by new election districts (1885) which more faithfully mirrored population distribution. The reforms embodied in the Franchise Act of 1884 led for the first time to a rough semblance of universal manhood suffrage. As recent research has emphasized, the combined effect of these changes still left a great many Britons outside the pale of the Constitution.[9] Nevertheless, whatever the considerable defects and

[7] On the situation before 1884, see H. J. Hanham, *Elections and Party Management.*

[8] David Butler, *The Electoral System in Britain Since 1918*; William B. Gwyn, *Democracy and the Cost of Politics in Britain*; H. J. Hanham, *The Reformed Electoral System in Great Britain, 1832–1914*; Cornelius O'Leary, *The Elimination of Corrupt Practices in British Elections, 1868–1911.*

[9] Neal Blewett, "The Franchise in the United Kingdom, 1885–1918," *Past and Present*, no. 32 (1965), 27–56; Hugh Clegg, Alan Fox, and A. F. Thompson, *A History of British Trade Unions*, pp. 269–271; H.C.G. Matthew, R. I. McKibbin, and J. A. Kay, "The Franchise Factor in the Rise of the Labour Party," pp. 723–750.

7

anomalies remaining in the electoral system, by 1885 "the word 'Reform' no longer naturally denoted 'Electoral Reform.' "[10] The electoral process, formerly an institution for reformers *to* attack, had now become an avenue *of* attack.

The period under discussion also witnessed the modernization of another important element in British politics, the party system. Political parties replaced factions built around notables as the accepted nuclei for organizing a Government within Parliament.[11] This development inevitably affected the individual Member of Parliament, downgrading him from an independent center of authority and criticism to a much diminished role as defender of the party leadership. Divisions within Parliament accordingly followed party lines to a much greater extent than before. In another respect, the partisan environment of Westminster took on a marked resemblance to the contemporary pattern. Then, as now, two parties divided the bulk of the popular vote, but they frequently had to rely for their parliamentary majority upon tacit alliances with assorted minor parties. It was during this period, moreover, that the three major parties of modern British political history—Liberal, Labour, and Conservative—first achieved representation in the same Parliament. As questions of distributive justice began to force their way onto the political agenda, the partisans staked out positions that sound familiar to the observer of British politics in the post-1945 setting.

For all these reasons, then, the period of British politics bounded by 1885 and 1910 merits sustained study. It presents an opportunity to examine problems of major interest to students of voting behavior and to do so in a broader historical context than is customary. The study is further warranted by the inability of scholars to achieve anything approaching consensus on the salient features of political life during the period. Indeed, as scholarly interest in the

[10] Butler, *Electoral System*, p. 1.
[11] D.E.D. Beales, *The Political Parties of Nineteenth Century Britain* (London: Historical Association, 1971).

period has deepened, disagreement has intensified to a point where virtually every claim or generalization generates a counter-argument. This description is particularly apt for the two main topics addressed in the study, the contours of electoral cleavage and the source of long-term change in party fortunes.[12]

Contemporary observers seem to have treated political parties not as collections of voters sharing a considered attachment to basic political values nor as floating masses of individuals responding like Pavlovian dogs to the bribes offered by party leaders. Much like modern political scientists, they recognized that party coalitions were often based on shared social characteristics and fortified by the dead hand of tradition. As one MP wrote,

> To many persons party symbols and party associations have taken the place of all party meaning [so] that to vote "blue" or to vote "yellow" has become the traditional practice in many families. . . . The answer of not a few to all solicitations is "my father always voted 'blue' (or 'yellow') and so did my grandfather, and so shall I."[13]

What groups were significant in binding voters to their parties? According to the conventional wisdom expressed in many modern accounts of the period, religious or denominational differences provided the basic line of political demarcation. The electoral arena is portrayed in these accounts as a context in which the protagonists fought out battles which had their origin in Reformation-era conflicts. The kinds of issues which provoked partisan conflict, it is argued, have a quaint tone when compared to the characteristically modern rhetoric of class conflict.

Other scholars reject this religious interpretation, however, and describe party competition under the Third Reform Act as a relatively straightforward clash of economic

[12] Full references for these arguments are presented in Chapters 2–3.
[13] Cited in *Bradford Constitutional Yearbook* (Bradford: H. H. Tetley, 1904), p. 79.

interests. The proponents of this alternative perspective regard the pre-1918 party system as a somewhat more primitive version of the class-stratified configuration that has characterized post-1945 Britain. Perhaps, to consider yet another logical possibility, these contrasting views can be reconciled. If class and religion overlapped to a considerable degree, it would make sense to treat them not as competitive sources of cleavage but as mutually reinforcing influences on voter behavior.[14] We must also entertain the possibility that a variable which has not thus far figured prominently in British historical election analysis—such as region—exercised a considerable impact on voter alignments. The merits of these competing claims can be assessed in part through a systematic analysis of voting patterns—a major task of this study.

If the nature of electoral stability under the Third Reform Act has proved so difficult to gauge, the problem of change has generated even more disagreement. The rise of the Labour Party at the expense of the Liberals, a trend first suggested during the period, has been described by one reviewer as a subject likely to replace the rise of the gentry as the foremost problem in modern British political development. This transformation of the party system has been attributed to all manner of forces: changes in the basis of electoral cleavage, bad tactics by Liberal strategists, the increasing structural differentiation of industry, reapportionment of constituencies, the growth of secularism, the extension of the franchise in 1918, wartime disagreements among the Liberal leadership, etc. These factors are not all equally amenable to verification with the methods favored here; but because many of them are based upon unproven claims about voting behavior, the systematic anal-

[14] Derek Urwin, "Towards the Nationalisation of British Politics? Party Politics, 1885–1940" (Paper presented to the conference on "Wahlerbewegung in der europäischen Geschichte," Historische Kommission zu Berlin, May 1978).

ysis of electoral data from the pre-1918 period may contribute significantly to clarifying the debate.

These empirical disputes among students of British political development tie into some broader theoretical issues that concern specialists in political sociology, voting behavior and political parties. By paying due regard to these issues, an intensive study of Britain may contribute to theoretical development in the field of political behavior. For example, the social analysis of voting has spawned many useful insights about the process by which social divisions impinge upon voting and considerable speculation about hierarchies of cleavage. The British data offer an opportunity to refine and test some of these insights for a period for which survey data are unavailable. The general phenomenon of change in party systems can also be advanced by examining trends in British voting. The electoral history of many nations seems to be marked by an alternating series of stable party configurations followed by an abrupt period of electoral discontinuity in which stable allegiances are disrupted and new party coalitions emerge. The periods of electoral stability, which have been described variously as "party systems" and "sociopolitical periods," tend to exhibit a characteristic political agenda, a high degree of persistence in mass voter alignments and a relatively fixed distribution of the vote.[15] In explaining why such stable systems seem to give way to rapid decomposition and reformulation, researchers have speculated about the role of factors such as new political issues, demographic changes, alterations in the legal-institutional structure of elections, and generational displacement in dissolving a seemingly stable pattern of political conflict. The process of electoral change in Britain can thus be regarded as another potential inci-

[15] Walter Dean Burnham, "Party Systems and the Political Process," in *The American Party Systems*, ed. William Chambers and Walter Dean Burnham, 2nd ed. (New York: Oxford University Press, 1975), pp. 277–307; Everett C. Ladd, *American Political Parties* (New York: W. W. Norton, 1970).

11

dence of a recurring phenomenon and be treated as a "case" in the study of the transformation of party systems.

APPROACH

One problem with the existing literature, as we have just seen, is that scholars have given radically different answers to a number of basic questions. Such disagreement alone warrants further study of the period. Equally important, existing studies have failed to capitalize fully upon modern techniques of electoral analysis. To remedy that omission requires a new kind of study with methods suitable to the analysis of mass politics.

Without doing too much violence to their unique qualities, previous voter studies of the period can be placed into four categories: single election studies, works of electoral geography, intensive local profiles, and, a more recent development, historical survey research. Four of the eight general elections fought during the period have been the subject of monographs similar to the Nuffield College series on post-World War II British elections.[16] These single election studies characteristically examine the record of the Government that called the election, its fortune in by-elections, the kinds of issues raised during the campaign, the tactics of interest groups and candidates, and the general pattern of the returns. In the typical works of electoral geography which were popular early in the twentieth century, the authors mapped the results of elections and commented upon the spatial distribution of party support and the relationship between party vote and parliamentary rep-

[16] D. C. Savage, "General Election of 1886 in Great Britain and Ireland" (Ph.D. thesis, University of London, 1958); Mary E. Y. Enstam, "The 'Khaki' Election of 1900 in the United Kingdom" (Ph.D. thesis, Duke University, 1968); A. K. Russell, *Liberal Landslide* (Newton Abbot: David and Charles, 1973); M. Charlita Brady, "The British General Elections of 1910" (Ph.D. thesis, Fordham University, 1947); Neal Blewett, *The Peers, the Parties and the People*.

resentation.[17] Recent work in the genre has utilized more sophisticated techniques to explore the relationship between constituency voting patterns and aspects of social structure.[18] It is difficult to characterize works in the third division of historical voting research, intensive local profiles of particular areas or constituencies.[19] The questions which motivate such studies are often quite specific to the locale under investigation, which might range from a single constituency or city to a large region. With some notable exceptions, the authors of these studies use the traditional techniques of narrative history. In recent years, scholars have attempted to harness the techniques of public opinion research to historical inquiry.[20] By probing the memories of the elderly during in-depth interviews, scholars have helped to elucidate features of the period which were evident only to persons who witnessed events for themselves.

Each of these approaches has made a distinctive contribution to furthering our understanding of political life between 1885 and 1910; the present study, which is built upon its predecessors, will incorporate such techniques where appropriate. But this survey attempts to overcome the limitations of scope and method which characterize the existing body of research. First, the investigation is compre-

[17] J. E. Baines, "Parliamentary Representation in England Illustrated by the Elections of 1892 and 1895," *Journal of the Royal Statistical Society* 59 (March 1896), 38–118; Edward B. Krehbiel, "Geographic Influences in British Elections," pp. 419–432; E. N. Mozley, "The Political Heptarchy," *Contemporary Review* 97 (April 1910), 400–412; S. Rosenbaum, "The General Election of January, 1910, and the Bearing of the Results on Some Problems of Representation," *Journal of the Royal Statistical Society* 73 (May 1910), 473–511.

[18] Michael Kinnear, *The British Voter*; Henry Pelling, *Social Geography of British Elections, 1885–1910*.

[19] Some examples include P. F. Clarke, *Lancashire and the New Liberalism* (London: Cambridge University Press, 1971); Christopher Green, "Birmingham's Politics, 1873–1891," *Midland History* 2 (Autumn 1973), 84–98; Janet Howarth, "The Liberal Revival in Northamptonshire, 1880–1895," *Historical Journal* 12 (March 1969), 78–118.

[20] David Butler and Donald Stokes, *Political Change in Britain*; Paul Thompson, *The Edwardians* (Bloomington: Indiana University Press, 1975).

hensive in its coverage of the period. Unlike the single election studies, and most local surveys and geographical analyses, it deals with voting behavior over the entire twenty-five years of the period and, on occasion, extends the analysis to cover developments well beyond 1910. This scope is essential if the study is to pay proper regard both to the durability of party alignments and the forces working for change. The scope is further broadened by the attempt to examine developments throughout all of Great Britain. Rather than allow local peculiarities to dominate the inquiry, an attempt is made to discover patterns with more general applications. Second, the study takes advantage of modern advances in the ecological analysis of voting behavior.[21] These new methods certainly do not rule out impression and insight nor do they provide a set of facts which mysteriously "speak for themselves." But modern quantitative analysis provides more explicit standards of inference than conventional historiography and permits systematic comparisons of the power of various explanations. A study with these features should advance our knowledge of the period and provide conclusions which are themselves available for additional testing and further development.

The centerpiece of this work is a quantitative analysis of the relations between various social forces and the patterns of party support in general elections from 1885 to 1910. The units of analysis consist of sets of parliamentary constituencies that were combined until their boundaries corresponded closely to the units for which census data were enumerated. From the census material and miscellaneous sources, we have extracted tangible measures of the social forces which have been cited as important factors in structuring the aggregate vote. By using a variety of statistical

[21] For the most advanced techniques, see Lawrence Boyd and Gudmund Iversen, *Contextual Analysis* (Belmont, Cal.: Wadsworth, 1979); several examples can be found in Mattei Dogan and Stein Rokkan, eds., *Social Ecology*.

techniques, primarily regression analysis, we can measure with some precision the predictive power of the social variables and the extent and manner of their relationship to the political variables.

These particulars do not apply to all phases of the analysis. In some instances, the political variables were derived from the results of local government elections, and some of the social variables under investigation had to be collected from data sources which went far beyond the bounds of 1885 and 1910. A more important limit was my recognition that "electoral data are only the outward and visible sign of an invisible political situation which has to be intuitively apprehended in the light of many variables, not all of which are numerical ones."[22] Therefore, to make sense of the statistical patterns which emerged from the quantitative analysis, we will take advantage of the techniques associated with conventional historiography. Thus, the findings of intensive studies in selected locales are cited if they illuminate a problem. Similarly, illustrations and examples are brought forward in support of arguments that cannot always be verified in a manner that satisfies the strict standards of empirical social research. In an area so open to investigation, an area in which the proper questions have not yet been identified nor the necessary concepts specified with any degree of precision, the combination of traditional historical method with the techniques of modern social science seems the most promising avenue for advancing knowledge.

Despite its attempt at inclusiveness, there is a great expanse of ground on which this research does not tread, or treads with an exceedingly light foot. Consider the very interesting questions that have been raised by scholars who regarded political parties primarily as organizations. The well-known works by Ostrogorski, Lowell, and McKenzie, for example, detail the distribution of power within parties,

[22] John Vincent and M. Stenton, eds., *McCalmont's Parliamentary Poll Book*, p. x.

the mechanisms for adjudicating disputes within the organization, the evolution of party structure, and relations between the top leadership and the troops situated in local outposts.[23] The agenda for many modern inquiries was set by the kinds of problems pursued in these classic works. Similarly, by treating political parties as governing coalitions, scholars have provided rich insights into the Byzantine intrigues which occur within governments, the development of new leadership groups, great struggles over party policy on contentious national issues, and other aspects of political life which so fascinate students of "high politics."[24]

This study, though it certainly cannot overlook these problems, concentrates more fully upon the "third face" of political parties—their function as mass coalitions in the electorate. Rather than emphasize the behavior of elites—activists, Cabinet ministers, officials, and the like—the study is concerned with the soft-spoken majority for whom politics meant only occasional outings to the polling station. Of course, the actions of the elites strongly conditioned the alternatives to which the masses responded, and the actions of the voters cannot be studied without some reference to the more exalted arena in Westminster. Still, such topics as campaign machinery, internal party schisms, and the passage of legislation will be discussed only insofar as they relate to mass political behavior.

CONTENTS

The two chapters which follow set the tone for the inquiry by reviewing research on voter alignments under the

[23] A. Lawrence Lowell, *The Government of England*, 2 vols. (London: Macmillan, 1920); Robert McKenzie, *British Political Parties*, 2nd ed. (London: Mercury Books, 1961); M. Ostrogorski, *Democracy and the Organization of Political Parties*, ed. Seymour Martin Lipset, 2 vols. (Garden City, New York: Doubleday-Anchor, 1964).

[24] A. B. Cooke and J. R. Vincent, *The Governing Passion* (Brighton: Harvester Press, 1974); Peter Stansky, *Ambitions and Strategies* (London: Oxford University Press, 1964).

Third Reform Act. These chapters examine the background and assumptions of the class and religious interpretations of the party system and evaluate the empirical evidence offered in support of each approach. The verdict for both interpretations is mixed. There is a good bit of impressionistic evidence about the importance of class and religious factors in British voting but not enough hard data to permit a thorough assessment of the explanatory power of these social forces.

The difficulties encountered in evaluating the structure of the vote under the Third Reform Act stem primarily from the limited availability of social and political data. Chapter 4 is thus devoted to the factors which have hampered systematic ecological analysis of elections in the period. Because of recent advances in the study of voting behavior, these factors need no longer prevent the kind of electoral analysis which might resolve debates about the influence of various social forces on the vote. The chapter presents details about research strategy and concludes with an example of the procedures used in the remainder of the study.

Using the new techniques, Chapters 5 and 6 examine the effects of class and religion on voting in the general elections between 1885 and 1910. Chapter 5 is concerned principally with the mechanisms by which class and religion came to exert so much power upon the behavior of voters. The statistical testing discussed in Chapter 6 demonstrates that the power of the social forces varies dramatically with the manner in which class and religion are operationalized. The indicators are associated with different conceptions of the variables which posit distinctive modes of influence on the vote. These chapters also consider variations in alignment over time and across space within Britain.

On balance, the findings of the electoral analysis suggest the primacy of religious influences before World War I. Though social class was usually associated with the voting pattern, the class cleavage seems to have been politically relevant for only a small core of the electorate. This finding raises major questions which are addressed in subsequent chapters. Chapter 7 attempts to penetrate the denominational basis of the party systems by examining the role of religion in forming the social consciousness of the electorate in the late Victorian-Edwardian period. Chapter 8 goes a step further as it attempts to understand the decline of this traditional party system in the years after 1910. How and why did a party system underpinned by religious differences give birth to a new system in which social class became the chief characteristic defining the party coalitions? The key to resolving this question, it is argued, is the recognition that significant changes in social practice, particularly in institutions which play a major role in the socialization process, may substantially alter social consciousness and reverberate in the political system.

The concluding chapter recapitulates the findings and draws out the implications of the study for subsequent research on party systems in other polities.

CHAPTER 2

Class Politics without Class Parties?

... it is not probable that the distinction between the political parties and the social classes can be maintained in contemporary society. The classes are gradually becoming transformed into parties.[1] —*Emile Boutmy (1904)*

Pulzer's dictum—"Class is the basis of British party politics; all else is embellishment and detail"—expresses a consensus about the social basis of partisan conflict in post-1945 Britain.[2] Without exception, the pioneering postwar studies of British voting behavior found social class to be the principal line of political demarcation. Though it can easily be overdrawn, this portrait reflects a great deal of truth.[3] Recent studies conducted with sophisticated ecological techniques have confirmed that the class composition of constituencies has been the single most powerful influence on the voters' party choice since World War II.[4] Measured at the individual level through opinion surveys, class determines the standing partisan allegiance of a high proportion of British respondents, a proportion much higher

[1] Emile Boutmy, *The English People*, trans. E. English (London: T. Fisher Unwin, 1904), pp. 231–232.

[2] Peter G. J. Pulzer, *Political Representation and Elections in Britain*, 3rd ed. (London: Allen and Unwin, 1975), p. 102.

[3] For some important qualifications, see Richard Rose, "Britain: Simple Abstractions and Complex Realities," in *Electoral Behavior: A Comparative Handbook*, ed. Richard Rose (New York: Free Press, 1974), pp. 481–542.

[4] William Miller, "Social Class and Party Choice in England: A New Analysis," pp. 257–284, and also his "Class, Region and Strata at the British General Election of 1979," *Parliamentary Affairs* 32 (Autumn 1979), 376–382; Jorgen Rasmussen, "The Impact of Constituency Structural Characteristics Upon Political Preferences in Britain," pp. 123–145.

than has been reported in most other nations for which survey data are available.[5] Despite the recent intensification of cleavages based on nonclass factors such as ethnicity and peripheral nationalism, social class has continued to exercise a considerable impact on British voting patterns.

How long has class been the ascendant variable in the British party system? Some scholars have argued that class first achieved a decisive role in the political system between 1885 and 1910. This chapter describes in some detail the class interpretation of British politics under the Third Reform Act and evaluates the evidence which has been adduced on its behalf. The evidence is sufficiently strong to warrant further study but not strong enough to justify drawing firm conclusions about the impact of class on voter alignments. Because of limitations in the major studies and disagreement in the findings, the case for the class interpretation must be regarded as yet unproven.

AN OUTLINE OF THE CLASS INTERPRETATION

From the accounts left to us by politicians, journalists, scholars, and political activists, it is clear that many contemporary observers perceived politics in late Victorian-Edwardian Britain as an exercise in class conflict. Like most political sociologists today, they treated elections largely as the democratic expression of the class struggle. Sir William Harcourt gave expression to that point of view when he wrote Lord Rosebery in 1894,

You desire to avert "the cleavage of classes." The hope on your part is natural but you are too late. The horizontal division of parties was certain to come as a consequence of household suf-

[5] Butler and Stokes, *Political Change in Britain*, 2nd ed. Mark Franklin and Anthony Mughan, "The Decline of Class Voting in Britain: Problems of Analysis and Interpretation," *American Political Science Review* 72 (June 1978), 523–534.

frage. The thin edge of the wedge was inserted and the cleavage is expanding day by day.[6]

Gladstone had recognized the same division in 1886 when he described the Irish Home Rule crisis in Britain as another case in which "the masses" sided with the Liberals against "the classes" and their Conservative spokesmen. The more conservative members of both parties were prone to deplore the introduction of "class interests" to the political agenda, attributing it to the continual expansion of the franchise and blaming it for lowering the moral tone in public affairs.[7] For the Conservatives, who had never wholeheartedly accepted Disraeli's "Tory Democracy," the development of universal manhood suffrage was perceived (wrongly, it turns out) as a threat to their very survival as a major political force.

At the heart of this interpretation was a widespread belief that a solid majority of working-class voters was invariably sympathetic to the Liberal party or its "Independent Labour" allies. The Conservative editor, J. St. Loe Strachey, referred in 1895 to the "almost universal 'general impression' that Gladstonianism is the natural creed of the working man" and admitted that

. . . the ordinary Unionist of means like the ordinary Gladstonian of means is inclined to believe that at present the working man is naturally a Gladstonian. The thing has been said again and again by his opponents, and he has no means of disproving it by personal enquiry. He is inclined to think that the working man must do what is so largely expected of him and become a Gladstonian.[8]

[6] Quoted in R.C.K. Ensor, *England, 1870–1914*, p. 33.

[7] "The lower class of voters care nothing and know less about political questions and their action in the polling booth is influenced only by what they think they can or cannot *get*." Letter from E. H. Villiers to C. P. Villiers, October 18, 1890, E. H. Villiers Correspondence, British Library of Political Science, London School of Economics.

[8] J. St. Loe Strachey, "Infringing a Political Patent," *The Nineteenth Century* 37 (February 1895), 208.

This impression seemed to be confirmed by the Liberal preponderance in industrial and urban seats. According to Edward Krehbiel, an American student of British electoral geography, "it is true as a fundamental principle that the laboring classes are radical in tendency and vote with the Liberal or Labor parties."[9] Though writing from an altogether different perspective, Friedrich Engels agreed that the English working class had been ever since its enfranchisement "the tail of the 'Great Liberal Party.' "[10] When Charles Trevelyan contended in 1922 that "the World War has brought a wholesale transference of the working-class vote from Liberalism to Labour," he gave further currency to the assumption that the prewar working class had been attached solidly to the Liberal party.[11]

If we are to believe contemporary accounts, this Liberal-oriented working class was confronted in the electoral arena by a Conservative-minded middle class. Indeed, the Conservative orientation of the British middle class seemed too obvious to require much comment. Sidney Webb referred offhand to the Conservatives as "essentially the party of wealth and privilege" and loyal Tories did not dissent from this characterization, describing theirs as "the party of stucco respectability."[12] As early as 1874, in commenting on the

[9] Krehbiel, "Geographic Influences," p. 430.

[10] Friedrich Engels, *The British Labour Movement* (London: Martin Lawrence, 1934), p. 33. For a similar opinion by another British Marxist, see the comments of E. Belfort Bax in *Liberalism and Labour* (London: Twentieth Century Press, n.d.), p. 18.

[11] Charles Trevelyan, *From Liberalism to Labour* (London: George Allen and Unwin, 1921), p. 22. Many postwar commentaries also gave the impression of a wholesale switch in party allegiance by the working class. See M. Beer, *A History of British Socialism*, vol. II (London: George Allen and Unwin, 1953); Hamilton Fyfe, *The British Liberal Party* (London: George Allen and Unwin, 1928), p. 133; Walter Inman, "The British Liberal Party, 1892–1939," p. 368; T. L. Jarman, *Socialism in Britain* (London: Victor Gollancz, 1972), p. 66; A. J. Anthony Morris, *Parliamentary Democracy in the Nineteenth Century* (Oxford: Pergamon Press, 1967), p. 26.

[12] Sidney Webb, *Socialism in England*, 2nd ed. (London: Swann Sonnenschein, 1893), p. 122; William J. Wilkinson, *Tory Democracy* (New York: Columbia University Press, 1925), p. 247.

next to last general election held under the Second Reform Act, the radical Frederic Harrison found in the voting patterns clear evidence "that the middle-classes have gone over to the enemy bag and baggage."[13] An American scholar, Edward Porritt, called attention in 1895 to the increasing significance of social stratification in British politics:

Middle class England is rapidly becoming Conservative; a glance at the election returns from the cities with large suburban populations shows that . . . the representatives of these middle-class communities still acting with the Liberals in the House of Commons are likely to become fewer as each General Election comes around, and as the democracy becomes more assertive and more demanding.[14]

The main elements of Conservative voting strength, Krehbiel affirmed, were "property owners" and "the man of means."[15]

Local observers spoke the same language, associating party fortunes with the social composition of the population. For example, the Wolverhampton Liberals expressed little optimism about their chances of holding the western division of the city because the constituency was "simply an extension of villadom."[16] A Conservative candidate for Wolverhampton West reinforced that impression when he campaigned in 1910 as "a businessman seeking to represent a business constituency."[17] The Wolverhampton Liberals found their most reliable electoral support in the industrial districts of the southern and eastern parliamentary divisions: "It is well known that Sedgeley and Coseley are radical to the backbone. At Sedgeley a timorous Whiggism and a

[13] Cited in Paul Adelman, *Gladstone, Disraeli and Later Victorian Politics* (London: Longman, 1970), p. 86.
[14] Edward Porritt, "The Break-up of the British Party System," *Annals of the American Academy of Political and Social Science* 5 (January 1895), 504.
[15] Krehbiel, "Geographic Influences," p. 431.
[16] Edith H. Fowler, *The Life of Henry Hartley Fowler, First Viscount Wolverhampton* (London: Hutchinson, 1912), pp. 186–187.
[17] Election address of Albert Bird, Gladstone Library, National Liberal Club (election addresses for January 1910, Vol. 2).

selfish Toryism are regarded with equal detestation . . . by the workingmen who compose almost entirely the electorate."[18] Even in Brighton, hardly a bastion of left-wing politics, the acknowledged backbone of Liberalism was "the Radical workingman."[19] The Brighton Conservatives attempted to combat these tendencies by sponsoring the speaking tour of a Conservative workingman brought down from London. When his meetings were disrupted by unruly crowds, the Conservative newspaper was moved to denounce the "freedom-loving, tolerant, Liberal British workingman who would not listen to his brother because he happened to be a Tory," thereby underscoring the traditional association between working-class voters and Liberal partisanship.[20]

These assumptions about voter loyalties have been echoed in much of the modern literature on British politics before World War I.[21] Peter Pulzer's standard account of British elections discussed the pre-1918 party system in explicit class terms: "Especially since the Second Reform Act [in] 1867, the further one went down the social scale, the more likely one was to find support for the party of the left (Liberal until 1914, Labour thereafter)."[22] More recent texts on British elections have more or less repeated this conclusion. Historians have been especially active in advancing the class interpretation of party alignments under the Third Reform Act. After studying the social geography of London constituencies from 1885 to 1910, Henry Pelling identified class as the major electoral factor in the metropolis, and he later characterized the Liberals under Gladstone as

[18] *Evening Express* (Wolverhampton), March 5, 1885, p. 2. See also the *Wolverhampton Chronicle*, November 24, 1897, p. 2.

[19] *Sussex Evening Times*, November 2, 1894, p. 2.

[20] *Brighton Gazette*, March 25, 1905, p. 5.

[21] See the summaries in two recent books about electoral politics in Britain: Geoffrey Alderman, *British Elections* (London: B. T. Batsford, 1978), pp. 148–152; Iain McLean, *Elections* (London: Longman, 1976), pp. 48–51.

[22] Pulzer, *Political Representation*, p. 102.

a working-class party in all but name, "as much of a workingman's party as the Labour party is today."[23] Studies of London using more refined measures of constituency social composition have supported Pelling's conclusion about the primacy of the class alignment. The case for class politics has been argued most forcefully by P. F. Clarke in his research on Edwardian Lancashire.[24] Clarke has sought to demonstrate that class had replaced religion as the ambit of party conflict in Lancashire well before 1918 and the onset of Liberal decline. The success of the Liberals in areas of high enfranchisement is cited as proof of the party's successful adjustment to class-stratified electoral politics.

Having sketched the class interpretation rather more boldly than is customary, it is important to acknowledge some of the qualifications that appear in the literature. All advocates of the interpretation admit that the progress of the class alignment was not uniform across the country. In some areas, conflicts over religion divided the working class internally and postponed the evolution of class-based electoral conflict.[25] Furthermore, most of these authors admit the existence of areas of strong working-class Conservatism. Some attribute the unexpected success of Conservatism in various large cities to the nefarious working of the electoral system, which effectively disfranchised many potential working-class voters, and to other unsavory practices involving force, fraud, and intimidation.[26] These deviations from the class alignment are more commonly attributed to peculiar local factors. Pelling observed that working-class support for Conservatism in London's East End grew out

---

[23] Henry Pelling, *Social Geography of British Elections, 1885–1910*, p. 57, and also his *Popular Politics and Society in Late Victorian Britain*, p. 17.

[24] Clarke, *Lancashire*, and also his "Electoral Sociology of Modern Britain," pp. 31–55.

[25] Lancashire is the prime example of this phenomenon. See David A. Roberts, "Religion and Politics in Liverpool Since 1900" (M.Sc. thesis, University of London, 1965).

[26] H. F. Moorhouse, "The Political Incorporation of the British Working Class: An Interpretation," *Sociology* 7 (September 1973), 341–360.

of resentment toward Jewish immigrants who competed with natives for the scarce employment available in the area.[27] Working-class Tories in Lancashire used the vote to express hostility to their Liberal employers while their counterparts in the Midlands acted against their "normal" tendencies for the opposite reason—to express solidarity with their civic-minded, Conservative business elite.[28] Pelling found that working-class Conservatives generally belonged to occupational groups that benefited from specific policies associated with Conservative governments.[29]

While all the authors thus acknowledge the phenomenon of cross-class voting and try to account for it, they clearly regard such areas as anomalous and assert, as a general rule, that the norm was a positive relationship between wealth and the propensity to vote Conservative. Despite the occasional exception, they would agree with P. F. Clarke that "class politics, in much their modern form, appeared in England before the First World War."[30]

We must also note the considerable confusion about the identity of the relevant class groupings. Even by the middle of the nineteenth century, the use of class terminology was far from uniform. To some observers, the "working class" comprised a diverse group of laborers: "wage earners," "the industrial classes," "hand workers," "democratic and oppressed interests," and "persons who might have reason to challenge the existing social order." Other references are more specific, equating the working class with the trade union movement or the "politically conscious" section of the manual laborers. When we try to define the middle class, we find a similar level of ambiguity. The synonyms include "the merchant class," "commerce," "business and the moneyed," "professional and commercial elements,"

[27] Pelling, *Social Geography*, pp. 42–46.
[28] James Cornford, "The Transformation of Conservatism in the Late Nineteenth Century," pp. 61–64.
[29] Pelling, *Social Geography*, pp. 425–426.
[30] Clarke, "Electoral Sociology," p. 51.

26

"the propertied," "wealth, position and the privileged order," and "the urban bourgeoisie."

We can discern at least three different conceptions of
"class" in this confusing welter of terms. The Weberian
emphasis on *socioeconomic status* is apparent in studies which
assign class position on the basis of levels of material comfort or deprivation. The distinction between manual and
nonmanual work seems concerned primarily with aspects
of *occupational prestige*. In the studies which equate the working class with industrial producers, we find the familiar
Marxist conception of class position as a function of the
occupational structure. The bulk of the studies seem to lean
toward the Weberian approach, but the distinction is not
always recognized when it comes time to construct indicators of constituency class composition. We shall have more
to say in Chapter 5 about measurement techniques in the
analysis of class-based voting.

THE RISE OF THE CLASS ALIGNMENT

To explain the development of class politics in Britain,
scholars have usually echoed Harcourt's judgment about
the franchise. Accepting the premise usually associated with
the opponents of electoral reform—that the adoption of a
democratic franchise must inevitably lead to political conflict over economic issues—scholars argue that groups
brought into the electorate used their new power to advance their perceived economic interests. The parties staked
out positions on these demands which tended, in the main,
to range them on different sides of the question. The association hardened over time as the parties became identified with the interests of the various social groups. The
resulting class-based party system has dominated British
political life ever since.

Of course, there are variations on this basic theme. Some
observers treat the process of electoral differentiation by
social class as an inevitable development in an advanced

industrial society. As concrete manifestations of class interests, political parties must react to changes in social structure and the level of enfranchisement.[31] But others are more careful to portray the development as contingent upon peculiar features of the British environment. Whatever the emphasis, most scholars regard the development of class lines as a concomitant of the extension of the franchise and the incorporation of new classes in the political system.

The process of social differentiation by parties began almost immediately with the Great Reform Act of 1832. In the party system of early Victorian Britain, the Tories represented the Land, the traditional source of influence in British government, against the ambitions of the emerging industrial capitalists whose claims were championed by the Whigs and their successors, the Liberals. Because this cleavage overlapped to a considerable extent the divisions between city and country and the religious conflict between adherents of the established Church and Dissenters, it would be correct to treat class (or perhaps "situs") as only one element in the formation of party alignments. Subsequent extensions of the franchise in 1867 and 1884 gradually led to the consolidation of both Land and Capital in the Conservative party and the emergence of the Liberals as the champions of the working class. John Stuart Mill professed to see this happening as early as the 1830s, but most accounts tie the clarification of class alignments to Gladstone's increasing radicalism over the Irish issue.[32]

According to Ensor, the Irish Land Acts passed in Gladstone's second Government (1880–1885) seemed to the propertied interest nothing more than an abject surrender by a weak government to a band of ruffians.[33] Raising fears

[31] H.R.G. Greaves, *The British Constitution*, 4th ed. (London: George Allen and Unwin, 1958), p. 111.

[32] Mill is cited in a work first published in 1835: Alexis de Tocqueville, *Journeys to England and Ireland*, ed. J. P. Mayer (Garden City, New York: Doubleday-Anchor, 1967), p. 72.

[33] R.C.K. Ensor, "Some Political and Economic Inter-Actions in Late Victorian England," *Transactions of the Royal Historical Society* 31 (1949), 17–28.

about the Liberals' will to resist further attacks on property, these acts prompted a considerable number of the more Whiggish Liberals to change to a Tory allegiance. This steady trickle assumed the proportions of a flood when the Grand Old Man announced in 1886 his support for a limited measure of Home Rule in Ireland.[34]

The effect of this announcement on the Liberals' social base has usually been obscured because it prompted the departure of Joseph Chamberlain, the most prominent representative of Radicalism in the party. Hence, in some accounts, Chamberlain's departure over the Irish issue is said to have delayed the advent of class politics in Britain.[35] It is now recognized that Chamberlain's defection was personal and that he did not carry with him (outside the Midlands, at any rate) large numbers of Radical MPs or voters.[36] The Liberals did lose what remained of their peerage, the Whig remnant, and large sections of the urban middle class—an event that had long been prophesied. Those who left Gladstone because of Ireland used the Liberal Unionist movement as a halfway house on the road to Conservatism, but the issue merely provided an excuse to leave a party that seemed increasingly out of touch with moderate opinion.[37]

The actions of the Liberal leadership after 1886 seemed to justify fears among disillusioned Liberals that their former party was prepared to pay any price to appease "Demos." The Radical element, succeeding to positions of considerable authority after the schism, boasted that the defections of the Whigs enabled the Liberals to become a party "almost exclusively identified with the particular in-

[34] This argument can be found in virtually every study of the period. See Ensor, *England*, pp. 206–207, 377–378.

[35] L. T. Hobhouse, *Liberalism* (1911; reprint ed., New York: Oxford University Press, 1964), pp. 112–113.

[36] T. W. Heyck, "Home Rule, Radicalism and the Liberal Party," pp. 66–91.

[37] Gordon Goodman, "Liberal Unionism: The Revolt of the Whigs," pp. 173–189; Maurice Woods, *A History of the Tory Party* (London: Hodder and Stoughton, 1924), p. 438.

terests of the working class."[38] This reorientation was essential to a party shorn of its middle-class base. As Engels put it unkindly in describing the motivation of the Liberals, "it is a question of catching the Labour vote if they intend to continue as a party."[39] Thus, in 1886 began a discernible shift of the Liberal party away from its traditional policies toward a far more activist and class-oriented position.

The first concrete manifestation of this move to the left was the "Newcastle Programme," which formed the basis of the Liberal campaign in the general election of 1892. The adoption of the program, which consisted of sections of Chamberlain's "Unauthorized Programme" that had been deemed too radical for inclusion in the 1885 manifesto, was cited as the major factor in winning the Liberals another turn in office. Despite the Government's weakness from 1892 to 1895, it managed to alienate the propertied classes even more by passing a revolutionary set of inheritance taxes. The disastrous general election defeats in 1895 and 1900 were attributed to the party's reluctance to go far enough in meeting working-class grievances and to the temporary aberration of working-class imperialism. By denouncing Chinese "slavery" in the Boer Republics and opposing the imposition of taxes on foodstuffs, the Liberals rode back into office in 1906 on the greatest electoral tide of their history. It was this election, Richard Shannon has written, that revealed "the reality of class and class interests as the major electoral determinant."[40]

Throughout the next nine years of government, the Liberals presided over an extraordinarily creative period in

[38] L. A. Atherly-Jones, "The New Liberalism," *Nineteenth Century* 26 (August 1889), 187.

[39] Engels to A. Bebel, July 5, 1892, in *Karl Marx and Frederick Engels on Britain*, 2nd ed. (Moscow: Foreign Language Publishing House, 1962), p. 572.

[40] Richard Shannon, *The Crisis of Imperialism, 1865–1915* (St. Albans: Paladin, 1976), p. 379. On the importance of 1906, see also G. N. Sanderson, "The 'Swing of the Pendulum' in British General Elections, 1832–1966," *Political Studies* 14 (1966), 358, and Esmé Wingfield-Stratford, *The Victorian Aftermath* (New York: William Morrow, 1934), pp. 212–213.

British statecraft. The Government introduced legislation that laid the groundwork for the modern welfare state and even extended recognition of trade union rights. The continuing drift to the left culminated in two general elections during 1910. By winning a majority of seats in January, the Liberals could claim mass sanction for the land taxes that had inspired the Lords' opposition to their 1909 budget. The second election, fought on the same "Peers vs. People" theme, confirmed the dominance of the Commons in the legislative process. In these elections, it is argued, economic issues were openly recognized as the legitimate stuff of party differences, and the results confirmed the status of the Liberals as the most powerful voice in British social democracy.[41]

These strategic moves were accompanied by a change in the party's intellectual orientation. To provide a basis for the new approach, Liberal thinkers formulated a modernized ideology that reconciled traditional Liberal values with the demands of an advanced industrial society.[42] Far more expansive about the proper scope of state activity than traditional Liberal thought, this "New Liberalism" or "Edwardian Progressivism" was propounded in a series of stimulating books written by C.F.G. Masterman, J. A. Hobson, L. T. Hobhouse, and others. The ideas of the New Liberalism were disseminated throughout the country in the pages of the *Manchester Guardian* and through the stump speaking of the two shining stars in the Liberal Government under Asquith, David Lloyd George and Winston Churchill. In terms of its voting strength, intellectual baggage and parliamentary competence, therefore, the Liberal party was

[41] For the views of contemporaries on the importance of class in the 1910 elections, see Alfred L. P. Dennis, "Impressions of British Party Politics: 1909–1911," *American Political Science Review* 5 (November 1911), 514–516; J. A. Hobson, "The General Election: A Sociological Interpretation," pp. 97–117.

[42] P. F. Clarke, *Liberals and Social Democrats* (London: Cambridge University Press, 1978); Michael Freeden, *The New Liberalism: An Ideology of Social Reform* (Oxford: Clarendon Press, 1978).

well-equipped for its role as the most important progressive force in British politics.

That, at least, is the portrait which emerges from advocates of the class interpretation. Our study is primarily concerned with the accuracy of this interpretation insofar as it relates to mass voting behavior. Does the available evidence about voting patterns support the picture that has just been sketched?

EVALUATING THE EVIDENCE

All but one of the systematic attempts to assess the relationship between class and party have dealt with parliamentary elections in London. In the earliest study, James Cornford investigated the hypothesis that the adoption of single-member constituencies in 1884, by concentrating voters in socially homogeneous election districts, facilitated the development of an electoral cleavage along class lines. To test the argument, he studied the relationship between per capita assessed valuation, a measure of constituency wealth, and the Conservative share of the parliamentary vote in 1885. The strong positive relationship embodied in a correlation coefficient of $+0.74$ suggested that in London "class was becoming the most important single factor in deciding political allegiance."[43] According to Cornford, London was the exemplar of a national trend in which, by comparison with elections under the Second Reform Act, the class alignment had become the dominant motif.

In his larger study of British elections from 1885 to 1910, Henry Pelling presented detailed data for constituencies within the borders of the London County Council.[44] To measure constituency wealth, Pelling used 1891 census data on the number of female domestic servants per hundred households. On the basis of the value of this measure, the constituencies were allocated to three categories: A (pre-

---

[43] Cornford, "Transformation of Conservatism," p. 37.
[44] Pelling, *Social Geography*, ch. 2.

dominantly middle class), B (mixed middle and working class), and C (predominantly working class). As the data in Table 2.1 show, the Conservative vote increased steadily with the value of the wealth indicator. This was true for all eight general elections of the period. Like Cornford before him, Pelling concluded that "class counted for more than any other factor in London elections."[45] Based on a more impressionistic analysis of urban constituencies outside the metropolis, he thought that the class/party relationship probably held throughout the country.

The primacy of class in voting was also argued by Paul Thompson in his study of London political life during the period.[46] Unlike Cornford or Pelling, who relied on surrogate measures of constituency social composition, Thompson attempted to estimate the actual working-class and middle-class shares of the electorate. For primary data, he relied upon the census of street blocks conducted by School Board visitors in 1889 and published in Charles

TABLE 2.1. Conservative Vote in London Constituencies
Grouped by Pelling's Categories, 1885–1910

Type of Constituency	1885	1886	1892	1895	1900
Category A—middle class	60.0	66.6	61.9	68.8	72.9
Category B—mixed class	50.6	57.5	51.6	57.4	63.2
Category C—working class	46.6	53.0	45.8	52.6	53.8

	1906	Jan. 1910	Dec. 1910	$\bar{M}$	N
Category A—middle class	56.1	63.6	65.5	64.4	(18)
Category B—mixed class	44.5	49.5	49.7	53.0	(15)
Category C—working class	42.2	46.8	45.6	48.3	(24)

Entries are Conservative-Liberal Unionist share of total vote.
SOURCE: Calculated from Pelling, *Social Geography*, Tables 1-3.

[45] *Ibid.*, p. 57.
[46] Paul Thompson, *Socialists, Liberals and Labour*, esp. Appendix A.

33

Booth's classic survey of social life in London. Apportioning the blocks to the appropriate parliamentary constituency, Thompson then estimated the working-class and middle-class electorates by taking fractions of the respective class populations in the election districts. According to Thompson, the number of electors predicted by this technique corresponded closely to the actual number of voters on the electoral registers. The constituencies were then collapsed into five groups, A to E, in which the middle-class proportion of the electorate increased from an average of 7.5% to 52.5%. The method just described was followed for 1885 to 1900 but revised somewhat for the period from 1900 to 1910. There are few details about the revised technique, but the four social groupings that emerged from the classification bear a strong resemblance to the five categories used for the first fifteen years of the study. The technique produced the results in Table 2.2. In all general elections, the Liberal vote declined with the increased concentration of middle-class electors. On the basis of the table, Thompson's findings appear to validate the conclusions drawn by Cornford and Pelling.

In the only study which attempted systematic coverage of all urban British constituencies, Neal Blewett presented data which lent additional support to the class interpretation of voting.[47] In those parliamentary constituencies which corresponded closely to boroughs, Blewett followed Pelling by assigning social status based on the number of female domestics per family. The raw data for computing the ratio were taken from the 1911 census. This technique was not particularly useful in the boroughs subdivided into a number of single-member constituencies nor for the many boroughs with boundaries that did not correspond closely to the constituency of the same name. To determine the appropriate classification in those circumstances, Blewett relied on social descriptions from the local press, the impres-

[47] Blewett, *Peers, Parties and People.*

TABLE 2.2. Liberal Vote in London Constituencies
Grouped by Thompson's Categories, 1885–1910

| | A. 1885–1900 | | | | | | |
	1885	1886	1892	1895	1900	M	N
Middle class electors average = 7.5%	53.0	50.0	55.3	48.4	45.6	50.5	(10)
Middle class electors average = 14.2%	51.2	46.3	52.0	45.0	42.6	47.4	(12)
Middle class electors average = 25.5%	50.7	44.4	49.5	45.5	38.3	45.7	(12)
Middle class electors range from 33 to 40%	44.6	44.3	44.5	37.3	36.0	41.3	(4)
Middle class electors average = 52.5%	39.3	32.5	40.0	34.2	28.6	34.9	(19)

| | B. 1900–1910 | | | | | |
	1900	1906	Jan. 1910	Dec. 1910	M̄	N
Working class = 90%	48.1	60.4	55.1	54.2	54.5	(15)
Working class = 80–90%	44.0	57.4	52.0	52.7	51.5	(12)
Working class = 60–80%	35.7	53.6	48.1	47.2	46.2	(12)
Working class less than 60%	28.1	45.5	41.3	37.2	38.0	(18)

Entries are Liberal share of total vote.
SOURCE: Thompson, *Socialists, Liberals & Labour*, Appendix A, Tables 3, 7. (Reprinted with permission.)

sions gleaned from Pelling's survey of British constituencies and, in his own word, "guesswork."[48] This process eventually produced three groups corresponding to Pelling's A, B, and C categories. The mean Conservative vote in these constituency groups, arrayed in Table 2.3, followed the

[48] *Ibid.*, p. 489.

TABLE 2.3. Conservative Vote in British Urban Constituencies Grouped by Blewett's Categories, 1885–1910

Type of Constituency	1885	1886	1892	1895	1900
Category A—middle class	57.1	65.0	60.3	64.3	65.8
Category B—mixed class	49.7	54.5	52.9	56.0	57.2
Category C—working class	46.2	50.2	48.5	52.9	54.1

	1906	Jan. 1910	Dec. 1910	M̄	N
Category A—middle class	53.6	60.5	61.8	61.1	(48)
Category B—mixed class	45.5	50.2	50.9	52.1	(107)
Category C—working class	41.0	44.7	45.8	47.9	(124)

Entries are Conservative-Liberal Unionist share of total vote.
SOURCE: Blewett, *Peers, Parties and People*, Appendix III, Table B. (Reprinted with permission.)

social composition, further confirming the importance of class in the pre-1918 party system.

These studies have greatly influenced subsequent interpretations of electoral life under the Third Reform Act. In criticizing them, it is appropriate to acknowledge their considerable contribution to our understanding of political life during the period. As the first systematic attempts to establish the contours of electoral life, the studies have supplied a useful corrective to those traditional accounts that portray the period before 1918 as a time when politics was exclusively a matter of ancient religious conflicts and elections were wholly innocent of class influences. Thanks to these works, scholars now recognize considerable continuity in political themes and voting patterns between the pre- and post-1918 eras. By challenging conventional wisdom and generating new controversies, the studies by Pelling and others have paved the way for this particular inquiry. That influence should be apparent in both the themes and methods of this book.

Because Blewett's classification technique involved quite

personal and subjective assessments of constituency social composition, it is difficult to raise criticisms or attempt to replicate the findings. The ultimate test of his arguments will have to wait until Chapters 5 and 6, which examine the relationship between social and political variables over all the constituencies in Britain. However, we can raise and test a number of possible criticisms against the other three studies. It should be noted that the most important evidence for the validity of the class interpretation will be the new data collected for this study and presented later in the book. Because the studies of Cornford, Pelling, and Thompson have done so much to shape the class interpretation of the period, it seems appropriate to test the conclusions with the same data and techniques used by these authors.

By concentrating exclusively on London, the city for which the richest data are available, the three studies under discussion may well have examined a deviant case. A number of peculiar social features of the city probably made it an inappropriate basis for generalization to the rest of Britain. As a city attracting a large number of migrants from the provinces and other countries, London lacked the strong community life that was usually associated with religiosity.[49] It was also unusual among British cities in the extent to which residential life was segregated by social class.[50] Both these factors—low rates of religiosity and high levels of social differentiation by area—would make the city an atypically fertile environment for the development of class-based politics. If so, as suggested at the outset of this discussion, it would then be dangerous to attribute patterns observed in London to the remainder of the country.

To examine this possibility requires comparing the level of class voting in London with the magnitude of the class alignment elsewhere. The data in Table 2.4 permit a com-

[49] Hugh McCleod, *Class and Religion in the Late Victorian City*.
[50] C.F.G. Masterman, *Heart of the Empire* (London: T. Fisher Unwin, 1901), pp. vi, 11.

TABLE 2.4. Index of Class Voting in British Urban Constituencies, 1885–1910

Type of Constituency	1885	1886	1892	1895	1900	1906	Jan. 1910	Dec. 1910	N
A. London									
Working class	53.4	47.0	54.2	47.4	46.2	57.8	53.2	54.4	(29)
Middle class	40.1	33.4	38.1	31.2	27.1	43.9	36.4	34.5	(17)
Index	*13.3*	*13.6*	*16.1*	*16.2*	*19.1*	*13.9*	*16.8*	*19.9*	
B. Other Cities									
Working class	53.8	49.8	51.5	47.1	45.9	59.0	55.3	54.2	(85)
Middle class	42.9	35.0	39.7	35.7	34.2	46.4	39.5	38.2	(27)
Index	*10.9*	*14.8*	*11.8*	*11.4*	*11.7*	*12.6*	*15.8*	*16.0*	

Entries are Conservative-Liberal Unionist share of total vote.
SOURCE: See text.

parison of the level of class voting in London and all other provincial cities combined. The level of class voting has been assessed by modifying the Alford "index of class voting" to fit areal data.[51] Alford measured class voting among survey respondents by the simple technique of subtracting the vote for left parties among middle-class respondents from the corresponding percentage among working-class voters in the survey. The remainder, which indicates the level of class polarization in voting, is equivalent to the slope in a regression equation using dummy variables. We have modified the index for areal data by using relatively homogeneous parliamentary constituencies instead of individuals as the unit of analysis. The "working class" and "middle class" constituencies in Table 2.4 consist of Blewett's A and C groups. For each election, the mean Liberal/Labour vote in the predominantly middle-class constituencies was subtracted from the Liberal/Labour vote in predominantly working-class districts.

The data confirm the suspicion that the use of London as a model prejudices the case for class politics from the outset. The London index of class voting for the entire period averaged three points higher than the level in the provinces. Only in a single election, 1886, did provincial

[51] Robert Alford, *Party and Society*, ch. 5.

voting adhere to class lines more closely than in London. The trend lines in Figure 2.1 also show that the progression of the class alignment followed different patterns. In London, class voting increased in a fairly uniform pattern over the entire period. In the provinces, by contrast, the plot of class voting over time more closely resembled a U-shaped curve. After a spurt in 1886, the index returned to 1885 levels for the next three elections, ascending again only in 1910. The crudeness of the technique leaves open a great many questions, but it does support the criticism that London voting cannot readily be generalized outside the southeast.

The three studies are subject to another criticism. Though asserting that class had become the major line of electoral cleavage, the authors demonstrated only that class was pos-

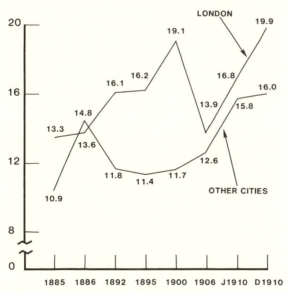

Figure 2.1. Plot of Class Voting in British
Urban Constituencies, 1885–1910

39

itively related to the vote. No attempt was made to compare the impact of class with other variables nor, even more basically, to demonstrate that the class/party linkage was strong. The conclusions about the *primacy* of class influence are simply not warranted by the data presented in the studies.

We will have to wait until Chapter 5 for a multivariate analysis of the impact of class against other predictors of the vote but can consider here the issue about the strength of the class/party relationship. One way to approach this issue is to determine, in statistical terms, the extent of co-variation between the measures of class composition of parliamentary constituencies and party shares of the vote. Cornford presented such data only for the election of 1885, and the other two authors, by grouping constituencies into socially similar categories, in effect hid the data necessary to test the explanatory power of social class on variations in voting behavior.

To test more adequately the relationship between class and the vote in London, we will attempt to replicate that section of Pelling's study which estimated the number of domestic servants per hundred households for constituencies.[52] Rather than grouping the constituencies and reporting only a category mean, we shall use the actual value of the class indicator to predict the partisan distribution of the vote. Pelling's social data, taken from Charles Booth's research in the 1890s, are superior to Cornford's 1881 data as a basis for categorizing constituencies during the period from 1885 to 1910. Because Thompson's data, methods,

[52] There are good reasons for doubting the validity of the index based on female domestic servants. Departing from traditional practice, the 1891 census included as domestic servants females (unmarried and otherwise unoccupied) who spent most of their time assisting with household duties. Recognizing that this classification might apply to many women who should not by any stretch of the imagination be regarded as domestic servants, the census authorities reverted to a more explicit definition in 1911. See the *1901 Census, England and Wales, General Report, Parliamentary Papers*, CVIII, 1904, Cd. 2174, pp. 76–77.

and findings so closely parallel Pelling's, a reanalysis of the latter's data will suffice to evaluate both studies.

The replication involves some guesswork because Pelling did not present the value of the social indicator for the constituencies nor, more importantly, reveal his decision rules for matching the constituencies to the registration districts used as units of enumeration by Booth. In the absence of such guidance, we decided to match constituencies to a corresponding registration district (or set of districts) only if the gross population disparity between the two units did not exceed 5%.[53] When the disparity exceeded 5%, the constituency was grouped in a multiconstituency unit that did fall within the tolerance limit. This procedure produced nineteen units with a single parliamentary constituency, ten units with two constituencies each, and six units with three constituencies. The census data collected by Booth were aggregated for these units as were the raw data for parliamentary elections. The registration district of Bethnal Green, comprising two constituencies by that name, had the lowest value on the index with only 3.05 servants per hundred families. At the other end of the social scale, the registration districts of St. George, Hanover Square (84.76), Hampstead (82.50), and Kensington (78.1) had the highest values.

Of the fifty-seven constituencies in London, all but ten fell into the same general category under this scheme and under Pelling's classification system. The discordant cases all involved constituencies in multiconstituency units that

[53] The social data appear in Charles Booth, *Life and Labour of the People in London*, 3rd ser. (1902–1904; reprint ed., New York: AMS Press, 1970) VI, 205–209. The description of London's constituency boundaries appears in schedules 4–6, *Redistribution of Seats Act, 1885*, 48 & 49 Vict., 1884–5, c. 23. The electoral data were taken from F.W.S. Craig, *British Parliamentary Election Results, 1885–1918*. Because of its huge nonresident vote, the City of London constituency was excluded from the analysis. Its inclusion as a unit with a value of only 20.80 on the servant index would have further reduced the association between the index and the Conservative vote.

Details of the boundary-matching scheme are available on request.

Pelling equated with subdistricts of registration units even in the face of enormous population discrepancies.[54] For example, it appeared that Pelling equated the Clapham division of the Battersea and Clapham constituencies with Clapham Parish even though the parliamentary constituency was over two times the size of the parish. Similarly, it seems that Pelling equated the constituency of Lambeth Norwood (population 68,411 in 1891) with the registration district of Norwood (population of 25,657). Rather than tolerate such substantial disparities, our replication merged these two constituencies into multiconstituency units that corresponded much more closely to the registration areas. The loss in number of cases seems well worth the gain in validity.

The results of regressing the Conservative share of the poll on the index measure, presented in Table 2.5, reveal what could best be described as a moderate relationship. The positive increment in the Conservative vote with an increase of one servant per hundred families varied from

[54] The discrepant units and the population disparity are:

Constituency	Registration units	Population ratio (c/ru)
Battersea & Clapham-Battersea	Battersea, E & W	65%
Battersea & Clapham-Clapham	Clapham	220%
Camberwell North	St. George, Camberwell	140%
Camberwell Dulwich	Camberwell; Dulwich	94%
Lambeth Norwood	Norwood	167%
Lambeth North	Lambeth Church, 1 & 2; Waterloo Road	73%
Hackney North	Stoke Newington; Stamford Hill; West Hackney	85%
St. Pancras East	Somers Town; Camden Town	126%
Finsbury East	City Road; Finsbury	107%
Islington West	Southwest Islington	70%

I must emphasize that I do not know for certain if these were Pelling's classifications, but it seems likely. Matching to these boundaries eliminates all the discordant cases and adds no new ones.

TABLE 2.5. Relationship of Conservative Vote to Index
of Female Domestics Per Hundred Families in London, 1885–1910

Year	Slope	Intercept	R²	N
1885	.24	46.7	.42	(35)
1886	.34	48.6	.39	(31)
1892	.20	46.9	.29	(33)
1895	.10	52.4	.19	(30)
1900	.23	54.4	.23	(29)
1906	.25	39.1	.34	(34)
1910, Jan.	.29	44.8	.39	(35)
1910, Dec.	.37	43.8	.39	(33)

SOURCE: See text and notes.

about one-tenth of one percent in 1895 to more than one-third of one percent in 1886 and 1910 (December). The servant index generally accounted for from one-fifth to two-fifths of the variance in Conservative voting. Against these statistics, it must be noted that the regression indicates high levels of Conservative voting in districts with low concentrations of domestic servants. The predicted Conservative share of the poll in a hypothetical unit with a value of zero on the social index ranged from 39.1% in 1906 to 54.4% in 1900.[55] To put these figures in context, it will help to compare the magnitudes with results of constituency regressions in more recent general elections. Miller has shown that a single social variable—the proportion of employers and managers in the population—explained from two-thirds to four-fifths of the variation in Conservative voting in the five general elections between 1964 and 1974 (October), roughly twice the variance accounted for by Pelling's social index.[56] Miller's analysis further indicates that a modern constituency without any employers or managers would give only 20% of its vote to the Conservatives—about half the figure for a constituency with no servants in the pre-1918 system. The differences between Pelling and Mil-

[55] This figure is the intercept in the regression equation, the value of the dependent variable when the independent variable equals zero.
[56] Miller, "Social Class and Party Choice," p. 276.

ler's social index prevents us from interpreting these findings too literally, but the figures at the very least call for caution before assigning primacy to class as an electoral force before 1918.

Another way to approach the problem of the strength of the class/party relationship involves a more direct (but less sophisticated) comparison of class influences in the pre-1918 and post-1945 party systems. Once again, the technique for making comparisons is the modified version of Alford's index of class voting. But instead of comparing London data with the provinces, the technique is applied to class voting in London constituencies for two periods: 1885 to 1910 and 1955 to 1970. By comparing class effects under the Third Reform Act with the level of class voting in the modern party system, we can get some idea about the relative importance that ought to be assigned to class influences in the late Victorian era.[57]

In this analysis, the social composition of pre-1918 constituencies was assessed by Thompson's estimate of the working-class electorate, a more precise scheme than the classification used by Pelling. For a constituency to be regarded as predominantly working-class, at least 90% of its population had to fall into that category. The constituencies placed into the middle-class group had at least one-third of their electorate in the middle class. As before, the index of class voting was determined by subtracting the combined Liberal-Labour vote in the middle-class group from the same figure in the working-class constituencies. The social composition of constituencies from 1955 to 1970 can be gauged directly from the sample census of parliamentary areas published in 1966.[58] The "working-class" constituencies include all those districts in which at least 79% of

[57] These data were first presented in Kenneth D. Wald, "The Rise of Class-Based Voting in London," pp. 219–229.

[58] The relevant information is published in David Butler and Michael Pinto-Duschinsky, *The British General Election of 1970* (London: Macmillan, 1971), pp. 360–361.

the *population* consisted of manual workers, and the middle-class constituencies were those with at least 52% in non-manual pursuits. The "left vote" for the more recent period includes only the Labour proportion.

Comparisons across such a wide time span and with admittedly crude procedures do not lend themselves to a definitive analysis of changing vote patterns. But the results in Table 2.6 are at least suggestive, and confirm that class had much less impact on voter alignment in the early period. The average index for 1885 to 1910 is only slightly more than half the equivalent figure for the five elections in the modern period. However class-based elections may have seemed to observers at the turn of the century, they did not even approach the level of class alignment evident from 1955 to 1970. This disparity can best be appreciated by considering extreme cases. Even in 1970, when the Labour party suffered substantial defections from its working-class base, the level of the index was much higher than it was in 1910, the year usually regarded as the apotheosis

TABLE 2.6. Index of Class Voting in London Constituencies, General Elections of 1885–1910 and 1955–1970 Compared

Predominant in Constituency *	Mean Left Vote**							
	1885	1886	1892	1895	1900	1906	Jan. 1910	Dec. 1910
Working class	54.4	48.2	55.2	47.9	45.0	61.7	54.4	56.0
Middle class	41.3	35.1	40.2	33.6	28.0	43.7	36.8	34.6
Index	*13.1*	*13.1*	*15.0*	*14.3*	*17.0*	*18.0*	*17.6*	*21.4*

	1955	1959	1964	1966	1970
Working class	74.7	70.0	73.2	79.5	72.3
Middle class	38.9	41.9	49.2	50.5	46.2
Index	*35.8*	*28.1*	*24.0*	*29.0*	*26.1*

* There are ten predominantly working-class constituencies for 1885–95, fifteen for 1900–10 and ten for 1955–70. The predominantly middle-class constituencies number twenty-three for 1885–95, eighteen for 1900–10 and thirteen for 1955–70.
** The "mean left vote" for 1885–1910 includes both the Liberal and Labour share of the vote. For the 1955–70 elections, only the Labour vote is included.
SOURCE: See text.

of class conflict in the Edwardian electoral system. So in one of the least class-based elections of the post-1945 era, voting followed class lines much more closely than it had in one of the most overtly class-oriented elections of the pre-1918 period. By modern standards, class had very little impact on the vote.

ANALYSIS OF LOCAL GOVERNMENT ELECTIONS[59]

Considering the ambiguities of existing research, it is best to consider the case for class politics under the Third Reform Act as "not proven." More direct doubt can be cast upon the class interpretation by the results of research on local government elections in five diverse English cities—Bradford, Brighton, Norwich, Reading, and Wolverhampton.[60] The research, conducted at a time when no standard compendium of parliamentary election results existed and the possibilities for ecological analysis of the period had not yet been recognized, points in the direction of the larger study presented in Chapter 5.

The choice of local government elections was dictated by necessity, particularly by the difficulty of obtaining useful data on the social composition of parliamentary constituencies. Because the electoral wards of local government were sometimes used as administrative areas, official and private sources frequently provided social data for the units. When analyzed and transformed by use of the appropriate statistical technique, such data can yield quantitative estimates of ward social status; these estimates can then be used to observe the relationship between social environment and party fortunes in local government elections.

Though dictated by necessity, the use of the local government arena can be defended on nonutilitarian grounds.

[59] For more information on this analysis, see Kenneth D. Wald, "Class and the Vote Before the First World War," pp. 441–457.

[60] On the characteristics of these cities, see Kenneth D. Wald, "Patterns of English Voter Alignment Since 1885," (Ph.D. thesis, Washington University, 1976), pp. 24–56.

Most importantly, there is good reason to believe that local contests generated the same structure of voter alignments which characterized parliamentary elections. Indeed, local partisans treated municipal elections as an opportunity to hone their organizations for impending parliamentary battles. The Liberal newspaper in Bradford reported that the municipal campaign of 1888 was widely regarded "as a sort of rehearsal for the Parliamentary conflict," and sources in Norwich described the local elections in that city as "a General Election in miniature."[61] In a letter to a local party official, the Conservative member for a Wolverhampton constituency advised the same attitude toward municipal elections: ". . . while maintaining the attitude of neutrality I have always observed in municipal politics, I may say that it seems to me the policy of contesting seats has to be considered with relation to the effect that may be produced upon our Parliamentary prospects *and nothing else.*"[62] Even in Brighton, where borough council elections were ostensibly nonpartisan, the *Sussex Evening Times* discovered that partisan politics "are in nearly every instance busily at work underneath."[63] As one would expect from these attitudes, the candidates for local honors, even if they stood without party labels, tended to be the same people who manned the party organization for general elections and sat upon the dais with parliamentary candidates at election rallies. With the same persons and organizations in command of electoral appeals, it was argued, the voters were bound to follow a common line in parliamentary and municipal elections.[64]

In some respects, local government elections were even superior to the parliamentary arena as an environment for

[61] *Bradford Observer*, October 26, 1886, p. 4; *Eastern Daily Press* (Norwich), November 3, 1889, p. 8.

[62] Alfred A. Bird to Charles Marston, October 10, 1912. A complete copy of this letter was made available to me by Dr. G. W. Jones.

[63] *Sussex Evening Times*, October 22, 1890, p. 4.

[64] J. Seymour Lloyd, *Municipal Elections and How to Fight Them*, rev. ed. (London: Vacher, 1909), p. 32.

examining the social basis of party conflict. Falling on a fixed date each year, local elections were less subject to the influence of temporary "Westminster issues" which might distort partisan allegiance. The local government electorate was larger than the parliamentary electorate and presumably more representative of mass opinion.[65] Moreover, local government elections were more open to candidates representing working-class interests. Unlike the parliamentary candidate, who had to lodge a deposit to cover the anticipated cost of the poll, the borough council aspirant had only to raise funds for his own campaign.[66] Thus the Labour party (or the forces that eventually coalesced into that party) was a powerful municipal force long before it gained significant representation in Parliament.

As in most of the London studies, the class indicator used in the analysis of local elections emphasized the material welfare of the election districts. Following procedures developed by Innes in his study of class fertility patterns, potential measures of wealth such as statistics of health, public assistance, tax assessments, population density, housing values, and the like were collected for wards in each of the cities.[67] The available statistics, which varied in quality and quantity by city, were assembled in matrix form and subjected to correlation analysis. The statistics which correlated at a high level (usually at 0.5 or better) were retained for inclusion in the final indicator of ward social composition.[68]

Two statistical transformations were essential. First, the statistics that survived the winnowing-out process had to

[65] Brian Keith-Lucas, *The English Local Government Franchise* (Oxford: Basil Blackwell, 1952).

[66] Charles Seymour and Donald P. Frary, *How the World Votes* (Springfield, Mass.: C. A. Nichols, 1918), II, 156.

[67] John W. Innes, *Class Fertility Trends in England and Wales* (Princeton: Princeton University Press, 1938).

[68] For full particulars, see Wald, "English Voter Alignments," pp. 111–128, and also his "The Development of Social Indicators for Historical Election Research" (Paper presented to the European Studies Conference, University of Nebraska—Omaha, 1976).

be converted to standard scores. This transformation put the various indicators onto a common measurement scale. Second, to ensure that all index components varied positively with wealth, some of the variables had their signs reversed. Once the statistics had been standardized and ordered to reflect a consistent interpretation, they were summed by ward. The final wealth index was the mean of the combined standard scores for each ward. Though averaging scores on the various statistics somewhat muddied differences between wards, this seemed a reasonable price to pay for a measure which recognized the multidimensionality of class. For the five cities, the poorest ward had a "wealth index" of − 1.8 and the most prosperous had a value of about + 2.0. The range of values for one of the five cities, Brighton, is indicated in Table 2.7.

The reliability of the measure was established by selecting the index components, where possible, from aggregated time-series data. This prevented yearly fluctuations from exercising undue influence on the index. The validity of the measure, guaranteed partly by the selection procedure, was further established by comparing the quantitative index with qualitative descriptions of wards gathered from the local press. For example, the Brighton newspaper boasted of the "aristocratic" wards that formed the city's outer ring.[69] These outlying wards—West, Montpelier, Preston, Preston

TABLE 2.7. Wealth Index for Brighton Wards

Wards	Wealth Index	Wards	Wealth Index
1. West	1.16	8. Lewes Road	− 0.23
2. Kemptown	1.14	9. Queen's Park	− 0.31
3. Montpelier	0.84	10. St. Nicholas	− 0.59
4. Preston Park	0.83	11. Pier	− 0.76
5. Preston	0.60	12. St. Peter	− 1.05
6. Regency	0.33	13. St. John	− 1.14
7. Pavilion	0.33	14. Hanover	− 1.16

[69] *Sussex Evening Times*, April 29, 1890, p. 4, and April 18, 1890, p. 3; *Brighton Gazette* November 2, 1907, p. 5.

Park, and Kemptown—stood well above the mean on the Brighton scale of wealth with an average index of + 0.9. As Table 2.7 indicates, they were in fact the top five wards on the wealth index. The brightness of the periphery contrasted sharply with the squalid interior, graphically characterized by the *Brighton Gazette* as "street after street of small dilapidated houses, studded here and there with little chandler's shops and beer taverns," populated largely by "the male loafer and female slut."[70] The wards which attracted special distaste from the *Gazette*'s correspondent— St. Nicholas, St. Peter, St. John, Hanover, and Pier—occupy the bottom five places in Table 2.7 with an average index of − 0.9. Similar patterns in the other cities suggest that the quantitative measure accurately mirrored the social composition of the wards.

The class indicators were entered as predictors of party support in regression equations, "party support" being defined as the mean percentage of the vote obtained by each party's candidates over the life of the ward. In Table 2.8, which presents the results of the analysis, the equations have been computed for all possible combinations of conflict with three parties. The equations contained dummy variables to account for local variations in partisanship. The final two columns present the number of wards that had at least one contest of the type (out of all ninety-six wards in the five cities) and the total number of elections in each category. Despite the frequency of unopposed returns, the analysis was based on nearly seven hundred different local contests.

Whether based on "slope" or "fit" measures of class-voting, the data in Table 2.8 do little to support the class interpretation. The flatness of the slopes suggests that the prewar party system was not class-based in the modern

[70] *Brighton Gazette*, September 28, 1905, p. 5; October 19, 1905, p. 4; November 3, 1906, p. 5; October 5, 1900, p. 5; November 1, 1902, p. 5; and October 26, 1905, p. 5.

TABLE 2.8. Relationship Between Wealth Index and the Vote in Local
Government Elections in Five English Cities, 1885–1910

Party	Slope*	Intercept	Multiple R^2 (%)	N of Cases Wards	N of Cases Elections
Conservative					
v. Liberal	2.0	36.9	10.3	85	412
v. Labour	1.8	37.1	6.5	45	107
v. Liberal and					
Labour	3.8	38.6	8.9	26	83
Liberal					
v. Conservative	− 2.0	47.5	10.3	85	412
v. Labour	2.3	39.7	26.5	31	69
v. Conservative					
and Labour	− 1.4	34.1	1.4	26	83
Labour					
v. Conservative	− 1.8	21.0	6.5	42	107
v. Liberal	− 2.3	27.7	26.5	31	69
v. Conservative					
and Liberal	− 2.3	27.3	2.3	26	83

* Except for three-party contests, the regression equations included dummy
variables to adjust the slope for local variations in partisanship.

sense of that term. This can best be appreciated by using
the regression equations to predict party support in hypothetical wards at the extremes of the wealth continuum.
Even when it was most sharply related to class lines (in
three-party contests) the Conservative vote in a poor ward
with an indicator of − 2.0 would differ from the party's
support in a ward with a + 2.0 wealth indicator by a mere
15%. That hardly constitutes a sharp line of cleavage. The
regression lines were not only flat; they also failed to predict
ward partisanship very accurately. In three-fourths of the
elections, the Conservative candidate was confronted by a
single Liberal or Labour opponent. Yet only about 10% of
the party variance in Conservative vs. Liberal contests and
7% in Tory vs. Labour contests could be attributed to the
wealth of the wards. Even when measurement difficulties
and the use of surrogate class indicators are taken into
account, these findings raise fundamental doubts about the
importance of class lines in voting before World War I.

SUMMARY

This chapter has examined a contention increasingly found in the scholarly literature on the development of the British party system—that the class alignment dominated elections as early as the Edwardian era. The studies cited in support of this interpretation suffer from a variety of problems that cast doubt upon their conclusions. In a direct test of the interpretation with local election data for five English cities, the class interpretation was quite thoroughly rejected. Considering the rather crude methods used in all these studies, we should not reject the class interpretation, but only hold it in abeyance until examining the more comprehensive and sophisticated analysis reported in Chapters 5 and 6. We must now turn an equally critical eye to the interpretation which most directly challenges the class perspective— the traditional religious model of party alignments under the Third Reform Act.

CHAPTER 3

Crosses on the Ballot?

For the explanation of electoral behavior both in our own country and abroad, we always have to pay attention first to the religious factor.[1]
—J. J. de Jong

Among the variables that define electoral coalitions in advanced societies, the "religious factor" has demonstrated a surprising degree of persistence. Political sociologists sometimes convey the assumption that "there is an irreversible trend in modern political societies toward class-based voting and therefore toward an increasingly well-defined economic division between parties."[2] Despite predictions that it was bound to lose its political relevance in the face of the economic cleavages generated by industrialization, religion has demonstrated remarkable vitality as a source of partisan differences in many economically advanced societies. Intensive survey-based studies of electoral cleavage patterns demonstrate that religion often competes on equal terms with class as a social basis for party coalitions.[3] From his reading of this literature, Philip Con-

[1] J. J. de Jong, *Overheid en onderdaan* (Wageningen, Holland: Zomer en Keunings, 1956), p. 160, cited in Arend Lijphart, "Religious vs. Linguistic vs. Class Voting: The 'Crucial Experiment' of Comparing Belgium, Canada, South Africa and Switzerland," *American Political Science Review* 73 (June 1979), 443.

[2] Leon Epstein, *Political Parties in Western Democracies* (New York: Frederick A. Praeger, 1967), p. 88.

[3] Richard Rose and Derek Urwin, "Social Cohesion, Political Parties and Strains in Regimes," pp. 7–67; Arend Lijphart, "Class Voting and Religious Voting in the European Democracies."

verse has concluded that "religious differentiation intrudes on partisan political alignments in [an] unexpectedly powerful degree wherever it conceivably can."[4] Even in an age of secularism, the religious variable continues to exercise a potent impact on political behavior.

Among modern societies, Britain seems to be one of the few exceptions to this generalization. This is not to deny the evidence that churchgoing and other measures of religiosity can somewhat mitigate the effects of class membership on individual voting behavior.[5] Furthermore, the generalization has to be tempered by recognizing that in parts of the United Kingdom where religious differences are rife, particularly Northern Ireland, the party battle reflects religious rather than class differences.[6] But in general, because of its overall religious homogeneity, Britain is frequently described as a nation in which the absence of deep-rooted religious differences fostered the development of a relatively "pure" class-based party system.[7]

This portrait clashes sharply with the historical tradition emphasizing the primacy of religious conflicts in British political development. Indeed, the stereotype of Britain as a society in which political divisions have nearly always followed class lines can be set against equally sweeping generalizations claiming that the historical pattern of British politics is incomprehensible unless perceived essentially as an expression of religious group conflict.[8] We are concerned in this chapter with the evidence for the persistence in late Victorian-Edwardian Britain of the religious alignment in mass voting behavior. A detailed exposition of the

[4] Philip E. Converse, "Some Priority Variables in Comparative Electoral Research," p. 734.

[5] Butler and Stokes, *Political Change*, 2nd ed., pp. 154–167.

[6] Richard Rose, *The Problem of Party Government* (Harmondsworth, Middlesex: Penguin Books, 1974), pp. 43–45.

[7] John Bonham, *The Middle Class Vote* (London: Faber and Faber, 1954), pp. 194–195; Carl J. Friedrich, *Constitutional Government and Democracy*, rev. ed. (Boston: Little, Brown, 1971), p. 297.

[8] E. R. Taylor, *Methodism and Politics, 1791–1850* (Cambridge: Cambridge University Press, 1935), p. 1.

religious interpretation, followed by an evaluation of the empirical evidence on its behalf, leads to a conclusion like the moral drawn from Chapter 2: There is good reason to suspect that religious factors played a role in the party system but no decisive evidence to confirm the supposition.

THE RELIGIOUS INTERPRETATION

The reader who delves into first-hand accounts of life before World War I cannot help but note the frequent references to religious influences on the vote. Unlike the typical situation on the continent, where political conflict was generated by splits between Catholics and Protestants or the warfare of clericals and unbelievers, the British religious cleavage manifested itself most readily as a schism within Protestantism. According to one retrospective analysis, British politics before 1914 took its tone from Milton, not Mill, reflecting the historical conflict between the Church of England and the Protestant denominations that had accepted the principles of the Reformation.[9] The nature of this conflict was summarized concisely by an observation attributed to the Bishop of Manchester: "I do not like what I find is the accepted maxim in Lancashire, that every Churchman is a Conservative and every Nonconformist a Liberal."[10]

The identification of the Church of England with Conservatism is at least as old as Macaulay's famous jibe at the state Church as "the Tory party at prayers." The identity of interests between Church and party was recognized as late as 1906 by the Anglican cleric who could still write rather matter-of-factly about "the opposition of the great majority of English Churchmen to the Liberal party."[11] The

[9] W. Haslam Mills, "Some Changes in British Public Life," *Nation* 17 (August 1926), 149–150.

[10] Quoted in Clarke, "Electoral Sociology," p. 46.

[11] Conrad Noel, *The Labour Party: What It Is and What It Wants* (London: T. Fisher Unwin, 1906), p. 3.

relationship was apparent throughout the country. An Anglican clergyman told his parishioners in Reading that their Church appeared to many as merely "an ornamental appendage to the Conservative government," a description that seemed credible in a city where the success of Conservative candidates in local elections correlated highly with the size of "the Church Party" in the wards.[12] A Yorkshireman discerned the same connection when he spoke disparagingly of the "Tory-cum-Liberal Unionist-cum-Church party."[13] In perhaps the most sweeping characterization of the period, a speaker told a meeting of Nonconformists that "the Church was synonymous with unmitigated Toryism, and if the Church were disestablished Toryism would vanish into thin air."[14]

Even more people agreed on the linkage between Nonconformists and the Liberal party. A modern writer has recalled that any Nonconformist who admitted to a Conservative loyalty before World War I was treated as a social deviant.[15] As one who fell into that category, Austen Chamberlain recalled the period before 1918 as a time "when to say of a man that he was a Nonconformist was almost to predicate that he was a Liberal."[16] The converse was equally true. "To talk of the Liberal Party without Nonconformists," a dissenting minister wrote, "is precisely the same thing as to talk of the Unionist Party without Conservatives."[17] The historic Liberalism of Bradford and Norwich was generally attributed to their Nonconformist traditions; a Conservative candidate in Wolverhampton put down his three consecutive defeats to Nonconformist influences in

[12] *Reading Observer*, August 6, 1904, p. 3. On the "Church Party," see *Ibid.*, November 7, 1903, p. 3 and November 5, 1904, p. 2.

[13] *Bradford Observer*, November 1, 1888, p. 7.

[14] *Ibid.*, October 29, 1890, p. 7.

[15] T. M. Parker, "Religion and Politics in Britain," *Journal of Contemporary History* 2 (October 1967), 129.

[16] Quoted in Hamilton Fyfe, *The British Liberal Party* (London: George Allen and Unwin, 1928), p. 47.

[17] Quoted in Blewett, *Peers, Parties and People*, p. 229.

the constituency.[18] The national leaders of the Free Churches, with everything to gain by exaggerating their contribution to the party, did all they could to sustain the impression that Nonconformity constituted the backbone of Liberal voting strength.[19]

This religious division, so it seems, was a more potent source of political differences than the division of social classes. In areas such as Yorkshire and South Wales, where working-class political cohesion was especially noteworthy, observers have argued that common religious traditions provided the basis for political consensus.[20] More commonly, the absence of class alignments was associated with internal divisions of the working class along religious lines. Throughout Lancashire and Ulster, Conservative success among working-class voters was attributed to electoral mobilization along Catholic-Protestant lines.[21] The less violent sectarian split within Protestantism, Keir Hardie argued, accounted for the difficulty faced by socialists who wanted to mobilize working-class voters on an economic basis. He wrote in 1910:

Up to the present the two parties have been able to divide the electors into two almost evenly divided halves. . . . What is it that keeps them divided? They are at one on Labour questions. They all want to enjoy the full fruits of their toil. Many of them are good Trade Unionists and stand together when on strike. What

[18] *Bradford Observer*, February 6, 1884, p. 5; *Ibid.*, January 4, 1886, p. 7; A. D. Bayne, *A Comprehensive History of Norwich* (London: Jarrold and Sons, 1869), p. ix; L. S. Amery, *England Before the Storm, 1896–1914* (London: Hutchinson, 1953), p. 276.

[19] Stephen Koss, *Nonconformity in Modern British Politics*. One leader, Robertson Nicoll, told the *British Weekly*, "Take the Nonconformist Party out of it, and there is no Liberal Party." Cited in Anthony King, "Some Aspects of the History of the Liberal Party in Britain, 1906–1914," p. 42.

[20] G.D.H. Cole, *British Working Class Politics, 1832–1914* (London: George Routledge, 1941), pp. 119–120; Ensor, *England,* p. 222; E. P. Thompson, "Homage to Tom Maguire," pp. 276–316.

[21] Stanley Salvidge, *Salvidge of Liverpool* (London: Hodder and Stoughton, 1934).

is it that divides them at the poll? One goes to church on Sunday and another to chapel. That and nothing more.[22]

Socialists seemed to enjoy their greatest success when they could fuse political action with revivalist enthusiasm.[23]

The political importance of religious factors before 1918, so evident to persons who lived through the period, has also been noted by a variety of modern observers. In a recent study of Anglican-Methodist relations, one author expressed this understanding succinctly: "It is often assumed that Church (of England) means Tory and that Chapel means Whig (or, in due course, Liberal). This is a good rule when writing about the seventeenth century, and is generally valid for the last quarter of the nineteenth century."[24] A study of the Liberal Government of 1905 to 1914 concluded along the same lines that religious forces were paramount in forming the political agenda:

British politics in the twentieth century are incomprehensible unless religion is reckoned as one of the major factors in party allegiance. The Conservatives stood for the Church of England and the Liberals for Nonconformity—the Baptists, the Congregationalists and the various Methodist connections. Church-vs.-chapel was a more potent public issue than capital-vs.-labour.[25]

In concluding his study of party development at the turn of the century, another scholar contended that "the Conservative-Liberal split was still much more clearly tied to the Anglican-Nonconformist division than to struggles between middle- and working-classes."[26] It would probably not be an exaggeration to describe the denominational

[22] James Keir Hardie, *My Confession of Faith in the Labour Alliance* (London: Independent Labour Party, 1910), p. 3.

[23] Henry Pelling, *Origins of the Labour Party*, 2nd ed. (London: Oxford University Press, 1965), pp. 125–144.

[24] Anthony Armstrong, *The Church of England, the Methodists and Society, 1700–1850* (Totowa, New Jersey: Rowman and Littlefield, 1973), p. 160.

[25] Colin Cross, *The Liberals in Power, 1905–1914* (London: Barrie and Rockliff, 1963), p. 5.

[26] D.E.D. Beales, *The Political Parties of Nineteenth Century England* (London: Historical Association, 1971), p. 21.

interpretation of political parties as the dominant strain in the historical literature on the political system of 1885-1910.

Before examining its genesis, we should take note of several qualifications and ambiguities in the literature on the religious interpretation. Most authors recognize the importance of political divisions within the major religious groups. The multifarious tendencies that coexisted uneasily in the state Church—ritualism, Evangelicalism, Christian Socialism, Tractarianism, etc.—had political equivalents that frequently diminished Anglican cohesion in party politics.[27] Given the numerical preponderance of Anglicans in the British population, it could hardly have been otherwise, for a party supported by all Anglicans would have won every general election with huge parliamentary majorities. The Conservatives did well in the period—but certainly not that well. The single largest element of Protestant Nonconformity, the Methodist connection, was also diverse in political leanings. The smaller sects which seemed to imbibe Liberalism as part of their creed were balanced by the Wesleyans, the largest Methodist denomination, who remained close to the established Church in liturgy, ritual, and church structure. Some evidence suggests that a large segment of the Wesleyans maintained the founder's preference for the Conservative party, but it is difficult to tell if that alleged tendency reflected the pull of religious tradition or class influences.[28] At any rate, the discussion of religious group propensities is just that—a matter of *tendencies*.

The Catholic community in Britain is also somewhat ambiguously placed in the religious interpretation. The conditions under which the Church of England split from Ca-

[27] Ian Bradley, *The Call to Seriousness* (London: Macmillan, 1977), p. 174.

[28] Horton Davies, *The English Free Churches*, 2nd ed. (London: Oxford University Press, 1963), pp. 155–157. The *Methodist Times* estimated in 1886 that one-third of Methodist votes went to Conservative candidates. See John K. Lindsay, "The Liberal Unionist Party Until December 1887" (Ph.D. thesis, University of Edinburgh, 1955), p. 204.

tholicism almost guaranteed enmity between the state Church and the Church of Rome in England. If Conservatism was the natural party of Anglicans, then Catholics were likely to support whatever alternatives were available. The historical legacy of Catholic hostility to Conservatism was reinforced after 1886 by the Irish question on which the Catholic population in Britain, overwhelmingly of Irish descent, was ranged against Conservative policy. The resemblances between Anglicanism and Catholicism could also push Catholics in the other direction. On questions involving religious education in the schools, for instance, the Catholics were much more disposed to accept the Conservative preference for state support of sectarian schools than the secular solution which Nonconformists impressed on the Liberal party. On issues with cultural overtones such as drink and Sabbatarianism, the Catholics' preference for individual choice often put them at loggerheads with Liberals who wanted piety enforced by the law.[29] On balance, the Irish issue probably was the decisive factor, but the relations between Catholics and Liberals were never without tension.[30]

EXPLAINING THE RELIGIOUS FACTOR

To account for the political role of religion in British politics of this period, most scholars have adopted what might best be described as an interest group interpretation. In this approach, political parties are conceived as agencies that seek for reasons of sympathy and expedience to advance the interests of particular religious groups through the political process. As a party becomes the traditional champion of a particular denomination, the connection be-

[29] See the statement by the Canon of Wolverhampton in Wolverhampton and District, Inc., Licensed Victuallers' Friendly and Protective Society, *Jubilee Banquet, 1889* (Wolverhampton: Plimmer and Co., 1889), pp. 32–33.

[30] Pelling, *Social Geography*, p. 50.

60

tween the two may be strengthened by the development of shared values.

Thus, it has been argued, the original division between Whigs and Tories reflected the historic competition between Dissent and the Church of England, and the cleavage based on these competing interests dominated British politics well into the twentieth century.[31] Whatever the ebb and flow of particular issues, the constant theme in political life was Conservative opposition to Whig-Liberal efforts to remove Nonconformist disabilities.[32]

A Whig initiative in 1828 was required to repeal the Test and Corporation Acts which had reserved civil life exclusively for Anglicans. To convert the legal right of Nonconformists to hold public office into a realistic prospect, the old unreformed electoral system first had to be replaced by a new structure that more fairly represented public opinion. The laws that facilitated the change received far more enthusiastic backing from Whigs than Tories. Similarly, the universities were opened up to Dissenters, thanks to the actions of various Liberal ministries. Through the efforts of Whigs or Liberals, the more strictly religious disabilities suffered by those who rejected the state Church were also diminished. Thus, Melbourne's administration conferred legal recognition upon marriages solemnized by non-Anglican religious rites. The Whigs and Liberals also granted relief to Nonconformists who had been obliged to contribute financially to the maintenance of the parish church.

By the beginning of the period which we are studying, the Nonconformist campaign had largely accomplished its objectives: Dissent no longer constituted a serious legal or

[31] Leslie Lipson, "The Two-Party System in British Politics," *American Political Science Review* 47 (June 1953), 353; George M. Trevelyan, *An Autobiography and Other Essays* (London: Longmans, Green, 1949), pp. 197–198.

[32] The details can be found in George M. Trevelyan, *History of England*, vol. III (Garden City, New York: Doubleday-Anchor, 1953), and David Thomson, *England in the Nineteenth Century* (Harmondsworth, Middlesex: Penguin, 1950).

political handicap.[33] Abandoning their defensive posture, Nonconformists moved into the attack on three major fronts—establishment, education, and entertainment. On each of these problems, the Nonconformists pressed their claims through the agency of the Liberal party and were resisted by a Conservative party which generally followed policies favored by the Church of England.

Under Gladstone's leadership in 1869, the Liberal Government had succeeded in disestablishing the Church of England in Ireland. The "unauthorized program" issued by radicals in 1885 called for similar action in Wales, another part of the United Kingdom where Anglicans clearly stood in a minority. The call for Welsh disestablishment, the policy of the National Liberal Federation since 1887, was incorporated into the Liberal program in 1892 and eventually pushed through the Commons (though not the Lords) by the Liberal Government in 1895. Though the most influential Liberals never called for disestablishment in England, where the Church could realistically be regarded as a "national" institution, the Conservatives were quick to argue that a Liberal victory would bring in its wake "disestablishment of the Church, godless education [and] Atheism."[34]

This issue played a particularly large role in the general election of 1885.[35] The Primrose League, Lord Randolph Churchill's ambitious attempt to revive Tory democracy based on traditional values, was especially active in warning Anglicans of the threat the Liberals posed to their church. According to one Conservative speaker, "the result of the forthcoming election would to a great extent foreshadow whether religion is hereafter to form a part of the statecraft of this realm."[36] This theme was continued throughout the

---

[33] T. Bennett, *Laws Against Nonconformity* (Grimsby: Roberts and Jackson, 1913).

[34] *Evening Express and Star* (Wolverhampton), November 17, 1885, p. 2.

[35] Alan Simon, "Church Disestablishment as a Factor in the General Election of 1885," *Historical Journal* 18 (December 1975), 791–820.

[36] *Reading Mercury*, November 7, 1885, p. 7.

entire period. During the 1906 campaign in Wolverhampton, Conservatives circulated phony placards urging votes for the opposition candidate on the grounds of disestablishment.[37] The Conservative canvassers in Reading allegedly spread rumors that the Liberals intended to demolish the parish church.[38] In the elections of 1910, Anglicans in Norwich were reminded by the diocese that the preservation of their religion was contingent upon the retention of the House of Lords.[39] Commentators in these cities and elsewhere thought that such claims may have been responsible for Conservative victories in various general elections.[40]

The parties were also ranged on different sides of the controversy about the control of elementary education.[41] Throughout the period, the education question was debated almost solely in religious terms, as if the only question was "to what extent religion should be taught in the schools, and whether it should be taught, putting the matter bluntly, by one set of bigots or another.[42] After considerable hesitation, Nonconformists had eventually come to terms with Forster's Education Act of 1870. The act created a system

[37] *Express and Star* (Wolverhampton), January 11, 1906, p. 2.

[38] *Reading Observer*, July 13, 1895, p. 5; September 15, 1900, p. 5; and January 13, 1906, p. 8.

[39] *Norwich Diocesan Gazette* 16 (January 1910), 4–5.

[40] Edith H. Fowler, *The Life of Henry Hartley Fowler, First Viscount Wolverhampton* (London: Hutchinson, 1912), p. 551.

[41] The debate on education is covered in Marjorie Cruickshank, *Church and State in English Education* (New York: St. Martin's, 1963); Stephen G. Platten, "The Conflict Over the Control of Elementary Education, 1870–1902, and Its Effect Upon the Life and Influence of the Church," *British Journal of Educational Studies* 33 (October 1975), 276–302; Alan Rogers, "Churches and Children–A Study in the Controversy over the 1902 Education Act," *British Journal of Educational Studies* (November 1959), 29–51; Benjamin Sacks, *The Religious Issue in the State Schools of England and Wales, 1902–1914* (Albuquerque: University of New Mexico Press, 1965).

[42] J. M. Kennedy, *Tory Democracy* (London: Stephen Swift, 1911), p. 200. At about the same time, Ramsay MacDonald referred to "the simple-minded condition of the average Member of Parliament when anything outside teetotalism or religious education is discussed." See his editorial in *Socialist Review* 1 (1908), 321.

of locally financed nondenominational primary schools, a system which supplemented but did not replace the system of central government grants to the "voluntary" schools maintained by religious groups. In practice, the Nonconformists turned their schools over to public control and concentrated their efforts on making the new School Board system irresistibly attractive. Using the Liberal election machinery, Nonconformists attempted to pack the elective school boards with supporters of the nondenominational system, a practice Anglicans resisted under Conservative leadership.[43] This issue came to a head in 1902 when the Conservative Government passed a new Education Act. To the horror of Nonconformists, the act put all elementary education under a common public authority and, much worse, financed both nondenominational and church-affiliated schools from local taxation. This blatant attempt to put the Church "on the rates" was a major factor in reuniting the Liberals after their bitter divisions over the Boer War.[44]

The question of entertainment, particularly the problem of alcohol, had also assumed the dimensions of a religiously based party issue. To the Nonconformist Conscience, alcohol was a social poison which, in the picturesque rhetoric of John Burns, "pollutes whatever it touches . . . enervates what it does not enslave . . . destroys slowly that which it does not degrade quickly."[45] Convinced that liquor was the major social problem, the Nonconformists pressed upon the Liberals a variety of schemes designed to induce a cer-

[43] Ensor, *England*, p. 146; Bryan Keith-Lucas, *The English Local Government Franchise* (Oxford: Basil Blackwell, 1952), p. 215.

[44] Ivor Bulmer-Thomas, *The Growth of the British Party System* (London: John Baker, 1965), 1, 161; Blewett, *Peers, Parties and People*, p. 27. For interesting information on the extent of electoral mobilization associated with the Education Act, see Michael Craton and H. W. McCready, *The Great Liberal Revival, 1903–1906* (London: Hansard Society for Parliamentary Government, 1966), p. 4.

[45] John Burns, *Labour and Drink* (London: Lees and Roper Trustees, 1904), p. 1.

tain degree of temperance through the law.[46] The party was variously harnessed to policies for Sunday closing of pubs, restrictions on licensing hours, the right of local option to deny new liquor licenses and withdrawal of liquor at public functions. The Conservatives, as befitted a party receiving substantial financial support from brewing interests, were associated with the traditional Anglican toleration for drink. This association was captured in an anecdote told by a former Conservative MP:

When I fought my first election as a Labour candidate in 1935 a woman said to me, "Call yourself a Socialist? Why you drink and go to Church, you're nothing but a Tory!" Thirteen years passed before I felt obliged to admit that my Yorkshire interlocutor was right and that I was "nobbut" a Tory. I crossed the floor of the House of Commons, and after a short period without party label, sat in the remainder of the Parliament as a Conservative."[47]

Needless to emphasize, the Liberals were not charmed by the "unholy alliance" of "Parsons and Publicans."

The tension between Nonconformists and Anglicans, manifested in conflict between Liberal and Conservative parties, probably reached a peak in the general elections of 1910.[48] For the Nonconformists, the Liberal assault on the House of Lords (also known as "The Beerage") marked an opportunity to pay back an institution that had persistently obstructed the removal of Nonconformist disabilities and prevented the passage of the social legislation they favored. Hence, militant Nonconformity was mobilized as if the fight against the Lords was the opening battle in a renewal of the English Civil War.[49]

---

[46] D. A. Hamer, *The Politics of Electoral Pressure* (Brighton: Harvester Press, 1977); David M. Fahey, "The Politics of Drink: Pressure Groups and the British Liberal Party, 1883–1908," *Social Science* 54 (1979), 76–85.

[47] Ivor Bulmer-Thomas, *The Party System in Great Britain* (London: Phoenix House, 1953), p. vi, n. 1.

[48] Kinnear, *British Voter*, p. 34.

[49] Blewett, *Peers, Parties and People*, pp. 343–349.

TESTING THE RELIGIOUS INTERPRETATION

No doubt because the impressionistic evidence has pointed so overwhelmingly to the importance of the religious factor, remarkably little has been done in the way of systematic analysis of denominational influences on voting behavior. Most scholars have inferred the existence of denominational forces from illustrative data. Thus, from an association between the party label of Members of Parliament and attendance at voluntary schools by county, Bealey and Pelling asserted that religious loyalties probably exceeded class and industrial factors as influences on the vote.[50] Leys, Moore, and Arnstein noted that petitions sent to Parliament and resolutions passed by constituency organizations dealt primarily with religious topics rather than with questions of distributive justice.[51] Blewett's conclusions about the religious factor in 1910 rest heavily upon his analysis of the denominational affiliation of parliamentary candidates, a mode of analysis also favored by Koss.[52] A number of more qualitatively oriented studies, particularly of Lancashire, have also emphasized the primacy of religion as the basis for electoral coalitions.[53]

Of the two studies which test the religious factor directly and systematically, the most important is contained in the landmark survey study of the British electorate, *Political Change in Britain*.[54] In their chapter on the evolution of voter alignments, Butler and Stokes emphasized the im-

[50] Frank Bealey and Henry Pelling, *Labour and Politics, 1900–1906*, pp. 2–6. To judge by his later work cited in Chapter 2, Pelling changed his mind about this.

[51] Walter Arnstein, "The Religious Issue in Mid-Victorian Politics: A Note on a Neglected Source," *Albion* 6 (1974), 134–143; Colin Leys, "Petitioning in the 19th and 20th Centuries," *Political Studies* 2 (February 1955), 59–60; Robert Moore, *Pit-men, Preachers and Politics*, p. 159.

[52] Blewett, *Peers, Parties and People*, pp. 229–233; Koss, *Nonconformity*, pp. 227–236.

[53] A. H. Birch, *Small Town Politics*, pp. 21–22, 176–177; David A. Roberts, "Religion and Politics in Liverpool Since 1900" (M.Sc. thesis, University of London, 1965).

[54] Butler and Stokes, *Political Change*, ch. 7.

portance of denominational influences before the First World War:

> . . . it is hardly too strong to say that British politics, which had revolved so overwhelmingly around religion in the 17th century, were still largely rooted in religion in the 19th century. The Conservatives were accepted as the Anglican and High Church Party, while the Liberals were the spokesmen of disestablishment and dissent. The Conservatives were, moreover, the party of Ulster and the Protestant ascendancy in Ireland, and the sectarian element in the Irish struggle reinforced the imprint of religion on British politics.[55]

It was not until the bulk of the industrial working class entered the electorate in 1918, they argue later, that class differences became the main line of mass political conflict in Britain. To support this argument, the authors presented data from their 1963 sample survey of the British electorate. All respondents were classified by partisan self-image, social class, religious preference, and age. Within each age cohort (a group of voters entering the electorate at roughly the same time), the members of the sample were cross-classified by party preference and social class, with a control for religious affiliation. The table most relevant to the argument is reprinted here as Table 3.1.

From the data in the table, which show the partisan preference of Anglicans and Nonconformists who were old enough to vote before 1918, we can draw two important

TABLE 3.1. Reproduction of Table 6.6, *Political Change in Britain* "Partisan Self-Image by Class and Religion Within Pre-1918 Cohort"

	Church of England		Nonconformist	
	Middle Class	Working Class	Middle Class	Working Class
Conservative	82%	50%	46%	19%
Other	18%	50%	54%	81%

SOURCE: David Butler and Donald Stokes, *Political Change in Britain*, p. 130. (© 1976 by St. Martin's Press, Inc. and reprinted by permission.)

[55] *Ibid.*, p. 155.

conclusions. If class had been the dominant factor determining partisanship before 1918, there would have been little difference in the distribution of party loyalties for the two religious groups after the removal of class effects. Manifestly, this was not the case. Though class tendencies were evident, considerably more cohesion prevailed among religious denominations than classes. As expected from the traditional historical literature on the period, a majority of Anglicans from both classes identified with the Conservative party, and a Liberal or Labour majority existed among both middle and working-class Nonconformists. This evidence suggests that religious agreement indeed overrode class conflict in electoral behavior. By comparing the patterns evident in Table 3.1 with similar results for subsequent age cohorts, Butler and Stokes also demonstrated that the pre-1918 cohort was apparently the last electoral generation for whom religious influences were paramount.[56] In each subsequent cohort, the class factor increasingly differentiated the partisanship of coreligionists. Though it never entirely disappeared, religious affiliation clearly lost primacy as an electoral factor. Confirming the predictions based on the traditional interpretation of British politics under the Third Reform Act, these findings pose a major challenge to the class interpretation discussed in Chapter 2.

There is, however, a problem with the argument based on the Butler-Stokes data set. It stems largely from a certain confusion of purpose in Chapter 6 of *Political Change in Britain*. Butler and Stokes never seem certain if the evidence they present should be cited to demonstrate the legacy of nonclass influences on modern (1963) voting behavior or, as they seem to suggest at the outset of the chapter, to characterize the electorate as it behaved before 1918. If the data are to be used for the second purpose, which would make them more useful for our analysis, two features of

[56] *Ibid.*, pp. 160–166.

the analysis require revision. First, the dependent variable presented in Table 3.1, the respondent's party image in 1963, does not necessarily represent his political allegiance before 1918. Fortunately, the survey inquired if the interviewee had ever preferred another party and, if so, asked for particulars.[57] The variable based on first-remembered partisanship is better for characterizing the political loyalties of the cohort as they were distributed before 1918. Second, the pre-1918 cohort appearing in Table 3.1 included women, who of course were not enfranchised until 1918. To make the cohort more representative of the pre-1918 electorate, the female respondents should be dropped from the analysis. Because women are somewhat more likely than men to vote according to their religious identity, their exclusion is all the more important.[58]

Table 3.2 presents data on the relationship between class, religion, and first party preference for male respondents in the pre-1918 cohort.[59] All the variables have been coded

TABLE 3.2. Relationship Between Class and First Party Preference, Controlling for Religion, Male Respondents Only, Within Pre-1918 Cohort

	Church of England		Nonconformist	
	Middle Class	Working Class	Middle Class	Working Class
Conservative	75% (18)	34% (17)	58% (7)	9% (1)
Other	25% (6)	66% (33)	42% (5)	91% (10)

SOURCE: Author's analysis of data set 7250, ICPSR.

[57] This variable is VAR0490 in the data set supplied by the Inter-University Consortium for Political and Social Research. See *Study of Political Change in Britain, 1963–1970* (Ann Arbor: ICPSR, 1972), 1, 201.

[58] Seymour Martin Lipset, *Political Man*, pp. 275–278.

[59] This analysis uses ICPSR Data Set 7250 which is documented by the volume cited in note 57. The data were first pruned to the 2,009 respondents interviewed in 1963 by invoking VAR010 as a filter. The four relevant variables were coded exactly as described in the relevant sections of Butler and Stokes:

First   VAR0490   1—Conservative; 2, 3—Liberal, La-
partisanship   bour; 4, 5, 8, 9, 0—Missing

in the manner described by Butler and Stokes for their cross-tabulation in Table 3.1. Despite the small number of cases available for inspection, the figures unambiguously contradict the religious interpretation of the pre-1918 party system. Though religious loyalties do exercise some influence, the paramount line of political division clearly runs between social classes. The middle-class respondents, whatever their religion, mainly identified with the Conservative party, unlike the working-class voters in both religious groups who reported anti-Conservative majorities. If the figures in Table 3.2 can be taken as an accurate estimate of the sentiments of the pre-1918 electorate, it appears that the class alignment dates from well before the First World War.

But can the pre-1918 respondents be taken as representative of the pre-1918 electorate? For reasons which have nothing whatsoever to do with measurement errors attributable to faulty memory, the answer is probably no. The elderly voters surveyed for the British election study in 1963 were young men or women before World War I, relatively inexperienced electors who were not yet frozen into durable political identities by years of reinforcing behavior. Voters just entering the electorate are notoriously susceptible to new bases of partisan alignment and form a most unreliable benchmark from which to generalize to the larger population.[60] Hence, the data in Tables 3.1 and 3.2 cannot really provide any basis for evaluating religious factors before 1918. We still await a definitive analysis of the

Religion	VAR0920	1—Anglican; 3, 4, 5—Nonconformist; 2, 6, 7, 8, 9, 0—Missing
Class	VAR0979	1, 2, 3—Middle; 4, 5, 6—Working; 9, 0—Missing
Cohort	VAR1208	1—Pre-1918; 2, 3, 4, 9, 0—Missing

The data utilized in this publication were made available by the Inter-University Consortium for Political and Social Research. Neither Butler and Stokes nor the Consortium bears any responsibility for the analyses or interpretations presented here.

[60] T. Allen Lambert, "Generations and Change: Toward a Theory of Generations as a Force in Historical Process," *Youth and Society* 4 (September 1972), 21–46.

relative importance of class and religious factors during the period, an analysis which will have to use ecological techniques.

The second piece of evidence relevant to the debate was intended by the author as suggestive rather than definitive and must be evaluated in that spirit. In an essay reviewing several works of historical voting behavior, T. J. Nossiter showed that evidence presented in Michael Kinnear's *The British Voter* belied Kinnear's own assertion about the importance of the religious variable in the general elections of 1910.[61] Using Kinnear's data on the class composition of constituencies (derived from the 1921 census) and the membership of Nonconformist circuits in 1922 (collected from religious yearbooks), Nossiter regressed the Conservative vote in 1910 on the class and religious measures in fifty-four constituencies with constant boundaries over the period. Finding that both class and Nonconformity were positively related to the Conservative share of the vote, he concluded that "there is something seriously wrong with traditional explanations of religion and voting behavior at this time."[62]

Aside from the dangers in using post-1918 data to characterize prewar election districts, the most serious drawback to this analysis—and the most probable cause of the surprising finding—is the nature of Kinnear's religious data. As Miller has demonstrated, the number of Nonconformists in an area reflected both *sectarianism*, the aspect of religion in which Kinnear was interested, and a more generalized *religiosity* or adherence to the organized forms of religion.[63] Because of this dual property, the measure assumed high values in middle class areas with strong church life and was in fact positively correlated with the number of Anglican clergy per capita in 1931. The positive rela-

[61] T. J. Nossiter, "Recent Work on English Elections, 1832–1935," pp. 525–528.

[62] *Ibid.*, p. 528.

[63] Miller, *Electoral Dynamics*, pp. 112–113.

tionship which Nossiter observed between Nonconformity and 1910 Conservatism was probably due more to this religiosity effect than to alleged Conservative sympathies among Nonconformists. Indeed, Miller's data, showing the persistence of anti-Conservative leanings among Nonconformists in the interwar period even after controls for class effects, suggest that Nossiter's findings are a spurious function of the religiosity effect inherent in Kinnear's data.[64] So rather than closing the debate, the evidence presented by Nossiter raises a number of new issues.

SUMMARY

In the previous chapter, the case for class politics was adjudged "not proven." The same verdict should be applied to the religious interpretation that finds such a prominent place in much of the historical literature. The impressionistic evidence suggests a strong religious influence on voting but one that has so far not been confirmed nor denied by systematic analysis of electoral data. The next chapter considers some of the obstacles to an ecological analysis of British elections before World War I and discusses a strategy for overcoming them.

[64] William L. Miller and Gillian Raab, "The Religious Alignment at English Elections Between 1918 and 1970," pp. 227–251.

CHAPTER 4

The Methods of Analysis

To anyone familiar with modern techniques of electoral research and unfamiliar with British social and electoral data, it may seem incredible that scholars should resort to the circuitous methods of analysis described in preceding chapters. When the dispute over the electoral import of class and religion has an empirical basis, the obvious solution is a multivariate analysis of voting patterns. To solve similar disputes about voting behavior in other countries, scholars have used census data to determine the social composition of electoral districts and examined the spatial relationship between class and religious variables and the partisan distribution of the vote.[1] The predictive capacity of these variables is then taken as an indication of the importance of the cleavage base associated with each measure.

Because of a host of measurement problems, this procedure has not been applied frequently to the British context. In fact, the leading student of British voting patterns, so moved by the number of obstacles to ecological analysis, once doubted even the possibility of substantial progress in the field of historical psephology:

Students of . . . political ecology are particularly handicapped in Britain. Work of the sort done by Professors Siegfried and Goguel in France and by Professor Gosnell and Mr. Lubell in the United States has been impossible. . . . Therefore virtually nothing has been done to use official election returns to answer the first question about voting, "Who votes how?"[2]

[1] Duncan MacRae, "Religious and Socioeconomic Factors in the French Vote," *American Journal of Sociology* 64 (November 1958), 290–298.
[2] David Butler, "The Study of Political Behavior in Britain," in *Essays*

73

This verdict seems to have been decisive; except for the London studies cited above and Blewett's eclectic analysis, the historical study of British elections relied largely on nonsystematic modes of inquiry.

Thanks however to technical developments in the ecological analysis of voting behavior, the obstacles that once deterred researchers no longer seem so formidable. Utilization of these new techniques has made it possible to conduct a systematic quantitative analysis of electoral behavior under the Third Reform Act, an analysis that may help to resolve some of the controversies reviewed in Chapters 2 and 3. This chapter recounts the problems to be overcome and provides examples of the application of ecological techniques to data from the period of interest.

THE PROBLEM OF ECOLOGICAL ANALYSIS

Ecological analysis is essentially an attempt to relate behavior to the characteristics of the environment. It differs from most modern electoral research in the use of geographical areas rather than individuals as the units of analysis. In the more conventional methodology of survey research, a representative sample of electors is subjected to interviews that probe political attitudes and social characteristics. The relationships observed among the variables for the respondents are assumed to apply, within certain statistical limits, to the broader population from which the sample was drawn. In situations where individual-level data are unavailable, scholars have developed methods to explore the kinds of questions addressed by survey research with data collected at the level of election districts. By studying spatial relationships between social and political variables, researchers can draw conclusions about the social basis of party support. Though the rules for inference are subtle, ecological analysis often provides the only oppor-

on the Behavioral Study of Politics, ed. Austin Ranney (Urbana: University of Illinois Press, 1962), p. 211.

tunity for systematic analysis of past elections.[3] In a way, ecological analysis makes it possible to converse with the dead.

Once regarded as a second-best kind of approach, clearly inferior to modes of analysis based on individual-level data, ecological analysis has recently come into its own. One major source of its "rehabilitation" has been the discovery that environmental factors often compete equally with or even outweigh individual characteristics as determinants of behavior. If behavior is structured by the environment, it clearly makes sense to adopt as a primary level of analysis the geographical area that constitutes the environment. The renewed interest in ecological analysis also stems from an increased understanding of ecological techniques. Statistical problems of inference that once seemed insuperable have been shown to be less limiting than once was thought. Armed with richer theories of human behavior and better understanding of statistical techniques, scholars have increasingly turned to ecological analysis for a better understanding of past elections.

In its most basic form, the ecological analysis of elections requires only the existence of social and political data of reasonable quality for common areal units. If the analysis is to assume a historical dimension, the unit boundaries should be relatively constant over time and the variables available continuously for the time-span of the study. On almost each of these requirements, the British electoral system posed formidable obstacles. Indeed, if they had wanted to design an electoral system for the express pur-

[3] A useful introduction to the subject is in P. J. Taylor and R. J. Johnston, *Geography of Elections* (Harmondsworth, Middlesex: Penguin Books, 1979), pp. 78–92. For more complex treatment, see Lawrence H. Boyd, Jr. and Gudmund R. Iversen, *Contextual Analysis: Concepts and Statistical Techniques* (Belmont, Ca.: Wadsworth, 1979); Dogan and Rokkan, *Social Ecology*; and Laura Irwin Langbein and Allan J. Lichtman, *Ecological Inference*, Sage University Paper Series on Quantitative Applications in the Social Sciences, no. 07-001 (Beverly Hills, Calif.: Sage Publications, 1976).

pose of frustrating social analysis, the persons responsible for the conduct of elections could not have improved much on the structure and conventions in force in Britain before World War I.

Departing from the practice common in most advanced societies, the British system of government was not based on common political and administrative boundaries. Motivated by a laudable desire to guard the secrecy of the ballot—a wise precaution in the days when "influence" still prevented complete independence in the voting booth—British electoral law forbade the report of election returns at any level below the parliamentary constituency. Democracy's gain was a loss for empirical social research. Because the parliamentary constituency was not an administrative unit nor, before 1918, invariably based on smaller administrative units, the information available from the decennial census was not presented for the same areal units that supplied political data. The bulk of census data was usually reported instead for a confusing welter of areas—counties, boroughs, poor law unions, urban sanitary districts, parishes, etc.—which frequently subsumed and often ignored altogether the boundaries of parliamentary constituencies.[4] Although the situation improved after World War I, it was not until the publication of sample census data for constituencies in 1966 that researchers were provided with detailed social data for politically meaningful units. From the outset, then, historically oriented researchers have been handicapped by the provision of census data for one set of districts and political data for others.

Beyond the problem of boundaries, the census data available for Britain do not seem to meet fully the needs of historical election analysis. Nowhere have census schedules been composed primarily to enable social scientists to test their hypotheses, but the British census seems even less helpful than most. In many countries, the census author-

[4] Vivian D. Lipman, *Local Government Areas, 1834–1945* (1949; reprint ed., Westport, Conn.: Greenwood Press, 1976).

ities inquired periodically about the religious affiliation of the population, and the churches supplied a variety of material on religious practices in the political units. After the furor generated by one attempt to conduct a census of worship in 1851, successive British governments have avoided making official inquiries into the religious propensities of their citizenry.[5] The less direct measures of religious preference collected by the government and private sources were rarely aggregated at the level of parliamentary constituencies. Even if such measures could be matched to constituencies, the danger remains that most indicators of denominational strength confuse sectarianism with religiosity, a situation likely to confound interpretations of religious and class effects on voting.

The possibility of misleading ecological correlations due to the class-based distribution of religious institutions is exacerbated considerably by the relatively poor quality of class data in the census volumes. The most logical source of such information, data on occupations, did not always distinguish clearly between industrial sector and occupational status. For example, it is not easy to distinguish in the pre-1911 censuses between managerial and manual workers in the steel industry, yet dividing lines of status within industry are commonly regarded as having major political relevance. The imprecise coding schemes in force before 1911 have prompted at least one leading authority on historical demography to express his opinion that the areal data published in the printed census volumes cannot be used with any confidence to determine the class structure of a community.[6]

Even if the researcher manages to overcome the obstacles due to boundaries and the quality of census data, another problem remains to which Butler himself has drawn atten-

[5] M. Drake, "The Census, 1801–1891," pp. 15–19.
[6] W. A. Armstrong, "The Use of Information About Occupation," in *Nineteenth Century Society*, ed. E. A. Wrigley (London: Cambridge University Press, 1972), p. 214.

tion—the validity of election returns as a measure of public opinion.[7] In double-member constituencies where each elector has two votes, the possibility of ticket splitting complicates a straightforward interpretation of the aggregate results. More seriously, because of several anomalous features in British election law, it is necessary to distinguish between the resident population of a constituency and the authorized electorate. Until the abolition of plural voting in 1948, the law authorized the vote on grounds of both occupation and property ownership. An individual was entitled to a vote in a constituency where he did not reside if he owned a specified amount of property in the district. Though not counted as part of the constituency population in the residentially based census, he was nevertheless part of the voting population. This tendency toward lack of correspondence between census population and electorate was further accentuated by restrictive franchise laws and the inequitable system of voter registration which effectively debarred a large number of working-class males.[8] To the extent that the social composition of a constituency was unrelated to the registered electorate, it is possible to attribute fallaciously voter behavior to the social groups who lived within the district but did not vote.

Little wonder that in the face of these serious obstacles few scholars had braved the historical analysis of British elections.[9] The logjam has finally been broken by an imaginative project on post-1918 British electoral behavior.[10] The techniques developed in that study are generally ap-

[7] David Butler and James Cornford, "United Kingdom," pp. 330–351.

[8] Neal Blewett, "The Franchise in the United Kingdom," pp. 27–56.

[9] For some earlier (limited) attempts to overcome some of these problems, see A. J. Allen, *The English Voter* (London: English Universities Press, 1964), and Wilma George, "Social Conditions and the Labour Vote in the County Boroughs of England and Wales," *British Journal of Sociology* 2 (September 1951), 255–259.

[10] Miller, *Electoral Dynamics*. Some of the journal articles by Miller and his colleagues provide greater detail and will be cited elsewhere.

plicable to the period before the First World War and therefore deserve careful exposition.

The most serious obstacle to political ecology, the boundary problem, became less severe after the redistribution of seats in 1918. From that point on, parliamentary constituencies usually respected the boundaries of the administrative units of local government—rural districts, urban districts, wards, county boroughs, administrative counties, plus the unique metropolitan boroughs in London. As these were also the units for which census data were reported, it was necessary only to aggregate the administrative units until they corresponded to the constituencies for which political variables were also available. In practice, this usually amounted to apportioning urban constituencies to the boroughs in which they belonged and then collapsing all remaining constituencies into residual counties. The relatively unchanging boundaries of British local government permitted Miller to construct 161 units with constant boundaries from 1918 until 1974.[11] With census data and election returns aggregated at a common unit, it was possible to undertake a comprehensive ecological analysis.

Miller also managed to derive meaningful measures of social composition from the decennial census. To estimate the religious composition of the "surrogate constituencies" described above, he made use of the 1921 and 1931 census data specifying the number of Anglican, Catholic, and "other" clergy for census areas. As he noted, constructing a measure from this type of data is akin to taking the distribution of naval commanders by sector as an estimate of naval strength.[12] The measure can nevertheless be defended on two grounds. First, in a political system in which the interests of the churches bulked large on the public agenda, the

[11] W. L. Miller, Gillian Raab, and R. Britto, "Voting Research and the Population Census, 1918–1971: Surrogate Data for Constituency Analysis," pp. 384–411. This detailed exposition of the matching scheme includes a demonstration that the level of aggregation (constituency, borough, county) does not introduce serious measurement errors.

[12] Miller, *Electoral Dynamics*, p. 110.

clergy frequently served as key agents of mass mobilization. Though adherents of a denomination may not have been distributed in precisely the same proportion as clergy, the latter were probably decisive in converting inchoate religious sentiments into tangible patterns of behavior. One would thus expect the distribution of the clergy to coincide with the strength of denominational influences on the vote. Second, the measure is also defensible on grounds that it avoids confusing sectarianism with religiosity, a weakness which characterizes the measure of church membership developed by Kinnear. A figure based on clergy per capita can differentiate between simple religiosity, which would manifest itself by positive values for the regression coefficients for all denominations, and sectarianism, a quality indicated if the signs on the coefficients differ from one denomination to the next. To capture sectarian effects alone, the clergy of a particular denomination were taken as a proportion of all clergy in the unit. Any distortion caused by the correlation between religiosity and class could be further corrected by entering a class variable as a predictor in the statistical analysis.

The latter type of correction was possible thanks to improvements in coding occupational data in the 1931 and 1951 censuses. Whatever their particular characteristics, the coding schemes in those censuses made fundamental distinctions between those who controlled the workplace—principally owners and managers—and those who were subordinate to them. This distinction corresponds nicely to the concept of social class inherent in one of the major theoretical traditions about class influences on voting. More importantly, the concentration of the "controllers" in a constituency seems to be the dominant force in molding the political outlook of the electorate, both through the force of sheer numbers and indirectly through the mechanism of social contact.[13] These occupational measures were sup-

[13] Miller, "Social Class and Party Choice," pp. 257–284.

plemented with census data tapping the differences in occupational prestige between manual and nonmanual labor and measures of social deprivation appropriate to a status-oriented conception of social differentiation.

Most of the problems of election returns as indicators of public opinion had been eliminated by 1918 or early in the interwar period. To deal with cross-party voting in double-member constituencies, which were finally eliminated in 1945, it was necessary only to consult the detailed breakdown of voting patterns provided in the local press. The plural vote was abolished altogether in 1948, though its significance had diminished well before then by the adoption of a virtually universal system of manhood suffrage. The franchise reforms of 1918 had also brought about a virtual identity between the male population enumerated in the census and the parliamentary electorate, thereby diminishing the prospect of misleading correlations. Thus, after a subtle probing of the available data, Miller was able to obtain for common areal units a time series of parliamentary election results, social class profiles, and estimates of religious propensities. The techniques followed in this prodigious effort offer opportunities to students of historical voting behavior in Britain and elsewhere. They are especially useful in systematically analyzing the contours of electoral behavior during the period of the Third Reform Act.

TECHNIQUES FOR ECOLOGICAL ANALYSIS, 1885–1910

The application of these techniques to the data available for the pre-1918 period has made it possible to examine empirically the influence of social class and religion on voting under the Third Reform Act. Some of the problems that once seemed so formidable turned out upon investigation to constitute only minor irritants, and others were overcome through the direct application of new techniques described above.

Boundary Matching. The boundary problem proved to be a less severe obstacle than expected. The Parliamentary Commissioners who apportioned constituencies in 1884 obviously took great pains not to cross the recognized boundaries of local government. As a result, the constituencies carved out of the major urban centers generally coincided with the boundaries of urban sanitary districts, the major unit of urban local government until 1888 and the unit by which the most valuable census information was still reported in 1891. The remaining nonborough constituencies were allocated within counties and could thus be collapsed to county residual units.

The matching procedure was complicated somewhat by the reorganization of local government in 1888. Under the new system, the major urban centers became county boroughs, units with considerably enhanced powers of self-government. Subsequent censuses reported most of the important social data for these urban counties. The boundaries of the new units did not always follow the outline of the old urban sanitary district—which had generally been the basis for urban constituency apportionment in 1884—but the correspondence was usually close enough to warrant treating the county boroughs as surrogate constituencies. Borough constituencies which could not be amalgamated to an urban unit were included in the county residual.

Taking advantage of this opportunity, the parliamentary constituencies established in 1884 were matched to the administrative boundaries of local government used as areas of enumeration in the census of 1891.[14] The matching pro-

[14] Information on the matching scheme is available on request from the author. The data sets will eventually be made available to other scholars through the Inter-University Consortium for Political and Social Research.

cedure for 1891 produced a total of 115 surrogate constituencies, 50 borough units and 65 county remainders.[15] Full details about the surrogate units which resulted from matching are presented in Table 4.1. As a general rule, borough constituencies were treated as coterminous with local government areas (urban authorities of 50,000 or more) when the population disparity between the two areas did not exceed 5%.[16] The vast majority of surrogate units were well within this tolerance, hardly surprising since parliamentary constituencies were usually based on local government authorities. Bristol was the major conurbation that could not be matched under these rules; among the smaller boroughs, Brighton, Halifax, Leicester, Merthyr Tydfil, Middlesbrough, Oldham, Southampton, Sutherland, and Wolverhampton had to be merged with county constituencies in the county residual.

Of the four population censuses conducted near or within

TABLE 4.1. Units of Analysis Based on 1891 Census Areas

	Number Surrogate Units	Number Constituencies
England		
Counties	41	303
Boroughs	43	132
Wales		
Counties	13	32
Boroughs	1	1
Scotland		
Counties	11	53
Boroughs	6	16
Total	115	537

[15] Considerable difficulties arose in matching for Scottish constituencies. Many of the borough constituencies in Scotland were combinations of cities and towns taken from different counties. This forced the merger of several counties into what might best be regarded as super residual units.

[16] Of course, a net population disparity could camouflage much higher gross differences, but there is no evidence that this was a significant problem. The disparities almost always involved either a constituency that took in some of the surrounding area or one which failed to incorporate some outlying development.

the period, that of 1891 was clearly the optimal choice for matching parliamentary constituencies to enumeration areas. The 1891 census reported data for urban sanitary districts and registration counties, the basic areas used in drawing constituency boundaries in 1884, and so minimized boundary disparities between political and administrative units. More importantly, the 1891 census reported a much more detailed occupational breakdown for urban areas than was available in either 1901 or 1911. The 1891 census was preferred over the 1881 alternative, which also provided detailed urban profiles, because 1891 was closer to the midpoint of the period under study. (The consequences of "aging" data on the analysis will be explored later in the chapter.)

Social Data. The development of common "sociopolitical" units was the first requirement for ecological analysis. The quality of analysis using these units depends to a large extent on the social and electoral data available for them. Obtaining high-quality social data proved much easier than expected.

As will become evident in Chapter 5, the term "religion" denotes a complex phenomenon with a variety of empirical referents. At the individual level, religious commitment can be defined on a continuum ranging from nominal adhesion to more rigorous displays of attachment. The variations in form of religious expression are reflected in the diversity of "religious" statistics at the community level, leaving the analyst with a choice among different indicators of religious behavior.

The census of 1891 enumerated Anglican, Roman Catholic, and "other" clergymen by counties and urban sanitary districts. These data can be used to construct the same per capita clergy distributions that Miller found so valuable in his post-1918 analysis. Though such measures are most useful as a gauge of capacity for mobilization, they are presumably related to the distribution of religious adherents in the population.

Churchgoing is certainly an important manifestation of religious commitment. The religious census of 1851 provided statistics of attendance at worship for the major denominations.[17] The units of enumeration for that census were close enough to the boundaries of our surrogate units to permit common aggregation. Though such data were a half-century old by 1900, there do not appear to have been radical changes in the geographical distribution of denominations in the interim.[18]

The religious controversies in education provide several potential measures of the denominational composition of the surrogate units. The 1851 religious census also collected information on the provision of facilities for elementary day and Sunday instruction. These figures were broken down by denominations, permitting the construction of statistical measures of denominational strength. Similar measures can be constructed from central government data on enrollment in public and denominational elementary schools, published intermittently after 1870.

Another source of religious data, largely overlooked in previous research, is the unofficial survey of local education authorities published in 1903.[19] This project, sponsored by the National Council of Evangelical Free Churches, includes statistics on the religious affiliation of local education committees at the turn of the century. These data can yield additional estimates of denominational strength to supplement the measures gleaned from government statistics.

[17] The religious census of 1851 (*Parliamentary Papers*, 1852–1853, LXXXIX [1690]; *P.P.*, 1854, LIX [1764]) has been reprinted in vols. X and XI in Irish Universities Press, *British Parliamentary Papers, Population* (Shannon: Irish Universities Press, 1970).
[18] Hugh McCleod, "Class, Community and Region: The Religious Geography of Nineteenth-Century England," in *A Sociological Yearbook of Religion in Britain 6*, ed. Michael Hill (London: SCM Press, 1973), p. 45.
[19] Thomas Law, *The Education Act at Work* (London: National Council of Evangelical Free Churches, 1903).

Though it has not dealt with problems of reliability and validity, this quick listing indicates that the measurement of religious sentiment is at least possible. Far from scarcity, the researcher confronts an abundance of data which allows the construction of a variety of religious indicators. Precisely because "religion" constitutes a multifaceted phenomenon, these multiple measures should permit a sensitive analysis of the impact of religion upon political behavior.

The concept of "social class" is no less ambiguous than religion, encompassing differences among individuals based on social prestige, material well-being, workplace autonomy, and other dimensions. There is agreement that occupation is the major determinant of class position in industrial societies. Can the census data on occupations tap stratification patterns within the surrogate units?

As noted above, the census of 1891 provided extremely detailed occupational profiles for the surrogate units. Despite some problems and ambiguities, these data can be used as a guide to the class composition of the units. For example, it is customary in modern research to divide the population into manual and nonmanual segments, equating the former with "the working class." Other scholars insist on making finer gradations within the corps of manual workers, partitioning on the basis of skill levels or workplace conditions. Though the 1891 occupational data are often not as precise as one might wish, they do allow the researcher to make these same distinctions. The coding scheme for the 1891 census is thus sufficient to gauge the class composition of the surrogate constituencies.

Electoral Data. Like the problems of boundary matching and constructing social indicators, the task of assembling useful partisan profiles can be accomplished with the available data. One major problem cited above was the difficulty of interpreting election results in the multimember constituencies. This proved less daunting than imagined thanks to the detailed breakdown of ballots in double-member constituencies provided in Craig's invaluable compendium of election results for 1885 to 1918.[20] The information in these detailed analyses reveals certain recurrent patterns which can be used to apportion voters to party coalitions. As a general rule, the vast majority of electors cast straight-party votes so there is little difficulty in discerning the partisan structure of the aggregate vote for those few units in which no detailed breakdown is available.

Similarly, the problem of fallacious ecological correlations due to class bias in the electoral system seems more formidable in theory than in practice. The number of plural voters has generally been reckoned at about one-half million. Though such voters could tip the scales in a single constituency, especially if it contained a largely nonresidential business district, the effects of the extra votes are minimized by aggregating all the votes in urban constituencies into a single metropolitan district. To address the bias against working-class participation, it might be advisable to include only workers in skilled occupations as part of the industrial workforce, thus depressing the measure of working-class concentration in units with large numbers of semi- and unskilled laborers. It is doubtful if even this correction is absolutely necessary. Even if the measure of industrialization overstates potential working-class electoral power by including workers without the vote, it probably does so to the same degree over all constituencies. In these circumstances, the measure of industrialization will bear a linear relationship to the concentration of working-class voters in the population. As long as the measure reflects a consistent relationship to the distribution of enfranchised workers, it will serve its primary purpose for the statistical analysis.

With these problems proving less serious than expected, the electoral profiles could be constructed for the surrogate units. The constituency electoral data from Craig were ag-

[20] Craig, *Parliamentary Election Results.*

gregated to yield a file corresponding to the surrogate units created under the boundary matching scheme of 1891. The electoral data file was then merged with the file containing social variables from the census of 1891 and other sources. The composite file then contained social variables from 1891 and the complete electoral history of each unit, the sum of votes for parties at each general election of the period.

AN EXAMPLE OF THE TECHNIQUES IN ACTION

The application of these new techniques should permit, for the first time, a systematic appraisal of the character of electoral politics under the Third Reform Act. As a way of illustrating the possibilities of ecological analysis with the techniques described above, this section presents an example of the kinds of electoral analyses which the methods facilitate. No claim is made that the results presented here should be regarded as definitive. The intent is not to settle the disputes described in earlier chapters but only to illustrate the mode of analysis to be employed in the remainder of the book. The provisional results do lead directly to the subject matter of the remaining chapters, the evolution of voter alignments in the late Victorian-Edwardian party system.

Among its other goals, this study is designed to determine the contours of partisanship in pre-1918 Britain, particularly the relative influence of class and religion on voting patterns. With that intent, the appropriate statistical technique is a multivariate regression analysis of election results. The units of analysis for this preliminary presentation will be the 115 surrogate constituencies matched to census districts in 1891. The dependent variable, the sum of Conservative or Liberal Unionist votes taken over the entire cast vote, was not calculated for units which went uncontested in a particular election. For this reason, the number of units included in the analysis varied from only 49 in

1900 to 111 in January 1910. The mean value of the dependent variable ranged from less than 43% in 1906 to approximately 51% in 1900.[21]

To measure the social composition of the units, we have calculated measures from the detailed occupational breakdown provided for counties and boroughs (actually urban sanitary districts) in the census of 1891. The religious measures were constructed by taking the number of Anglican, Catholic, and other (read Nonconformist) clergy as a percentage of the total population. This is not the only available measure of religion but will suffice for purposes of illustration. The class measure is an estimate of the concentration of industrial workers in the occupied population. Specifically, the numerator was calculated by subtracting from the sum of males aged ten and older the total number of males in that age group in nonindustrial classifications (professional, domestic, commercial, agricultural, unoccupied) and those in industrial occupations not directly involved in production or extraction (such as dealers in industrial products, persons engaged in board and lodging, construction workers, etc.). The goal was to produce an estimate of the number of persons working in factories or under factory-like conditions. This sum, taken over the number of gainfully employed workers, ranged from 18% to 78%.

These measures of class and religion were entered into a regression equation to predict the level of Unionist voting. The variables were not entered in a stepwise procedure but in such fashion that the coefficient measures the direct impact of each predictor on the Unionist vote with all other variables held constant. The entries in Table 4.2 are standardized regression coefficients, commonly known as beta

[21] The data from Craig (see n. 20) were supplied to me in machine-readable form by the Social Statistics Laboratory at the University of Strathclyde. The file is described in "Codebook of British Election Results, 1885–1918," mimeographed (University of Strathclyde, n.d.). I have checked and corrected the file and persons interested in obtaining it should contact me for further information.

weights or semistandardized slopes.[22] The coefficients marked by asterisks were at least twice the size of their standard errors, the customary mark of significance in analyses with nonsample data.

The results of the analysis in Table 4.2 generally conform to expectations. The proportion of Anglican clergy bore a positive (but intermittently significant) relationship to Conservative and Liberal Unionist voting in all eight general elections. There was a more consistent and a much stronger *negative* association between the Nonconformist presence and Conservative-Liberal Unionist voting. The Unionist vote also declined with the proportion of industrial workers in the population, a relationship which (excluding the Liberal disasters in 1895 and 1900) grew stronger over the period. Taken in concert, the four predictors of social structure explained from one-fourth to one-half the variation in voting. This power is hardly inconsequential when viewed either

TABLE 4.2. Regression Analysis of Conservative-Unionist General Election Votes, 1885–1910, Matched to 1891 Units

Election	Prop. Anglican Clergy (b)	Prop. "Other" Clergy (b)	Prop. Catholic Clergy (b)	Prop. Industrial Workers (b)	Multiple R^2	N of Cases
1885	.26*	−.41*	.26*	−.17	.30	105
1886	.26	−.44*	.23	−.23	.26	58
1892	.09	−.53*	.16	−.24*	.26	90
1895	.26*	−.54*	.21	−.06	.30	71
1900	.25	−.46*	.41*	−.08	.32	49
1906	.22	−.35*	.10	−.22	.20	98
1910, Jan.	.19*	−.58*	.20*	−.42*	.51	111
1910, Dec.	.21	−.46*	.34*	−.54*	.54	70

* Indicates coefficients significant at .05 level.

[22] Though unstandardized coefficients are generally preferred in ecological analysis, differences in scale make it impossible to compare the relative weight of different variables. For conflicting points of view on this question, see Langbein and Lichtman, *Ecological Inference*, pp. 33–38, and John L. Hammond, "New Approaches to Aggregate Electoral Data," *Journal of Interdisciplinary History* 9 (Winter 1979), 473–492.

against other ecological studies or, for that matter, against survey data.

The only anomaly was the small but consistently positive relationship between Catholicism and Conservative voting. This would have been expected only in 1885, when Catholics in Britain had been urged by their Nationalist leaders to vote Tory.[23] In 1886 and after, the Liberal commitment to Home Rule apparently brought the Catholics solidly into the Liberal coalition. Given what we know about the low rate of Catholic enfranchisement and the dynamics of political life in areas most heavily populated by Catholics, it seems best to interpret this anomaly as a textbook example of fallacious ecological correlations. Catholics did not vote Conservative but their presence inspired an anti-Liberal reaction among working-class Protestants. The regression coefficient should probably be understood as the bonus to Conservatism associated with the anti-Catholic backlash. In terms of ratios, the Conservatives usually gained more from the anti-Catholic reaction than from the direct presence of Anglicanism.

As these suggestive results demonstrate, the data and methods collected for this study can provide important information about British electoral politics under the Third Reform Act. How much confidence can we place in these results? Any statistical analysis of elections is fraught with potential errors due to a variety of technical problems. The most likely source of error for this type of inquiry, the problem of unreliable data, requires a comment.

In a study which examines relationships subject to change over time, it is particularly important to establish that observed relationships are not affected by chance fluctuations in statistical measures. The age of data used to construct the independent variables poses a real threat to the integrity of the findings. Most of the social data were collected in the mid-Victorian period or from the census of 1891. Are

[23] C.H.D. Howard, "The Parnell Manifesto of 1885 and the Schools Question," *English Historical Review* 57 (January 1947), 42–51.

such data relevant to the social composition of areas in 1910? If, for example, the analysis were to reveal a steady decline in the relationship between Nonconformist clergy per capita in 1891 and the Liberal vote in successive general elections, that might be due either to a decline in the political influence of denominationalism or to the inadequacy of 1891 census data in describing the religious geography of 1910.

In principle, the reliability of the 1891 data could be assessed by comparing the relationship between the 1891 social measures and the vote with a similar statistical analysis using measures from the census of 1911. Unfortunately, because of changes in local government boundaries between censuses, no such direct test is possible.[24] The only available alternative is to compare a statistical analysis using the 1891 units and data with a similar analysis in which the parliamentary constituencies are regrouped to correspond to the 1911 census boundaries and the independent variables are abstracted from the 1911 census enumeration.

Though such a comparison sounds much like the direct comparison we desire, it introduces some potential error not due to unreliability. Some difference in results is likely because of the changes in aggregation necessitated by boundary revisions. The analysis will also be affected by changes in the coding and availability of occupational data in the two censuses. The 1891 measure of industrialization was based on the extensive occupational profiles available for each unit. The 1911 measure was abstracted from a much less detailed summary of occupations and one which reflected a somewhat different coding scheme.[25]

---

[24] Boundary changes needed to rationalize local government areas frequently extended boroughs far beyond constituencies originally based on 1884 local government areas. An extension of the county borough of Newcastle on Tyne produced a 20% gross population disparity between the borough and constituency of the same name in 1911. The reorganization of local government in London completely defeats any attempt to create units with constant boundaries from 1885 to 1910.

[25] See Table 15(A) in *Census of England and Wales, 1911*, vol. X-1, p. 386.

Paradoxically, these elements of noncomparability between data sets matched to the 1891 and 1911 census boundaries could make a comparative statistical analysis extremely valuable. If class/party relationships looked quite similar in both data sets despite the three potential sources of difference, that would be a strong argument for the reliability of the 1891 data. It would suggest that variations in the age of the data, in the units of aggregation, and in occupational classification had only a negligible effect on the statistical analysis of voting. Such a finding would greatly enhance confidence in the substantive conclusions of an analysis.

Table 4.3 presents the results of a correlational analysis of class/party relationships for the 1891 and 1911 data sets.[26] In both cases, the dependent variable is the Unionist share of the total vote and the independent variable is the proportion of the male workforce engaged in industrial labor. The religious measures were excluded because they are not available for boroughs in 1911. Besides the date of collection for the social data, the two data sets differ in the boundaries of the surrogate units and the occupational coding schemes.

Happily, the analyses tell a very similar tale about the structure of the vote. The mean correlation between the proportion of industrial workers and the Unionist vote share

TABLE 4.3. Correlation Between Proportion Industrial Workers and Conservative-Unionist Vote Using 1891 and 1911 Units and Data for General Elections, 1885–1910

Units	1885	1886	1892	1895	1900	1906	Jan. 1910	Dec. 1910	M̄
1891	−.27	−.28	−.10	−.06	−.15	−.28	−.32	−.44	−.24
	(93)	(83)	(92)	(89)	(80)	(92)	(93)	(88)	
1911	−.37	−.29	−.08	−.06	−.17	−.26	−.26	−.44	−.24
	(86)	(75)	(85)	(82)	(70)	(85)	(86)	(81)	

Table entries are Pearson correlation coefficients.
Units were excluded only if all constituencies were uncontested.

[26] Because of their special problems of aggregation (see n. 15), the Scottish units were excluded from the analysis.

93

is −0.24 for both sets of data. Like the *magnitude* of the coefficients, the *pattern* of the relationship over time is virtually identical across data sets. Both analyses show a curvilinear pattern with class influences peaking at the ends of the period. These results are all the more encouraging for what they do *not* show. If the age of the data were a major influence on the results, the magnitude of class/party correlations would vary positively with the proximity of the election to the census. In the case of 1891, the correlations ought to decrease as the social data become obsolete. For the other set, we would expect the reverse, a steady increase in the coefficients across time as the elections "converged" on the social data gathered in 1911. Neither trend is apparent. The 1891 occupational data produced the same magnitude of correlation in 1906 as in 1885 or 1886. For the 1911 data set, the two elections most removed in time from the 1911 census had higher class/party correlations than all but one other election.

The minor discrepancies which do emerge probably owe more to boundary or coding differences than to unreliable data. On this evidence, therefore, we can be confident that the findings are not an artifact of the particular census, units, or coding scheme but a reflection of the "real" social forces underlying the vote.

SUMMARY

Recent advances in the methodology of historical election analysis offer considerable promise to students of late-Victorian politics. This chapter has demonstrated how these new techniques can be applied to data for elections from 1885 to 1910, yielding evidence about the contours of voter alignments before the First World War. In applying these techniques, we shall be guided by expectations based in part on a large body of data relating the choice of party to elements of the social structure. The next chapter reviews that literature with an eye toward the mechanisms by which social differences become lines of partisan cleavage.

CHAPTER 5

Voting and Social Structure: Conceptual Problems

The historical debate over the social basis of British electoral coalitions has been conducted largely in isolation from contemporary research on mass political behavior. The scholarly discourse reviewed in Chapters 2 and 3 has emphasized features specific to Britain rather than made use of concepts derived from the study of other political systems. The absence of a conceptual orientation has kept from the debate important theoretical insights that might help resolve some of the issues; it has also meant that scholarly investigations of the British experience have not contributed much to knowledge about the general relationship between voting and social structure. This chapter seeks to integrate the study of British electoral patterns from 1885 to 1910 with the broader concerns of contemporary electoral sociology. By raising conceptual questions about the structure of mass voter alignments, the chapter paves the way for the empirical analysis of British electoral cleavages in Chapter 6.

THE IMPORTANCE OF CONCEPTS

In the research on interparty conflicts in democratic nations, political parties are usually regarded as the institutional expression of structural cleavages in society. Guided by the theoretical formulations of Lipset and Rokkan, students of political sociology have attempted to account for cross-national variations in the social bases of party systems.[1] The logic of this research rests on the assumption that political parties function principally as advocates for the interests of specific constituencies. The analysis of electoral cleavages should reveal which of a series of potential social conflicts are most salient to an electorate.[2]

Though complex societies may be divided internally along any number of axes, Lipset and Rokkan suggest that most party systems are built on four major lines of social conflict, cleavage structures which result from major choice points in the modernization process. The historic struggle for power between churches and the advocates of a secular state left an imprint on modern political systems in the form of electoral conflict based on religious affiliation. Electoral divisions between workers and owners reflected the economic antagonisms first generated by industrialization and the factory system of production. In some nations, party systems still carry the mark of strains associated with the "national" revolutions, the migration of authority from the periphery to the center; if the distribution of ethnic subcultures coincided with the center/periphery split, this territorial dimension may also represent a clash between dominant and subordinate ethnocultural groups. Finally, the process of modernization produced conflicts between rural and urban groups, a sectoral division still affecting the structure of party alignments in some political systems.

As Lipset and Rokkan recognize, there is no guarantee that social conflict along any of these cleavage lines will necessarily be represented in the party system. Before a social cleavage can affect the party system, certain institutional features must be present. Differences in the devel-

[1] Seymour M. Lipset and Stein Rokkan, "Cleavage Structures, Party Systems and Voter Alignments: An Introduction," in *Party Systems and Voter Alignments*, pp. 1–64.

[2] For the most systematic analysis of social conflicts underlying cleavage structures, see Rose and Urwin, "Social Cohesion," pp. 7–67.

opment of these institutional thresholds might account for cross-national variations in the partisan representation of social conflicts. Indeed, Lipset and Rokkan suggest that national differences in the form and sequence of electoral cleavage structures constitute a prime topic for future research on mass voter alignments.

Though considerable attention has been paid to identifying the relevant social cleavages in various nations, scholars have said less about the microlevel mechanisms which account for the role of social factors in electoral decision-making. What forces generate political self-consciousness among persons sharing a common religious identity or membership in the same social class? How do individuals come to select a particular attribute as the basis for defining their political identity? To ask these questions is to raise even more basic questions: What do we mean by concepts such as "social class" or "religion"? What factors account for the precise location of political dividing lines within communities?

These questions have theoretical and empirical importance. Without a clear and unambiguous conceptualization of a particular cleavage, it is impossible to choose intelligently among alternative measures to test the electoral power of the social conflict. As research has repeatedly demonstrated, decisions about concepts will powerfully affect the results of empirical analysis. Drawing the line of demarcation between the middle and working class at a particular juncture represents a statement about the perceived reality of social structure and, as has been amply confirmed in several studies, the location of that line will strongly affect the level of observed class polarization in voting.[3] The same is true for religion; alternative measures of religious com-

---

[3] For Britain, see Michael Kahan, David Butler, and Donald Stokes, "On the Analytical Division of Social Class," *British Journal of Sociology* 17 (June 1966), 122–132; Miller, "Social Class," pp. 257–284. For a comparative perspective, see Carl Stone, "Class and Status Voting in Jamaica," *Social and Economic Studies* 26 (September 1977), 279–294.

mitment are associated with different levels of religious influence on voting.[4] Our task, therefore, is to conduct a review which makes explicit the reasoning about the modes of class and religious effects on voting. Such a review will guide the empirical analysis of British elections for 1885 to 1910 by suggesting what kinds of measures are appropriate indicators of the social forces under investigation.

MODES OF CLASS VOTING

The description of elections as "the expression of the democratic class struggle" reflects the abiding concern of political scientists with class differences in mass voting behavior.[5] Though most often associated with political life in Western Europe and Scandinavia, class voting has been examined in political contexts as diverse as North America, South America, Asia, and the West Indies. From a large and growing body of research, it is evident that the level of class polarization in voting may vary a good deal from one political system to the next and across space and time within a single system.[6] The research further suggests that the electoral impact of class may be diminished by other sources of conflict and by the nature of the political alternatives offered to the electorate.[7] Furthermore, the level of class voting seems to depend in part on the transmission of subjective class consciousness by mediating structures in the voter's personal environment.[8]

The problem of class voting is essentially a problem of

[4] J. M. Bochel and D. T. Denver, "Religion and Voting: A Critical Review and a New Analysis," pp. 205–219.

[5] Dewey Anderson and Percy E. Davidson, *Ballots and the Democratic Class Struggle* (Stanford, Calif.: Stanford University Press, 1943).

[6] The classic study here is Robert Alford, *Party and Society.*

[7] Reeve Vanneman, "U.S. and British Perceptions of Class," *American Journal of Sociology* 85 (January 1980), 769–790.

[8] Charles L. Prysby, "Neighborhood Class Composition and Individual Partisan Choice: A Test with Chilean Data," *Social Science Quarterly* 56 (September 1975), 225–238.

collective action.[9] In societies where ascriptive character-istics do not confer legal advantages, social classes are con-structs and class-based voting is a specific instance of a more general process of group formation.[10] This process re-quires that a set of individuals with something in common, a *quasi-group* in Dahrendorf's phrase, recognizes its collec-tive interest and undertakes concerted action to advance it.[11] In the context of social classes, this process involves the transition from *inequality* to *stratification*, the organiza-tion of society into bounded subcommunities based on eco-nomic criteria.

The giants of social theory were particularly interested in the problem of group formation. Both Marx and Weber, for all their differences, recognized the conditional rela-tionship between inequality and group action and at-tempted to specify the conditions which prompted mem-bers of quasi-groups to act together in pursuit of common objectives.[12] Rather than treat social classes as mere ana-lytical categories designated by a researcher, they insisted that "class" was a meaningful term only when it described a real pattern of social relationships, a point of view which continues to influence many students of society.[13]

The literature of collective action, heavily influenced by

[9] See Kenneth D. Wald, "Stratification and Voting Behavior: Electoral Cleavage in Britain Under the Third Reform Act."

[10] There is a long and venerable tradition of group analysis in political science. For applications to voting, see Philip E. Converse, "Group Influ-ence in Voting Behavior," (Ph.D. thesis, University of Michigan, 1958).

[11] Ralf Dahrendorf, *Class and Class Conflict in Industrial Society* (Stanford, Calif.: Stanford University Press, 1959), p. 179.

[12] Reinhard Bendix, "Inequality and Social Structure: A Comparison of Marx and Weber," *American Sociological Review* 39 (April 1974), 149–161; Lee Benson, "Group Cohesion and Social and Ideological Conflict," *American Behavioral Scientist* 16 (May 1973), 741–767; Bryn Jones, "Max Weber and the Concept of Social Class," *Sociological Review* 23 (November 1975), 729–758.

[13] For a review of the debate between "nominalist" and "realist" views of class, see Dennis Wrong, "Social Inequality Without Stratification," in *Structured Social Inequality*, ed. Celia Heller (New York: Macmillan, 1969), pp. 513–520.

the masters of social thought, is richest in theories about the broad social conditions which spawn social movements and in microlevel research about the traits which dispose individuals to join newly born collective movements of social protest. There is much less research about the crucial middle-level problem of mobilization, the recognition of group status by members of a particular economic aggregate; but there is enough commonality among theorists of collective behavior, group dynamics, social interaction, reference groups, and political mobilization to suggest a framework for the analysis of voting as a form of collective action.[14]

We have identified from these sources an intuitive hierarchy of factors which seem to facilitate group action, a rubric which here includes voting. This hierarchy represents a series of thresholds, a crucible through which a quasi-group must pass before it is likely to emerge as a "real" group with a propensity for collective action. This framework, as befits its patchwork character, is incomplete, lacking, for example, any reference to the many external factors that may interrupt the process of group formation. Nevertheless, the framework still offers a useful starting point for analysis of group formation, particularly class

[14] In constructing the framework, I have been most influenced by Benson, "Group Cohesion"; Oscar Glantz, "Class-Consciousness and Political Solidarity," *American Sociological Review* 23 (August 1958), 375–383; Michael Hechter, "Group Formation and the Cultural Division of Labor," *American Journal of Sociology* 84 (September 1979), 293–318; George C. Homans, *The Human Group* (New York: Harcourt, Brace and Co., 1950); Clark Kerr and Abraham Siegel, "The Inter-Industry Propensity to Strike," in *Industrial Conflict*, ed. Arthur Kornhauser, Robert Dubin, and Arthur M. Ross (New York: McGraw-Hill, 1954), pp. 189–212; Seymour Martin Lipset, Martin Trow, and James Coleman, *Union Democracy* (Garden City, New York: Doubleday-Anchor, 1956); D. Lockwood, "Sources of Variation in Working Class Images of Society," *Sociological Review* 14 (November 1966), 249–267; R. S. Neale, *Class and Ideology in the Nineteenth Century* (London: Routledge and Kegan Paul, 1972); Bertell Ollman, "Toward Class Consciousness Next Time: Marx and the Working Class," in *The Politics and Society Reader*, ed. Ira Katznelson (New York: David McKay, 1974), pp. 305–328; Charles Tilly, *From Mobilization to Revolution* (Reading, Mass.: Addison-Wesley, 1978).

cohesion, in the realm of electoral behavior. Such analysis of how and why people learn to act in common is essential to understanding the varying relevance of social classes to political conflict.

As the first condition of group formation, there must be some minimal recognition of group status by the members, a perception that they share common traits which somehow set them apart from others. This may be nothing more than a feeling by members of the economic aggregate that their position in life is partly determined by membership in the group. Without at least a recognition of social differentiation, no higher form of group awareness or solidarity is likely to emerge.

For group cohesion to develop beyond this point, the next essential element is within-group interaction. The increased familiarity bred by social interaction promotes a higher level of group awareness and reinforces the propensity of members to confine their social interchange within the bounds of the group. Sharp boundaries between groups facilitate within-group interaction. The sharper the boundaries, the more intense the interaction and the more pervasive the influence of the group on the outlook and ideas of its membership. Common life experiences, born of this sustained interaction, may even promote the formation of a world-view so distinctive that the group develops into a subculture, a process that many observers think describes the reality of working-class life in Britain.

Even with a distinctive class subculture, the prospect of concerted class action is conditional because some members may respond to recognition of their common fate by opting out and going it alone. When group boundaries are weak, enough individuals may be inspired to seek individual mobility so that a common group strategy is undermined. But when the boundaries are sharp enough to discourage individual escapes, group members are more likely to perceive that their situation will not change without a pooling of strength, an application of collective will. Therefore the next required step in the process of group formation is a recognition by members of the group that their situation is not likely to be improved or ameliorated by individual action.

The last stage is the development of an organizational capacity, which both reinforces and directs the sense of class awareness. Organizations such as labor unions educate their membership about political options, communicate messages about the importance of concerted action and demonstrate by their very existence the possibilities of effecting change through organizational effort. The membership may be brought to see that their condition is the product of public policy and will change only if public policy is redirected. It follows from the preceding that strong organizations are most likely to emerge endogenously in environments strongly conducive to group formation.

This framework is only suggestive and cannot possibly convey the subtleties of group formation or the many variations in the process, but it still provides a useful way to think about the specific case of group formation in the context of voting. Consider, for example, two men in late nineteenth century Britain. The one, a London dockworker, recently moved to the city from a country village in search of work and opportunity. Lacking skills or any control over the labor market, he is thrown into a daily struggle for survival that pits him against other men in equally desperate straits. He must move constantly in search of work and cannot develop any sustained involvement with a meaningful community. On the other hand, we may consider the coalminer in South Wales who lives in the same house where he was born and works in the mine where his father also labored. The geographical isolation of the mining community means that his social interactions are largely confined to other mining families. He becomes deeply imbedded in a community which continually reaffirms its integration by festivals, customs, habits, etc.[15] These two

[15] John Benson, *British Coalminers in the Nineteenth Century* (New York: Holmes and Meier, 1980).

profiles are extreme cases, overdrawn for the sake of presentation, but they describe some of the variety to be found in working-class existence during the period of our study. There can be little doubt that the condition of the dockworker militated against the development of a group consciousness. There may have been some protean sense of commonality with other dockers but no sustained interaction and no incentives likely to encourage his cooperation with men who were his competitors for scarce labor. Not surprisingly, the history of the London dockers is a story of intermittent outbursts of protest but no sustained organizational effort to change conditions. The prototypical miner, by contrast, lived in an environment strongly conducive to the formation of a collective outlook and communal action in politics, communities which were in the vanguard of the labor movement in Britain and elsewhere.

Utilizing the framework just developed, we may predict the level of class-based voting among several quasi-groups defined by their role in the production process.[16] These overlapping groups, which consist entirely of manual workers, are arranged in order of their predicted level of left-wing voting:

1. unskilled workers
2. manual workers
3. skilled workers
4. industrial workers
5. organized workers

The predicted level of left-wing cohesion, which rises as we go down the list, is based on judgments about the extent to which each group satisfied the conditions of group formation. This intuitive ranking will eventually be confronted with data.

Unskilled workers are frequently treated as a potential

[16] This categorization implies that production-based cleavages are the most potent form of economic conflict. For an alternative view, see Patrick Dunleavy, "The Political Implications of Sectoral Cleavages and the Growth of State Employment: Part I. The Analysis of Production Cleavages," *Political Studies* 28 (September 1980), 364–383.

source of political radicalism on the assumption that their deprived condition will generate a common political strategy aimed at redressing inequality.[17] Based on the framework of group formation, this seems most unlikely. The unskilled laborers constituted a recognized social grouping, the "roughs," but their conditions of life and work militated against the development of any higher level of group consciousness:

> The ever-pressing demands of the stomach, the chronic uncertainty of employment, the ceaseless shifting nature of the casual-labour market, the pitiful struggle of worker against worker at the dock gate, the arbitrary sentence of destitution, and the equally arbitrary cascade of charity provided no focus for any lasting growth of collective loyalty upon which a stable class consciousness could be based. Brought up to treat life with the fatalism of the gambler, the casual poor rejected the philosophy of thrift, self-denial, and self-help preached to them . . . but, by the same token, they rejected qualities, which, for different reasons, were also essential to the strength of the labour movement.[18]

This combination of rootlessness, lack of social integration and dependency, leading to an outlook of resignation and apathy, typifies workers "in various kinds of service occupations, in non- (or rather pre-) industrial jobs, those working in small-scale 'family enterprises,' and in agricultural employment.[19] Rather than respond with a concerted political counterattack, such workers acquiesced and politically proved highly susceptible to antiliberal themes and candidacies. The memoirs of many labor pioneers contain some variant of Keir Hardie's lament that "it is the slum vote which the socialist candidate fears most."[20]

---

[17] Lipset, *Political Man*, p. 239.

[18] Gareth Stedman Jones, *Outcast London* (Harmondsworth, Middlesex: Penguin, 1971), p. 344.

[19] Lockwood, "Sources of Variation in Working Class Images," p. 253.

[20] James Keir Hardie, *From Serfdom to Socialism* (London: George Allen, 1907), p. 26. For similar opinions, see C.F.G. Masterman, "Politics in Transition," *Nineteenth Century* 63 (January 1908), 11–12; W. T. Stead, "The General Election in Great Britain," *American Review of Reviews* 41 (February 1910), 179.

Though skilled workers constituted a heterogeneous sub-set of the working-class population, historians have invested them with a much higher propensity to undertake group action. Such workers often experienced enough residential stability to form tight and durable social networks. Mutual awareness, heightened by constant interaction, bred an active communal life and a highly differentiated organizational structure. Beyond this point, there is considerable disagreement about the direction which this stratum took in politics. Some scholars have referred to an "aristocracy of labour" composed of skilled artisans in the best-paid and most secure trades. This artisan elite, portrayed by some scholars as a self-satisfied, individualistic and complacent group, is said to have exerted an extremely conservative influence on the direction of working-class protest.[21] Yet others maintain that the skilled workers were the vanguard of the working-class, the source of the most dynamic pressure for social change.[22] To a remarkable degree, these conflicting views differ not on what the skilled workers actually *did* but upon whether their activity promoted or retarded revolutionary action. With a relatively inclusive conception of collective action to include voting for reformist parties, we assign the skilled workers a likelihood of collective action greater than the *Lumpenproletariat* but less than other economic formations. The manual workers, a category which includes both the skilled and unskilled, should place somewhere between them in terms of electoral cohesion.

With the industrial workers, we move to a group with much greater likelihood of group-based political behavior. Large-scale factories provided the characteristic methods of production in advanced capitalism. Many observers recognized the potential for social change which these factories represented. The industrial production process segregated the workers both residentially and on the shop floor, thus

---

[21] Eric Hobsbawn, *Labouring Men* (London: Weidenfeld and Nicholson, 1964), pp. 288–289.
[22] Pelling, *Popular Politics*, pp. 56–61.

promoting a high and constant level of worker interaction. Taught the need for cooperation by the very act of production, factory workers developed a high level of communal solidarity. The best description of the process of group formation among them comes not from Marx but from Michels:

> The mechanized large-scale factory operates like a model school of solidarity on the tightly-concentrated working force . . . the eternal close contact of working side by side to which the individuals are exposed in the factory; the ease with which workers get to know each other and talk to each other created by this process (on the way home or in the saloons); these encourage in the worker's soul the growth of a new feeling which is based no longer solely on technological but also on economic solidarity. . . . Thus the modern production process itself embeds in the mentality of the proletarian the seed of that complicated and curious plant designated by the social psychologist as Class Consciousness . . . [23]

The irony, as Marx noted frequently, was that the working class, the key agent in the attack on capitalism, was called into existence by process of capitalist production itself. In some cases, the physical concentration of industry facilitated the development of an entire network of social organizations which encapsulated the workers, enmeshing them in a subculture conducive to the development of an anti-capitalist world-view.[24] That solidarity was also expressed as electoral cohesion on behalf of leftist political parties.

Certain industrial environments were more likely than

[23] Robert Michels, "The Origins of Anti-Capitalistic Mass Spirit," in *Political Sociology*, ed. S. N. Eisenstadt (New York: Basic Books, 1971), pp. 498–499.
[24] Maurice Zeitlin and James Petras, "The Working-Class Vote in Chile: Christian Democracy versus Marxism," *British Journal of Sociology* 21 (March 1970), 21-22; Brian H. Smith and José Luis Rodriguez, "Comparative Working-Class Political Behavior," *American Behavioral Scientist* 18 (September 1974), 73; Robert H. Hill, "Sources of Variation in the Class Consciousness of the British Working Class" (Ph.D. thesis, Brown University, 1978). See also the essays in Martin Bulmer, ed., *Working-Class Images of Society*.

others to generate a strong sense of "working-classness." Environments especially favorable to the development of a common political orientation were often characterized by the presence of strong labor organizations. In the period of this study, the prime candidates for unionization were shipbuilders, miners, textile workers, printers, and carpenters. Most of these trades had in common a pattern of production which brought workers together in homogeneous communities and cut them off from influences operating outside the community. This pattern, an even purer form of the syndrome which Michels associated generally with industrialization, has been described as an "occupational community."[25] In such communities, Lockwood notes, the value of mutual assistance is constantly invoked to sustain group cohesion:

... communal sociability has a ritualistic quality, creating a high moral density and reinforcing sentiments of belongingness to a work-dominated collectivity. The isolated and endogamous nature of the community, its predominantly one-class population, and low rates of geographical and social mobility all tend to make it an inward-looking society and to accentuate the sense of cohesion that springs from shared work experiences.[26]

The high propensity for collective action in such communities, indicated by a ready embrace of trade unionism, should also promote an impressive degree of electoral solidarity.

Most existing studies on class-voting under the Third Reform Act have utilized measures of material comfort which are probably most sensitive to the concentration of unskilled workers and the poor. The class measures based on social indicators, such as Pelling's female domestic ratio and Wald's wealth index, are useful for characterizing the level of poverty or material comfort within geographical

---

[25] Robert Blauner, "Work Satisfaction and Industrial Trends in Modern Society," in *Labor and Trade Unionism*, ed. Walter Galenson and Seymour Martin Lipset (New York: John Wiley, 1960), pp. 339–360.
[26] Lockwood, "Sources of Variation in Working Class Images," p. 251.

areas but do not seem capable of distinguishing more precisely among subgroups within the working class. Fortunately, the occupational groups which we have been discussing in this chapter can be detected in the census data, and their concentration can be calculated for the surrogate units created by matching census units to parliamentary constituencies. The ecological analysis of relationships between party support in elections and occupational structure should provide a better understanding of the role of class differences in voting before the First World War.

RELIGION AND VOTING

The need for precise conceptualization of the religious factor was demonstrated convincingly in Bochel and Denver's critical analysis of British research on religion and voting. Their own examination of denominational voting, unusually precise and rigorous in measuring religious commitment, disclosed a "striking relationship between denomination and electoral behavior," a connection stronger than expected on the basis of conventional wisdom about political life in modern Britain. If a careful delineation of the religious factor revealed such strong denominational effects on voting in a supposedly secular age, similar care in conceptualization and measurement might reveal even stronger behavioral consequences for religion in the late Victorian-Edwardian era, an age for which religious cleavage was claimed to be "the single most important factor in structuring the vote."[27]

At first glance, it may seem easier to measure religious forces than social classes. Religious groups, as that term is usually interpreted, are organized formally as voluntary organizations. An individual may "opt out" of religious groups whereas it is not really possible to avoid the class

[27] John T. S. Madeley, "Protestantism and the Politics of Protest," *Acts, 15th International Conference on Sociology of Religion* (Lille, France: C.I.S.R., 1979), p. 187.

structure. Yet this ease of delineation is only apparent because "religion" encompasses both more and less than formally organized churches. Research on the phenomenon of confessional voting suggests that religion, broadly conceived, may exert an impact through four channels, all of which can be measured with the available data for Britain. We consider here the nature of each channel.

Religion as Interest Group. In much of the relevant literature, religions have been treated as interest groups, organized institutions which enter politics in order to further or oppose policies which might affect their standing as corporate bodies or masses of individuals. The denominations form attachments to political parties which, for reasons of sympathy and expedience, champion their interests in the political arena. The party may sponsor legislation to protect the status of an established church or intervene to prevent discrimination against a small sect.

In countries with a single dividing line between believers and secularists, the dominant religion is often represented by a clerical party.[28] In their attempt to preserve religious prerogatives from state encroachment, parties of this type often come into direct conflict with socialist movements. Religious-based parties also function in some settings as movements of defense for minority religions. Following the historical example of the *Zentrum* in pre-Hitler Germany or Muslim parties in India, these parties may seek to protect persons outside the state church by advocating separation of church and state. Such a role has also been played by liberal parties which enjoy support from the nonreligious or voters belonging to disfavored denominations.[29] The spectrum of religious parties also includes a type organized

[28] See Michael P. Fogarty, *Christian Democracy in Western Europe, 1820–1953* (South Bend, Indiana: University of Notre Dame Press, 1957).

[29] Geoffrey K. Roberts, "Religion and Political Liberalism in the German Federal Republic" (Paper presented to the Workshop on Religion and Politics, European Consortium for Political Research, Brussels, 1979).

by fundamentalists and zealots to protest modernism and the decline of religious influence in secular affairs.[30]

Though the grounds of debate have varied from one country to the next, some of the fiercest wars engaging these religious parties have been fought over the question of education. The British debate over religious control of primary education had parallels in both Belgium and France.[31] Though that particular issue has been removed from the political agenda in most countries, the clash of interests continues over social issues such as divorce, abortion, feminism, and forms of behavior traditionally proscribed by the dominant theology. The intensive activity which surrounds these issues—the high degree of effort expended in lobbying, parliamentary negotiations, and mass electoral mobilization—is indistinguishable from the sorts of behavior usually associated with an interest group model of the political process.[32]

As we observed in Chapter 3, the British experience of religious-based parties is often described in terms which are compatible with this tradition of group analysis. Thus, the initial division of Whigs and Tories is often traced to early competition between Anglicans and Dissenters. The lines of political conflict are said to have maintained a religious basis even as the Whigs eventually begat the Liberals and the Tories evolved into the modern Conservative party. The historical literature associates the Conservatives with the interests of the Church of England in matters such as education, establishment, and endowment and similarly views

[30] James W. White, "Mass Movement and Democracy: Sokagakkai in Japanese Politics," *American Political Science Review* 61 (September 1967), 744–750.

[31] Vernon Mallinson, *Power and Politics in Belgian Education, 1815–1961* (London: Heinemann, 1963); Bernard Brown, "Religious Schools and Politics in France," *Midwest Journal of Political Science* 2 (May 1958), 160–178.

[32] George Moyser, "The Political Organization of the Middle Class: The Case of the Church of England," in *The Middle Class in Politics*, ed. John Garrard et al. (Farnborough, Hampshire: Saxon House, 1978), pp. 262–293.

the Liberal party as the political expression of the Non-conformist movement for political and social emancipation.

Religion as Subculture. Another relevant framework treats the link between religion and politics as a facet of communal solidarity, an aspect of identification with a social group. The individual's attachment to a particular party is simply an outgrowth of his identification with the habits and values of the socially defined environment, part of a web of affiliations in which he is immersed from childhood. Religion is the cement which holds the community together, and political parties are the basis for asserting those values when the community interacts with the world outside its borders.[33]

This approach has been based on studies which show that the link between religion and politics varies with the level of social involvement in the life of the denomination.[34] It is the individuals most thoroughly integrated in the sub-community who are most likely to demonstrate the tendency to cast their votes along denominational lines. For its most strongly attached adherents, the religious group constitutes not just another secondary institution in which membership is claimed but a more embracing source of individual identity—in short, a subculture. In its most ex-

[33] Charles H. Anderson, "Religious Communality and Party Preference," in *Research in Religious Behavior*, ed. Benjamin Beit-Hallahmi (Monterey, Calif.: Brooks-Cole, 1973), pp. 336–352; Gary Easthope, "Religious War in Northern Ireland," *Sociology* 10 (September 1976), 427–450; Scott Greer, "Catholic Voters and the Democratic Party," *Public Opinion Quarterly* 25 (Winter 1961), 611–625; John Meisel, "Religious Affiliation and Electoral Behaviour: A Case Study," in *Voting in Canada*, ed. John C. Courtney (Scarborough, Ontario: Prentice-Hall of Canada, 1967), pp. 144–161; Michael W. Suleiman, "Elections in a Confessional Democracy," *Journal of Politics* 29 (February 1967), 109–128.

[34] For a good discussion on this point, see D. A. Kemp, *Society and Electoral Behaviour in Australia* (St. Lucia, Queensland: University of Queensland Press, 1978), pp. 202–212, and William P. Irvine and H. Gold, "Do Frozen Cleavages Ever Go Stale? The Bases of the Canadian and Australian Party Systems," *British Journal of Political Science* 10 (April 1980), 187–218.

treme form, as a sect, the religious group may encapsulate the life of the member, virtually shuttering off access to behavioral cues which emanate from the environment outside the subcommunity. The same tendency to dominate the perspectives of its membership is manifested in less intense fashion by religious collectivities that do not make such monopolistic claims upon the lives of the membership.

Affiliation with a religious group may breed a distinctive political outlook. Based on structured and semiprojective interviews with a sample of devout French Catholics, Michelat and Simon have reported the existence of a communal ideology which leads to a fierce rejection of left-wing politics:

In their opinion, communism represents a threat to the individual, who is himself indissociable from the communities he belongs to, and above all, from the enlarged "ego" of the family, defined as the place of privileged affective relations, a *foyer* (hence the connotation of warmth), a basic unit, a protective enclosure. The family is inseparable from the moral and religious values on which it is founded and which it transmits, as well as from the material heritage that makes its existence and durability possible on both the physical and the symbolic levels. Spiritual values, family values, freedom, individuality, and property are therefore inseparable. If these values were to be rejected, man's condition would be reduced to that of an animal. Communism is perceived as a violent threat to this cultural complex; it represents the masses (dangerous because they are selfish and can be manipulated) versus the individual.[35]

Susceptibility to this outlook varies positively with the level of religious commitment and, as is demonstrated conclusively, the linkage has direct behavioral consequences.

Three factors seem to promote a common political culture among the community of believers. In the first instance, the religious group may dominate the socialization process of its adherents, molding their political and social

---

[35] Guy Michelat and Michel Simon, "Religion, Class and Politics," *Comparative Politics* 10 (October 1977), 166.

outlooks. The continued involvement of individuals in the life of the group exposes them to a stream of messages which confirm the ideological tendencies in the subcommunity. Finally, the political orientation of the group is further reinforced among individuals by continued social interaction with like-minded group members.[36] Thus, the greater the involvement with the religious group, the more the individual is exposed to the political outlook of the membership and the greater the likelihood of behavioral conformity.

Some studies of the British experience treat religious groups as subcommunities engaged in political conflict. On a rather grand scale, Israel used the concept of subcommunity to describe the contending coalitions in the English Civil War.[37] According to his analysis, the Revolution is best understood as a clash between "two distinct sub-societies" which developed divergent cultural norms covering virtually every sphere of life. The subcultures were built around the religious symbols and practices of the Church of England, on the one hand, and the Puritan congregations, on the other. On a less grand scale, Moore applied a similar framework to his analysis of political life in the late nineteenth century.[38] Using the case of a Durham mining valley, he attempted to explain why villages with bifurcated social structures maintained striking degrees of political cohesion well into the Edwardian era. The evidence suggested that a culture of Methodism permeated village life, and its emphasis on individual rectitude, expressed in part through a commitment to the Liberal party, prevented the emergence of political cleavage organized around class interests. Though less concerned with political life, McCleod has shown how the same conditions existed in the more complex en-

[36] H. J. Hanham, "Politics and Community Life in Victorian and Edwardian Britain," *Folk Life* 4 (1966), 13.

[37] Herman Israel, "Some Religious Factors in the Emergence of Industrial Society in England," *American Sociological Review* 31 (October 1966), 589–599.

[38] Moore, *Pit-men*.

vironment of London.[39] He identified a set of encompassing subcommunities built around a religious core. Such
groups could become the basis for social and political action.

This approach has also been used by political scientists
to explain cross-class voting by church members. It has been
argued in several studies that a communal identity based
on religious association outweighs class influences, leading
to a unified stance in the political arena. As part of their
acquisition of group norms, working-class congregants ac-
quire the political outlooks typical of their mostly middle-
class coreligionists.[40] Because the religious community plays
such an important role in their social self-definition, these
working-class adherents come to choose it as the pole of
political reference.

Religion as Belief System. Another approach to be considered here looks at religions primarily as sources of political
values which may be expressed through the agency of a
political party. This framework, which has been applied
most extensively to historical studies of American voting
behavior, assumes that the doctrines of a religion have implications for secular behavior.[41] Parties may develop an
association with the outlook of a particular denomination,
coming eventually to serve as vehicles for the application
of religious precepts to questions of public policy.[42]

[39] Hugh McCleod, *Class and Religion in the Late Victorian City.*
[40] Bochel and Denver, "Religion and Voting," p. 216.
[41] The major American studies include Ronald Formisano, *The Birth of Mass Political Parties* (Princeton, New Jersey: Princeton University Press, 1971); John L. Hammond, *The Politics of Benevolence*; Richard Jensen, *The Winning of the Midwest* (Chicago: University of Chicago Press, 1971); Paul Kleppner, *The Cross of Culture*, and also his *The Third Electoral System* (Chapel Hill, North Carolina: University of North Carolina Press, 1979).
[42] Religious values are often cited as major determinants of the political behavior of groups on opposite sides of the political spectrum. See, e.g., Lawrence H. Fuchs, "American Jews and the Presidential Vote," *American Political Science Review* 49 (June 1955), 385-401, and Anthony M. Orum, "Religion and the Rise of the Radical White: The Case of Southern Wallace Support in 1968," *Social Science Quarterly* 51 (December 1970), 674–688.

In modern social science, "religion" has increasingly come to be defined less in institutional terms and more as a mode of reality construction. Because of the uniquely human capacity for self-consciousness, men are compelled to impose some form of sense and order on an otherwise inchoate universe. Religion, defined as "the construction of objective, morally binding, all-embracing universes of meaning," is a response to this need to interpret reality.[43] Through these constructed frameworks, man defines his relationship to fellow men and the powers beyond control; from them, man derives certain patterns of thought, habitual ways of behaving, and reacting.

Religion, in this sense, becomes relevant to politics because the comprehensive world-view associated with a denomination may contain elements pertinent to behavior in "secular" situations. This insight was first developed systematically in Max Weber's *Protestant Ethic and the Spirit of Capitalism*. A careful reading suggests that Weber was not interested strictly in docrine as a factor influencing behavior but rather in the interaction between the doctrine as expressed by the founder and the particular milieu in which the religion flourished. The doctrine, reworked and revised to fit the needs of an emerging social group, yields "the practical religion," a body of ideas claiming ancestry from the founder but in reality more a product of the adjustment of basic ideas to the "social, political and economic conditions of the time."[44] Thus the Puritans laid great emphasis on those aspects of Calvinism which endorsed values and forms of behavior supportive of capitalist enterprise. In Weber's words, what mattered was not "the ethical *doctrines* of a religion but that form of ethical conduct upon which *premiums* are placed." Puritanism encouraged a distinct code

[43] Peter Berger, *The Sacred Canopy* (Garden City, New York: Doubleday-Anchor, 1967), p. 176.
[44] David D. Laitin, "Religion, Political Culture and the Weberian Tradition," *World Politics* 30 (July 1978), 563–592.

of behavior, a mentality consistent with an economy built on capitalist principles.

As Weber identified the roots of economic behavior in religion, so other scholars have perceived connections between sacred values and political conduct. This has usually taken the form of finding ethical imperatives that are said to account for certain recurrent patterns of political behavior among members of a religious group. In one of the most ambitious of such analyses, Parenti studied the "political culture" embedded in the three great Western religions.[45] In his view, Catholicism, a religion of individual sin and personal salvation, discouraged attempts to solve social problems through collective action. Following other authorities on the subject, he argued that Judaism placed a much greater stress on this-worldliness and valued an active commitment to social justice as a factor in redemption. These contrasting theological positions were said to account for the conservative political orientation of Catholics and the liberal tendencies of Jews. The Protestant community, divided between fundamentalists and liberals, pursued two paths. Resembling Catholicism in its emphasis on heavenly rewards and personal responsibility, the fundamentalist wing is attracted to conservative politics. The liberal wing, committed to improving social conditions through the application of religious precepts, is receptive to the liberal political style.

In a similar analysis of religion in the Third World, Smith suggested that the form of political development in modernizing societies was likely to be shaped in major respects by the politically relevant elements of the dominant religious world-views.[46] The development of liberal democratic regimes in Latin America was inhibited by the emphasis

[45] Michael Parenti, "Political Values and Religious Cultures: Jews, Catholics and Protestants," *Journal for the Scientific Study of Religion* 6 (Fall 1967), 259–269.

[46] Donald Eugene Smith, *Religion and Political Development* (Boston: Little, Brown and Co., 1970), esp. ch. 6.

on hierarchy, authority, and absolutism in traditional Catholic social and political thought. Though less pronounced than Catholic doctrine, Islamic thought also stressed "obedience to the decrees of a sovereign God," leading to a submissiveness which devalues the participatory orientation necessary in democratic societies. By contrast, Hinduism and Buddhism are less attentive to constituted authority and seem much more likely to promote behavior consistent with the spirit of pluralist democracy. Though Smith is careful not to claim too much for religion, treating it as only one of several elements which contribute to political culture, he clearly perceives religious doctrine as an important influence upon behavior in political situations.

The nature of this linkage in the context of British politics has been explored most thoroughly in Michael Walzer's study of the political role of Puritan intellectuals.[47] The outlook of Puritanism, especially its emphasis on conversion and the importance of "right behavior," led most Puritans to a conception of politics as a venue for the realization of their ideals. This impulse was embodied in the theocratic state which Cromwell molded after the Revolution, and Puritan influences continued to operate long after the Restoration. In the period under study here, the Liberal party was actuated by the "Nonconformist conscience," the principle that "what was morally wrong could never be politically right." Nonconformist Liberals perceived their party as an agent of reforms that would promote the conditions conducive to individual regeneration—sobriety, Sunday quiet, the removal of temptation embodied in frivolous entertainment. These reforms were steadfastly opposed by Anglicans (and Catholics), under the aegis of the Conservative party, who accepted the inherent failing of man and called for individual liberty rather than state-regulated morality. The importance of religion as a source of political values has also been recognized by the

---

[47] Michael Walzer, *The Revolution of the Saints.*

scholars who argue that Wesleyan Methodism, with its doctrinal emphasis on social order, inhibited revolutionary tendencies among the nineteenth century working class.

Religion as Surrogate. Finally, to some observers, religion is relevant to politics only as a surrogate for some other form of "real" social conflict. For example, the religion of a low status group may become the basis for expressing collective identity as the group operates through religious institutions, its strongest organizational base, to pursue its political objectives. Similarly, the political cohesion of dominant religious groups may simply reflect the correlation between the pattern of religious affiliation and socioeconomic status. Though the political struggle appears to involve religious issues, religion is merely an idiom for expressing conflicts that have their basis in social, economic, or ethnic differences.

The basis for this approach is the recognition that religious commitments are not distributed uniformly in the social hierarchy; rather,

In all industrial societies, the attachment to the institutions and symbols of religion is decidedly greater among the dominant class than among the members of the subordinate class. Where the latter are drawn to religion, it is often through denominations or sects which differ significantly in belief from the religious institutions of the dominant class. It seems to be that under a class system, as against a traditional status order, man's worldly interests become too sharply opposed to be reconciled on the sacred plane. Hence the stratification of the secular order is frequently mirrored, albeit very imperfectly, in the stratification of the spiritual order.[48]

The class basis of religious affiliation sets up several possibilities for the relationship between religion and partisanship.

[48] Frank Parkin, *Class Inequality and Political Order* (St. Albans, Hertfordshire: Paladin, 1972), p. 71.

First and foremost, there is the possibility that religion and partisanship are essentially unrelated, their covariation rooted only in the common association of each with social class. In one of the first systematic studies of religious influences in American electoral politics, it was demonstrated that all but one of the major denominations could be ordered politically by their economic standing; several subsequent studies of political differences among and between religious groups in America show that the variation is explicable in terms of socioeconomic status.[49] These studies suggest that denominational political tendencies are simply a function of social inequality among denominations.[50]

Even if class differences account for political tendencies, minority groups may utilize their religious infrastructure as a base for political activity, promoting a "real" relationship between denomination and political behavior. To take another example from the United States, the black churches played a major role in the civil rights movement. As the only autonomous institutions in the black community, churches and their clergy supplied the leadership and support facilities in the drive for legal equality. Even today, when the atmosphere is less repressive, the church continues to serve as a major network for the mobilization of black political strength.

The same kind of approach is often encountered in studies of Jewish political behavior. The consistent political liberalism of Jews, which cannot be explained in strict economic terms, has frequently been interpreted as a response to status deprivation. Though acculturated and economically integrated, Jews retain something of a pariah status which keeps them in an outsider's role and disposes them to sympathize with movements for social and political

---

[49] Wesley Allinsmith and Beverly Allinsmith, "Religious Affiliation and Politico-Economic Attitude: A Study of Eight Major U. S. Religious Groups," *Public Opinion Quarterly* 12 (Fall 1948), 377–389.

[50] James Cornford has suggested that this might hold for Britain under the Third Reform Act in "The Transformation of Conservatism," p. 37, n. 2.

change.[51] The political cohesion of Jews reflects a sense of social marginality rather than anything inherent in Judaism.[52]

This perspective is apparent in some writings on British party politics. Due to Gladstone's conversion to the cause of Home Rule in 1886, the Irish Catholics of Britain are usually portrayed as the staunchest supporters of the Liberal party. From the "religion as surrogate" framework, this correlation of Catholicism and Liberalism was spurious, a function of the commitment of a poor colonial people, whose Catholicism was a facet of their oppression, to the pro-Irish policy of the Liberals under Gladstone. Similarly, the conflict of Catholic and Protestant within Northern Ireland has frequently been portrayed essentially as a battle about inequality fought through the medium of religious symbols.[53]

The framework has also been invoked to account for political differences between adherents of the Church of England and the Nonconformist denominations. In a stimulating book, Hechter argued that the distinctive role of religion in the voting patterns of Wales, Scotland, and the English rim was an expression of political solidarity by a colonialized working class.[54] Peripheral nationalism, generated by the subordination of the hinterland to the center, was *expressed through* the religious institutions of Nonconformity but *derived in the first instance from* economic exploitation. Within England, the often-noted importance of working-class Nonconformity and religiosity in the rise of popular socialism has been dismissed as merely a culturally

[51] Arthur Liebman, *Jews and the Left* (New York: Wiley-Interscience, 1979).

[52] On the concept of social marginality, see Kenneth D. Wald, "The Electoral Base of Political Machines: A Deviant Case Analysis," *Urban Affairs Quarterly* 16 (September 1980), 20–23.

[53] Liam DePaor, *Divided Ulster* (Harmondsworth, Middlesex: Penguin Books, 1971).

[54] Michael Hechter, *Internal Colonialism.*

conditioned mode of expression.[55] The chapel served as the training camp for young socialists because it was the only organizational model available to the working class. To treat religion as the causal factor, it is argued, is to miss the class cleavage which really inspired the drive for social change.

Like their counterparts in class analysis, the frameworks utilized to study religious-based voting provide guidance in identifying the mechanisms which convert sentiment into behavior. With these frameworks, we can proceed to develop statistical measures of religious and class forces and determine their contribution to structuring the vote during the period of the Third Reform Act.

[55] Thompson, "Tom Maguire," pp. 276–316.

CHAPTER 6

Voting and Social Structure: Empirical Analysis

The previous chapter described a series of conceptual approaches to the phenomena of class and religiously based voting. This chapter applies the approaches to British elections between 1885 and 1910. By confronting theory with data, we intend both to address historical questions about the development of partisan cleavages in Britain and to improve theoretical understanding of the relationship between voting and social structure.

MEASURES FOR ANALYSIS

As indicated in Chapter 4, several sources of data can be mined in the effort to construct measures of the various social factors thought to affect voting. All the class measures and several indicators of religious commitment will be constructed with data from the decennial population census. Several other data sources will provide additional measures of denominational strength.

In a historical study such as this, where the researcher must rely upon data collected by others and for purposes other than scholarly research, the problem of indicator validity is especially vexing.[1] The techniques commonly used

---

[1] For a good nontechnical discussion of validity, see Claire Selltiz et al., *Research Methods in Social Relations*, rev. ed. (New York: Holt, Rinehart and Winston, 1959), pp. 154–166.

in social research to establish that an indicator actually measures a particular property frequently cannot be applied in historical research. For several key concepts, we lack multiple measures which alone would permit a conclusive demonstration that a single measure taps an underlying dimension. The use of an indicator's predictive capacity as a measure of validity is even less appropriate. If, for instance, a particular measure of the working class fails to predict accurately the partisan distribution of the vote, it could mean that the measure was invalid; but the prediction failure might be due instead to the inadequacy of the theory which mandated selection of the variable or simply to the absence of class-related issues in an election. Given these problems, we shall have to defend most of the indicators on the grounds of face validity. Where possible, indicators will be validated with external evidence. In some instances, we will fashion indicators similar to those used by other scholars attempting to measure the same phenomenon. But there will be some indicators that can be supported only by arguing that it is reasonable to suppose that they capture the quality they are intended to identify.

Class Measures. The discussion of class-based voting identified a series of conditions likely to magnify the development of political cohesion and used those conditions to characterize the likelihood of common voting tendencies among certain occupational groups. Testing the predictions requires a measurement of the geographical concentration of the relevant occupational groups. As noted above, the occupational data from the 1891 census have been aggregated to match the surrogate units.[2] Despite some problems noted by demographers, the occupational data for this

---

[2] The occupational data appear in *Census of England and Wales, 1891*, C-7058, vol. III (London: HMSO, 1893; reprinted as vol. 23 in the "Population" series of the Irish Universities Press), and *Third Decennial Census of the Population of Scotland*, C-7134, vol. II, pt. II (Edinburgh: HMSO, 1893; reprinted as vol. 25 in the Irish Universities Press "Population" series).

period offer remarkable opportunities for social analysis. The roughly 350 occupational categories reported in the census actually divided the workforce more finely than is customary in even some of the best survey research available today.[3] These occupational categories can be sorted and aggregated to yield estimates of the size and concentration of the various economic groups whose political behavior is at issue.

The designation of an occupation as skilled or unskilled or as manual or nonmanual involves complex judgments about the nature of occupations and work. The difficulty is all the more acute when a single occupational category lumps together individuals of varying skills and income levels merely because they pursued a common trade. Despite these problems, the guardians of the British census began in 1911 an attempt to penetrate the class structure through the occupational statistics. The Registrar General graded the occupational categories of 1911 on a scale intended to measure skill level, occupational prestige, income, life-chances, and other manifestations of inequality.[4] By extending this scheme backwards, assigning the 1891 occupational categories to the 1911 grading scheme, sociologists have made it possible to derive from these occupational data meaningful measures of the various economic groupings required for this study.[5]

Unskilled workers comprised a large share of the econom-

[3] There were more than one-and-a-half times as many separate occupational classifications in the English-Welsh (348) and Scottish (368) census of 1891 as in the Butler-Stokes surveys, *Study of Political Change in Britain, 1963–1970*, vol. II (Ann Arbor, Mich.: Inter-University Consortium for Political Research, 1972), pp. 173–181.

[4] T.H.C. Stevenson, "Vital Statistics of Wealth and Poverty," *Journal of the Royal Statistical Society*, n.s., 91, pt. 2 (1928), 207–220.

[5] J. A. Banks, "The Social Structure of Nineteenth Century England as Seen Through the Census," in *The Census and Social Structure*, ed. Richard Lawton (London: Frank Cass, 1978), pp. 179–223. Compare Banks with W. A. Armstrong, "The Use of Information About Occupation," in *Nineteenth Century Society*, ed. E. A. Wrigley (Cambridge: Cambridge University Press, 1972), pp. 191–310.

ically active population in the 1891 census. Most of the unskilled were included in Class V of the 1911 social classification and we have taken the sum of persons in that grade as one measure of the concentration of the unskilled. Agricultural laborers, who certainly experienced the type of work situation likely to diminish collective consciousness, were not part of Class V but formed their own Class VIII. The second measure of the unskilled population adds the persons in Class VIII to the first measure. Both sums were then converted to proportions of the economically active male population.[6]

The Registrar General attempted to place *skilled manual workers* in Class III, the largest single grade in the 1891 census. We have followed that practice, taking the sum of workers in that classification as a proportion of the economically active population. This basis of classification is probably too gross to single out the putative "labour aristocrats."

The large, inclusive *manual worker* category included all occupations outside of Class I ("the upper and middle class") and Class II ("intermediate between the middle and working class"). Though Class II was rather vaguely described, the majority of occupations within it involved shopkeeping and dealing rather than any production-related work. This measure comprises a larger share of the workforce than any other economic variable in the analysis.

The social grading scheme did not separate *industrial workers* from other practitioners of manual labor, leaving that task to a later generation of social researchers. Fortunately, the census reports did define broad sectors and we focused our attention upon the "industrial" and "mining" sectors. In these two sectors, we attempted to identify and exclude all the occupations involving managerial and

[6] The economically active workforce excludes the census categories for persons retired from business, pensioners, persons "living on their own means," and "unclassifiable." The bulk of persons in the last category were persons under fifteen years of age attending school.

commercial tasks. Following Clark, our measure of industrial workers thus consists of the sum of nonexcluded occupations in the industrial and mining sectors, taken, as usual, over the base of economically active males.[7] Because of the failure of the census always to distinguish clearly between industry and occupation, this measure undoubtedly picks up a few of the supervisory and nonmanual employees associated with industrial enterprises. Nevertheless, it identifies the concentration of manual workers in factory or factory-like situations.

Finally, there is the problem of measuring the concentration of *organized workers*. No good ecological data exist on the extent of union penetration during this period, but we do have national figures on the level of unionization by occupational sectors.[8] The 1901 national density proportion (the number of organized workers as a proportion of the workforce) was applied to the relevant occupational categories in each unit, producing a measure of the workforce likely to be exposed to union influence.[9] This is by no means a direct estimate of union strength because there were undoubtedly significant regional variations in organization among certain trades. The figure represents instead an estimate of the concentration of those trades with the greatest nationwide propensity for union organization. In the absence of more direct data on the geographical concentration of unions, this estimate will have to suffice.

All these measures are broadly related to the idea of stratification, but they represent very different ways of conceptualizing inequality. Not surprisingly, they paint very different portraits of the class structure. As the data in

[7] Colin Clark, *The Conditions of Economic Progress* (London: Macmillan, 1940).

[8] H. A. Clegg, Alan Fox, and A. F. Thompson, *A History of British Trade Unions Since 1889*, pp. 466–468.

[9] The formula was: Unionization in 1901 = 0.21 × occupations in metal + 0.19 × occupations in mining + 0.08 × occupations in textiles + 0.10 × occupations in building + 0.12 × occupations in transportation + 0.03 × occupations in clothing + 0.17 × occupations in printing + 0.08 × occupations in wood.

TABLE 6.1. Description of Class Measures

	Mean	Standard Deviation	Minimum	Maximum
Nonagricultural laborers	.15	.04	.07	.26
All laborers	.23	.09	.09	.48
Manual workers	.76	.07	.56	.89
Skilled manual workers	.22	.08	.11	.48
Industrial workers	.44	.17	.18	.76
Organized workers	.09	.05	.03	.27

N = 115.

Table 6.1 show, the trade union measure is the most selective (mean value for all units = 0.09), and the indicator of manual workers is much more encompassing with a mean of 0.76. The measures differ in scale and, as shown by the spread of correlation coefficients in Table 6.2, they are also sensitive to the presence of different groups in the working population. The table gives us confidence that our approaches to stratification tap measures which are empirically as well as analytically distinct.

Religious Measures. It is best to admit at the outset the difficulty of finding operational measures appropriate to the four modes of religious influence on the vote. The subtlety of the approaches and their partial overlap would make it difficult to obtain empirical referents even if we

TABLE 6.2. Correlation Among Class Measures

	Non-agricultural Laborers	Manual Workers	Skilled Manuals	Industrial Workers	Organized Workers
All laborers	.02	−.10	−.41	−.74	−.56
Nonagricultural laborers	—	.14	.13	.07	−.11
Manual workers	—	—	.32	.62	.48
Skilled manual workers	—	—	—	.27	−.25
Industrial workers	—	—	—	—	.73

N = 115.

could collect our own data through survey research. The task is all the more daunting because we must rely upon information that was not collected to meet the needs of social scientists. Despite these problems, we have assembled a body of indicators that can reasonably be linked to the four approaches, permitting a quantitative analysis of the explanatory power of each mode. The indicators, discussed below, are described in Table 6.3 and correlated in Table 6.4.

The approach that treats religions as interest groups requires a measure corresponding to the organizational strength of the denominations. An appropriate measure would tap the capacity of the denomination to convert the sympathetic disposition of its adherents to active political work on behalf of policy objectives sanctioned by the church. Two sets of indicators seem adequate to the task. The first set, measures of clergy distribution from the 1891 census, recognizes that the clergy, by virtue of their position as denominational spokesmen, were well-placed to raise awareness about issues affecting the interests or the policy favored by church leaders. Narrative accounts of election campaigns from the period leave little doubt that the clergy recognized their strategic potential and often functioned as virtual party agents in attempts to mobilize adherents behind the church position. This was especially true when the vexing issue of education, which touched the interests of the churches directly, entered the political agenda. The occupational breakdown in the census of 1891 identified the number of Anglican, Roman Catholic, and "other" clergymen in each unit. By taking each figure as a proportion of the male workforce, we obtained estimates of the organizational strength of the Church of England, the Roman Catholic church, and the Nonconformist denominations.[10]

---

[10] In Scotland, the measure for the Church of England actually was constructed using only the clergy from the established Church of Scotland. The Nonconformist measure includes the clergy from the Free Church, United Presbyterians, Episcopalians, and "other religious bodies."

TABLE 6.3. Description of Religious Measures

	Mean	Standard Deviation	Minimum	Maximum	N
Anglican clergy	.0008	.0006	.00003	.003	(115)
Nonconformist clergy	.0005	.0004	.0001	.002	(115)
Catholic clergy	.00008	.00006	0	.0004	(115)
Anglican %, Ed. Comm.	.54	.14	.28	.92	(58)
Nonconformist %, Ed. Comm.	.41	.14	.04	.69	(58)
Catholic %, Ed. Comm.	.05	.06	0	.30	(58)
Anglican worship	.12	.05	.03	.25	(107)
Nonconformist worship	.15	.08	.05	.44	(107)
Catholic worship	.01	.02	0	.10	(107)
Anglican El. Ed.	.04	.02	.008	.08	(97)
Nonconformist El. Ed.	.01	.008	0	.06	(97)
Catholic El. Ed.	.003	.005	0	.03	(97)
Anglican Sunday School	.05	.02	.004	.10	(97)
Nonconformist Sunday School	.08	.07	.0007	.35	(97)
Catholic Sunday School	.003	.008	0	.06	(97)

See Table 6.9 for abbreviations.

This set of measures was used for purposes of illustration in Chapter 4.

The second set of measures of religions as interest groups indicates the success of the denominations in mobilizing to gain control of local education authorities. Under the Education Act of 1870, control over the municipal system of elementary education was vested in an elective school board. Elections to the board were essentially trials of strength

Table 6.4. Correlation Among Religious Measures

	2	3	4	5	6	7	8	9	10	11	12	13	14	15
A. Per Capita Clergy Distribution, 1891														
1. Anglican	.16	−.12	.69	−.48	−.51	.73	.06	−.43	.58	.04	−.33	.35	.10	−.33
2. Nonconformist	x	−.15	.32	−.12	−.48	−.16	.81	−.36	−.30	−.07	−.23	−.24	.63	−.19
3. Catholic	x	x	.01	−.31	.74	.01	−.20	.48	.04	−.14	.34	.12	−.12	.42
B. Local Education Authority Membership, ca. 1902														
4. Anglican	x	x	x	−.92	−.21	.69	−.11	−.29	.52	−.12	−.23	.41	−.48	−.16
5. Nonconformist	x	x	x	x	−.20	−.49	.26	−.04	−.37	.13	−.14	−.38	.39	−.19
6. Catholic	x	x	x	x	x	−.50	−.38	.82	−.33	−.03	.88	−.08	.21	.84
C. Attendance at Sunday Worship, 1851														
7. Anglican	x	x	x	x	x	x	−.24	−.34	.62	−.05	−.24	.49	−.33	−.27
8. Nonconformist	x	x	x	x	x	x	x	−.34	−.21	.05	−.24	−.16	.71	−.21
9. Catholic	x	x	x	x	x	x	x	x	−.15	.09	.66	−.06	−.08	.71
D. Attendance at Denominational Day School, 1851														
10. Anglican	x	x	x	x	x	x	x	x	x	.20	.04	.55	−.05	−.06
11. Nonconformist	x	x	x	x	x	x	x	x	x	x	.07	−.12	.24	−.06
12. Catholic	x	x	x	x	x	x	x	x	x	x	x			
E. Attendance at Denominational Sunday School, 1851														
13. Anglican	x	x	x	x	x	x	x	x	x	x	x	x	−.07	.21
14. Nonconformist	x	x	x	x	x	x	x	x	x	x	x	x	x	−.01

N's vary because of missing values.
Column 15 represents Catholic attendance at Sunday schools.

among the denominations that fought to control the kinds of religious doctrines imparted to children. The responsibility formerly vested in school boards was transferred in 1902 to committees of the local governing authority, the members appointed in due proportion to party strength on the authority. The vigorous denominational competition which had marked the boards was thereby simply transferred to the local councils. In a report on the working of the new act, a Nonconformist body presented data on the religious composition of the local authorities empowered to supervise elementary education.[11] We converted this data to proportions, yielding additional measures of the organizational strength of the Anglican, Catholic, and Nonconformist communities.

The concept of religious groups as subcommunities, encapsulating the lives of their members and promoting a common political orientation, suggests a measure of denominationalism built around the congregation. From this perspective, the church was the core organization in the lives of members of the subcommunity, not just a secondary social grouping. It provided the membership with opportunities for common prayer, intensive social interaction, and a host of ancillary activities not explicitly religious but nonetheless based on the denominational subcommunity. McCleod's study of London church life shows how, even in the generally secular environment of a cosmopolitan city, the congregation bounded the lives of its members.[12] So it seems appropriate to measure the concept by focusing on the churches and, more specifically, the distribution of denominational strength as revealed by statistics of worship.

The religious census of 1851, which marked the only occasion when the government sought to collect comprehensive data on religious practices in Britain, provided de-

---

[11] Rev. Thomas Law, *The Education Act at Work* (London: National Council of Evangelical Free Churches, 1903). Because of omissions, data from this source are available for only 58 English units.

[12] McCleod, *Class and Religion.*

131

tailed information on church attendance for most of our units.[13] We have apportioned churchgoers into Anglican, Catholic, and Nonconformist categories and divided each sum by the total population of the unit.[14] The figure represents attendance at either morning or evening services, whichever were best attended for each denomination.[15] The very considerable lapse of time between the 1851 census and the period of the study raises doubts about the validity of such measures. In the face of rapid social development— industrialization, population migration, etc.—do statistics about the distribution of denominational groups in mid-century supply an accurate guide to religious geography at the turn of the century? As the 1851 experiment was never repeated, no data which resolve that question authoritatively exist; but it is clear from a privately sponsored survey of church attendance in selected areas in 1881 that the intervening thirty years did not produce any dramatic

[13] The data on worship appeared in *Census of Great Britain, 1851* (London: HMSO, 1853), "Religious Worship in England and Wales," and *Census of Great Britain, 1851* (London: HMSO, 1854), "Religious Worship and Education, Scotland." These data can be found in vols. 10 and 11 in the "Population" series of the Irish Universities Press. Because of population growth, some of the borough units from the 1891 census were not enumerated separately in 1851, and these units have been coded as missing for all variables derived from the 1851 census.

[14] In calculating the Nonconformist attenders, we included Presbyterians, Congregationalists, Baptists, Quakers, Unitarians, Wesleyan and Primitive Methodists, Mormons, Jews, the Free Churches, and the various sects that were neither Anglican nor Roman Catholic. The "Anglican" measure in Scotland includes only the established Church of Scotland; the Presbyterians and Episcopalians are included as Nonconformists.

[15] The report on the census, prepared by Horace Mann, suggested four methods to calculate attendance so that individuals attending more than one service would not be counted separately for each service. We found from correlation that the four methods were largely indistinguishable (though the overall magnitude would of course differ). The statistic used in this book is based on attendance at whichever service was best attended for each denomination. Generally, this tapped morning services for Catholics and Anglicans and evening services for Nonconformists, although there was some variation from place to place. For the best discussion on the use of this data, see David M. Thompson, "The Religious Census of 1851," in *The Census and Social Structure*, pp. 241–286.

changes in the relative concentration of denominations by area.[16] Moreover, there are high correlations between the 1851 attendance figures and the distribution of clergy in 1891. This suggests a high level of stability in mass religious sentiments, fully consistent with Gay's reminder that conversion is usually a characteristic of individuals, not populations.[17]

In the final approach, religions are regarded as politically influential through their effects on the value system of adherents. Through a variety of techniques, the church attempts to inculcate in its adherents a set of beliefs with inescapable political implications. The process by which churches attempt to imbue their adherents with distinctive values is continuous and pervasive but probably reaches its most concentrated form in formal religious instruction. All the major British denominations maintained networks of Sunday schools and primary schools that included explicit instruction in church values. The National Society, the coordinating body for Anglican education programs, defined its task in missionary terms:

Our work is to teach children the facts of our religion, the doctrines of our religion, the duties of our religion. We teach them the facts of our religion, that they may be intelligent Christians, not ignorant as heathens; the doctrines, that they may not be Christians only, but Churchmen; the duties, that they may not be Churchmen only, but communicants.[18]

The role of religions as sources of political values will thus be gauged by measures of attendance at church-related educational institutions.

The relevant data can be found in the 1851 religious

[16] Hugh McCleod, "Class, Community and Region: The Religious Geography of Nineteenth-Century England," in *A Sociological Yearbook of Religion in England 6*, ed. Michael Hill (London: SCM Press, 1973), ch. 2.

[17] John D. Gay, *The Geography of Religion in England* (London: Duckworth, 1971), pp. 42–43.

[18] James C. Greenough, *The Evolution of Elementary Schools of Great Britain* (New York: D. Appleton, 1903), pp. 51–52.

TABLE 6.5. Correlations Between Measures of Class and Religion

	All Laborers	Nonagricultural Laborers	Manual Workers	Skilled Workers	Industrial Workers	Unionized Workers
A. *Per Capita Distribution, 1891*						
1. Anglican	.64	-.19	-.26	-.23	-.58	-.37
2. Nonconformist	.17	-.48	-.43	-.39	-.30	.07
3. Catholic	-.17	.19	.08	-.04	.13	.12
B. *Local Education Authority Membership, ca. 1902*						
4. Anglican	.57	-.05	-.19	-.18	-.53	-.38
5. Nonconformist	-.38	-.01	.09	-.05	.33	.18
6. Catholic	-.46	.14	.23	.20	.50	.51
C. *Attendance at Sunday Worship, 1851*						
7. Anglican	.61	.03	-.07	-.14	-.55	-.46
8. Nonconformist	.03	-.40	-.23	-.30	-.07	.26
9. Catholic	-.38	.40	.23	.17	.44	.24
D. *Attendance at Denominational Day School, 1851*						
10. Anglican	.38	.20	.15	-.01	-.20	-.19
11. Nonconformist	-.08	.36	-.10	.14	.06	-.01
12. Catholic	-.31	.29	.16	.10	.31	.24
E. *Attendance at Denominational Sunday School, 1851*						
13. Anglican	.35	-.06	.42	-.11	.03	-.06
14. Nonconformist	-.17	-.31	-.12	-.26	.24	.43
15. Catholic	-.33	.03	.24	.00	.43	.34

N's vary because of missing values.

census which inquired about enrollment in church schools offering Sunday and general primary education.[19] The students in these schools were apportioned to denominational groupings under the same classification system used for the worship statistics. So, following the same rules used in creating the church attendance measures, the sum of students in the major groupings was divided by total population. The time lag between these data and the period under study is in this case quite appropriate. As a very large contingent of the voters in elections between 1885 and 1910 were educated in the church schools that monopolized primary education until 1870, the 1851 data will correspond with the patterns of religious socialization in force when the voters were young. Though not as spectacular as the correlations between 1851 church attendance and 1891 clergy distribution, the coefficients measuring the relationship between 1851 school attendance and 1891 clergy are high enough to establish the validity of the education statistics. The differences may be due as much to the different aspect of religion being measured as to the validity of the indicators.

The discussion in Chapter 5 of the modes of religious effects on voting raised the possibility that religion was simply a surrogate for class effects. If so, the relationship between religion and partisanship should disappear with the introduction of controls for social class. We can test this interpretation by measuring the impact of religious variables in equations which include class controls. The data in Table 6.5, the coefficients of correlation between the class and religious variables, indicate that there was some overlap between economic structure and religious composition of the units but nothing like a complete identity. The table shows that Anglicanism was positively associated with the

---

[19] *Census of Great Britain, 1851* (London: HMSO, 1854), "Education, England and Wales," and *Census of Great Britain, 1851* (London: HMSO, 1854), "Religious Worship and Education, Scotland." See notes 13 and 14 for further details.

proportion of all laborers and negatively related to most of the remaining class measures. On the assumption that the measure of all laborers was sensitive to the concentration of farm workers and the other measures were associated with urban forms of production, the correlations suggest that Anglicanism had a rural base and declined with urbanization.[20] The geography of Catholicism had a reverse image, correlating negatively with the laborers measure and positively with most of the other class measures. On the whole, the distribution of Nonconformity was closer to that of Catholicism than Anglicanism, but there was greater variability depending on the particular measure of Dissent. The more sophisticated multivariate regression reported below will indicate how much of the relationship between religion and the vote is simply a function of economic differences between the denominations.

Some of these class and religious measures pinpoint rather small segments of the population which by themselves could exert relatively little direct impact on the vote. This does not invalidate the findings based on these measures because the vote decision is usually a function both of individual attributes and of social interaction patterns. Politically involved individuals usually cast only one vote, but they may influence many more through discussion, advocacy, canvassing, and other means of mobilization. If, then, the level of class-voting results both from individual attributes (one's class standing) and the pattern of primary group contacts (the likelihood of encountering a strongly persuasive Liberal coworker) a numerically small group may influence the aggregate vote division out of all proportion to its size. The models of group-based voting are thus not vitiated by the rather select nature of some of the groups whose concentration is measured.

[20] See K. S. Inglis, *Churches and the Working Classes in Victorian England* (London: Routledge and Kegan Paul, 1963), and E. R. Wickham, *Church and People in an Industrial Society* (London: Lutterworth, 1957).

Measures of the Vote. The dependent variable for the analysis is the sum of "Unionist" votes as a proportion of total votes in the constituencies of the surrogate units. The Unionist vote consists of the votes for all candidates identified as Conservative, Liberal Unionist, Unionist, and all independents who included one of those terms in their designations. Though some candidates might be difficult to classify in an age when party labels were more fluid, the vast majority of candidates presented no serious difficulties.[21] For this stage of the analysis, we assumed that the uncontested constituencies within a unit would not have altered substantially the aggregate partisan division of the vote in a surrogate unit. A more stringent decision rule, such as excluding any unit with even one uncontested constituency, would have so reduced the number of cases available for analysis that no reliable conclusions could have been drawn. Of course, in those rare instances when all the constituencies in a unit were uncontested, that unit was dropped from the analysis.

STATISTICAL ANALYSIS

To get some preliminary guidance from the data, each measure of class and religion was correlated with the Unionist vote in the eight general elections.

The analysis in Table 6.6 suggests that only three of the class measures were consistent with revisionist writing about the contours of the vote. In particular, the indicators which equated the "working class" with general laborers, non-agricultural laborers, and skilled manual workers performed contrary to expectations by correlating positively

[21] The classifications were derived from the machine-readable file of constituency results used in the compilation of Craig, *Parliamentary Election Results*. In revising the file, which is available from the Social Statistics Laboratory of the University of Strathclyde, I created a new category of "Independent Conservatives" consisting of Craig's categories for INDC, IC, FT, CFT, and UFT. The existing category of "Liberal Unionists" was enlarged to contain all candidates designated as LUFT.

TABLE 6.6. Correlation of Class Measures with Unionist Vote
in General Elections, 1885–1910

	1885	1886	1892	1895	1900
Nonagricultural laborers	.28	.26	.22	.23	.34
All laborers	.14	.11	.09	.05	.09
Manual workers	−.10	−.21	−.09	−.05	−.09
Skilled manual workers	−.03	.16	.20	.23	.15
Industrial workers	−.14	−.21	−.13	−.05	−.14
Organized workers	−.29	−.32	−.39	−.34	−.38
N =	(114)	(103)	(114)	(109)	(101)

	1906	Jan. 1910	Dec. 1910	Mean
Nonagricultural laborers	.13	.22	.25	.24
All laborers	.29	.29	.27	.17
Manual workers	−.15	−.13	−.30	−.14
Skilled manual workers	.07	.12	.06	.12
Industrial workers	−.26	−.30	−.38	−.20
Organized workers	−.40	−.51	−.49	−.39
N =	(114)	(115)	(108)	

with the Unionist vote in virtually all elections. The two
measures of general laborers had positive signs in all eight
elections, and the measure of skilled workers did so in all
but one election. The other three class measures had signs
in the predicted direction. The concentration of manual
workers and industrial workers was moderately and negatively associated with Unionist voting. The trade union
variable was even a stronger negative predictor of Unionism. Clearly, the definition of the "working class" makes a
difference in empirical analysis.

Table 6.7 presents similar coefficients for each of the
religious measures. The findings are broadly consistent with
the traditional religious model of the period. Of the thirty-
two coefficients representing the relationship between Anglicanism and the Unionist vote, thirty were in the expected
direction. Except for the measure of Sunday School attendance, all the Nonconformist measures were strong neg-

TABLE 6.7. Correlations of Religious Measures with Unionist Vote in General Elections, 1885–1910

Variables	1885	1886	1892	1895	1900	1906	Jan. 1910	Dec. 1910	M̄
A. *Per Capita Clergy Distribution, 1891*									
1. Anglican	.28	.24	.10	.09	.08	.30	.29	.35	.22
2. Nonconformist	−.37	−.35	−.49	−.49	−.42	−.27	−.46	−.37	−.40
3. Catholic	.25	.20	.19	.24	.36	.10	.20	.21	.22
B. *Local Education Authority Membership, ca. 1902*									
4. Anglican	.25	.13	.10	.07	.08	.30	.33	.37	.20
5. Nonconformist	−.40	−.19	−.16	−.22	−.22	−.28	−.35	−.42	−.28
6. Catholic	.37	.13	.14	.34	.32	−.04	.05	.12	.18
C. *Attendance at Sunday Worship, 1851*									
7. Anglican	.29	.30	.34	.26	.17	.39	.49	.42	.33
8. Nonconformist	−.45	−.46	−.59	−.58	−.50	−.38	−.54	−.46	−.50
9. Catholic	.24	.08	.18	.29	.29	.01	.07	.08	.16
D. *Attendance at Denominational Day School, 1851*									
10. Anglican	.30	.27	.24	.21	.22	.22	.30	.24	.25
11. Nonconformist	.02	.10	−.01	−.07	−.12	.09	−.08	−.08	.01
12. Catholic	.10	.08	.08	.12	.22	.23	.02	.03	.05
E. *Attendance at Denominational Sunday School, 1851*									
13. Anglican	.08	−.02	.12	.16	−.03	.14	.17	.07	.09
14. Nonconformist	−.28	−.35	−.55	−.48	−.36	−.42	−.59	−.46	−.44
15. Catholic	.15	.04	.04	.22	.16	−.07	−.02	.00	.07

N's vary because of missing values.

ative predictors of Conservatism. The Catholic indicators were, as a rule, modestly but positively associated with Unionism, a finding that will receive comment below. Simply comparing the magnitude of the coefficients in Tables 6.6 and 6.7 suggests stronger religious than class effects on the vote.

As instructive as they are, the findings from correlation analysis do not take account of interaction between predictors or provide estimates of the relative explanatory power of variables. To more fully understand the contours of voting requires a multivariate analysis. As a first step in that direction, we computed regression equations matching each set of religious indicators (n = 5) with each class indicator

139

(n = 6) in all eight general elections. Rather than present coefficients from the 240 regression equations that resulted, we have presented in Table 6.8A a summary of the predictive capacity of each measure.

In regressions with nonsample data, it is customary to evaluate the predictive capacity of a variable by comparing the unstandardized regression coefficient with its associated standard error. Coefficients at least twice the size of their standard errors are taken to be "significant" in the sense that they provide relatively accurate predictions of changes in a dependent variable. Following that custom, Table 6.8A reports the proportion of trials in which the coefficient for each independent variable was double its standard error.

TABLE 6.8. Summary of Coefficients Derived from Multivariate Regression Equations with Class and Religion as Independent Variables

	A. First Round (%)	B. Second Round (%)
Nonagricultural laborers	20	
All laborers	38	
Manual workers	78	53
Skilled manuals	15	
Industrial workers	63	53
Unionized workers	100	100
Clergy—Anglican	73	63
Clergy—Nonconformist	100	100
Clergy—Catholic	73	79
Ed. Comm.—Anglican	29	
Ed. Comm.—Nonconformist	29	
Ed. Comm.—Catholic	52	71
Worship—Anglican	54	17
Worship—Nonconformist	100	100
Worship—Catholic	35	
El. Ed.—Anglican	75	63
El. Ed.—Nonconformist	15	
El. Ed.—Catholic	27	
Sunday School—Anglican	8	
Sunday School—Nonconformist	94	96
Sunday School—Catholic	15	

Entries represent the percentage of equations in which the variable achieved statistical significance. See Table 6.9 for abbreviations.

Based on the multivariate analysis, the initial list of twenty-one predictors was reduced to eleven by excluding measures that were nonsignificant predictors in at least half the equations. Among the class measures, the indicators of unskilled laborers (total and nonagricultural) and skilled workers failed to meet that criterion and were dropped from subsequent analysis. This suggests that the counterintuitive findings for these variables in the correlation analysis (Table 6.6) were largely a statistical artifact. The winnowing process also eliminated seven religious measures including the Anglican and Nonconformist representation on local councils, Catholic church attendance, Anglican and Catholic Sunday School enrollment, and Nonconformist and Catholic day school enrollment. This leaves three indicators apiece for Anglicanism and Nonconformity and two measures of Catholicism.

With the weaker measures dropped, the next step was to rerun the regressions matching each remaining set of religious measures with the three indicators of class. This step was necessary to determine if some of the measures might have survived the initial winnowing only because they were matched against some extremely weak predictors. The results of the regression equations are summarized in Table 6.8B.

Based on this analysis, the predictor list was reduced further by eliminating another two measures. The indicator of Anglican church attendance, which had been significant in over half the initial regressions, was double its standard error in only one-sixth of the equations with the reduced set of predictors. We also dropped the measure of Catholic representation on local councils. Although it remained significant in two-thirds of the second round regressions, the measure was based on information for only about half the cases. This leaves one remaining Catholic measure, clergy distribution, which was a good predictor in nineteen of the twenty-four equations it entered.

The predictor list now contained just nine variables—three measures of Nonconformity, two measures of Anglicanism, one measure of Catholicism, and the three remaining measures of class. To compare the predictive power of these variables, we ran a new set of regression equations containing a single indicator for each religious grouping along with one of the class measures. As indicated by Table 6.9, six unique combinations of religious variables could be matched to the three class indicators in each of the eight elections. The last set of equations also contained variables designed to tap regional variations above and beyond class or religious effects. The three dummy variables represent peripheral England (the counties of the north, northwest, and southwest), Wales, and Scotland.[22]

Table 6.10 presents for each of these equations the values of the standardized regression coefficients and the proportion of the variance in Conservative-Unionist support explained jointly by all the independent variables.[23] The coefficients which did not achieve statistical significance as described above are listed as "NS" in the table.

The most important finding in the table relates to the dispute about the relative electoral impact of class and religious cleavages. To judge by the regression coefficients, religion had a much stronger electoral impact than social class. This interpretation can be established several ways. An analysis of the strongest variable in each equation shows that a religious predictor was more powerful than a class measure in 107 of the 144 analyses. The quantitative superiority of religious effects was especially pronounced in 1885, 1892, 1895, and 1906. If we restrict our attention to

[22] "Dummy" variables have only two values, 0 and 1. The coefficient represents the difference in the intercept for all units coded 0 and 1 on a particular dummy. Thus, in Table 6.14, the value of −0.55 for the Scottish dummy in 1885 (equation A1) indicates that the Unionist vote declined by about one-half of a standardized unit going from constituencies in central England to Scotland. This deviation is independent of class and religious differences between central England and Scotland.

[23] On the rationale for using standardized coefficients in ecological analysis, see John L. Hammond, "New Approaches to Aggregate Electoral Data," *Journal of Interdisciplinary History* 9 (Winter 1979), 473–492. Such measures were used in Miller, *Electoral Dynamics*.

TABLE 6.9. Form of Basic Equations

Form	Religious Combination	Class Variable	Region
A	Clergy—A, SS—N, Clergy—RC	1. Manual workers	Peripheral England
B	El.Ed.—A, SS—N, Clergy—RC		
C	El.Ed.—A, Worship—N, Clergy—RC	2. Industrial workers	Scotland
D	Clergy—A, Worship—N, Clergy—RC	3. Unionized workers	Wales
E	El.Ed.—A, Clergy—N, Clergy—RC		
F	Clergy—A, Clergy—N, Clergy—RC		

In subsequent tables, these equations will be identified by their form, i.e., F2 will indicate an equation with the three clergy measures and the proportion of industrial workers plus the regional dummies.

Abbreviations

A = Anglican; N = Nonconformist; RC = Roman Catholic

Clergy = Clergymen as a percentage of occupied male population, aged 10+, 1891

El.Ed. = Students in attendance at day schools as a percentage of total population, 1851

SS = Students in attendance at Sunday Schools as a percentage of total population, 1851

Ed. Comm. = Education Committee

Manual = Manual workers as a percentage of occupied male population, aged 10+, 1891

Industrial = Industrial workers as a percentage of occupied male population, aged 10+, 1891

Unionized = Unionized workers (1901) as a percentage of occupied male population, aged 10+, 1891

Peripheral England = Cheshire, Cornwall, Cumberland, Devonshire, Dorsetshire, Durham, Lancashire, Somerset, Westmorland, Wiltshire, Yorkshire.

Table 6.10. Basic Multiple Regression Equations, 1885-1910

Form	Independent Variables	1885	1886	1892	1895	1900	1906	Jan. 1910	Dec. 1910
A1	SS—Non	-.34	-.38	-.41	-.45	NS	-.39	-.55	-.33
	Clergy—A	NS	NS	NS	NS	NS	.21	NS	NS
	Clergy—RC	.27	.24	.22	.28	.31	.20	.29	.24
	Manual	-.29	-.36	-.24	NS	-.25	NS	-.15	-.28
	R²	.47	.46	.53	.48	.42	.39	.66	.52
A2	SS—Non	-.30	-.35	-.39	-.45	NS	-.37	-.50	-.32
	Clergy—A	NS	NS	NS	NS	-.30	NS	NS	NS
	Clergy—RC	.30	.28	.24	.29	.34	.22	.31	.28
	Industrial	-.29	-.31	-.25	NS	-.36	NS	-.27	-.35
	R²	.44	.39	.51	.47	.43	.38	.67	.51
A3	SS—Non	NS	-.35	-.35	-.38	NS	-.34	-.47	-.31
	Clergy—A	NS	NS	NS	NS	NS	NS	NS	NS
	Clergy—RC	.31	.29	.26	.31	.37	.23	.32	.30
	Unionization	-.32	-.24	-.30	-.26	-.44	-.23	-.28	-.32
	R²	.47	.39	.54	.51	.49	.40	.69	.52
	N =	(96)	(89)	(96)	(92)	(88)	(96)	(97)	(92)
B1	SS—Non	-.35	-.39	-.42	-.43	NS	-.45	-.59	-.36
	El.Ed—A	NS	NS	NS	NS	NS	NS	NS	NS
	Clergy—RC	.26	.23	.22	.29	.31	.20	.28	.23
	Manual	-.30	-.38	-.24	NS	-.23	NS	-.18	-.30
	R²	.48	.45	.53	.48	.42	.36	.64	.52
B2	SS—Non	-.30	-.34	-.38	-.43	NS	-.37	-.48	-.29
	El.Ed.—A	NS	NS	NS	NS	NS	NS	NS	NS
	Clergy—RC	.30	.29	.24	.29	.34	.22	.31	.29
	Industrial	-.22	-.31	-.18	NS	-.18	-.24	-.29	-.34
	R²	.44	.39	.50	.47	.39	.38	.68	.52

B3								
SS—Non	NS	−.35	−.34	−.35	NS	−.36	−.48	−.31
El.Ed.—A	NS	NS	NS	NS	NS	NS	NS	NS
Clergy—RC	.31	.29	.26	.32	.37	.23	.32	.30
Unionization	−.30	−.27	−.27	−.21	−.35	−.28	−.32	−.34
R²	.47	.38	.53	.50	.46	.39	.69	.52
N =	(96)	(89)	(96)	(92)	(88)	(96)	(97)	(92)
C1								
Worship—Non	−.49	−.39	−.38	−.55	−.28	−.34	−.30	NS
El.Ed.—A	NS	NS	NS	NS	NS	NS	NS	NS
Clergy—RC	.23	.20	.20	.24	.29	NS	.28	.21
Manual	−.30	−.39	−.25	−NS	−.23	−.20	−.22	−.35
R²	.52	.45	.52	.51	.44	.34	.56	.49
C2								
Worship—Non	−.52	−.42	−.41	−.56	−.31	−.35	−.31	−.28
El.Ed.—A	NS	NS	NS	NS	NS	NS	NS	NS
Clergy—RC	.26	.23	.22	.25	.31	.20	.31	.27
Industrial	−.28	−.34	−.25	−NS	−.21	−.32	−.39	−.43
R²	.50	.42	.52	.52	.42	.38	.64	.52
C3								
Worship—Non	−.47	−.38	−.35	−.52	NS	−.31	−.25	NS
El.Ed.—A	NS	NS	NS	NS	NS	NS	NS	NS
Clergy—RC	.28	.26	.24	.27	.34	.22	.33	.30
Unionization	−.31	−.29	−.31	−.23	−.34	−.32	−.39	−.41
R²	.52	.39	.54	.55	.48	.38	.64	.51
N =	(96)	(89)	(96)	(92)	(88)	(96)	(97)	(92)
D1								
Worship—Non	−.39	−.36	−.36	−.48	NS	−.30	−.29	−.24
Clergy—A	NS	NS	NS	NS	NS	.25	.24	NS
Clergy—RC	.23	.18	.20	.23	.30	.18	.27	.22
Manual	−.19	−.32	−.22	−NS	−.24	−NS	−.18	−.31
R²	.48	.42	.50	.47	.43	.37	.60	.53

145

TABLE 6.10 (cont.)

Form	Independent Variables	1885	1886	1892	1895	1900	1906	Jan. 1910	Dec. 1910
D2	Worship—Non	−.41	−.39	−.37	−.49	−.25	−.31	−.30	−.27
	Clergy—A	NS	NS	NS	NS	−.28	NS	NS	NS
	Clergy—RC	.24	.21	.22	.24	.33	.19	.29	.26
	Industrial	−.28	−.34	−.34	NS	−.39	−.30	−.38	−.45
	R²	.48	.40	.52	.48	.45	.39	.64	.54
D3	Worship—Non	−.36	−.36	−.32	−.44	NS	−.27	−.25	−.22
	Clergy—A	NS	NS	NS	NS	NS	NS	NS	NS
	Clergy—RC	.26	.22	.24	.26	.36	.21	.31	.28
	Unionization	−.29	−.24	−.32	−.25	−.42	−.25	−.34	−.37
	R²	.50	.38	.53	.51	.50	.39	.64	.54
	N =	(106)	(96)	(106)	(102)	(98)	(106)	(107)	(101)
E1	Clergy—Non	−.50	NS	NS	−.50	NS	NS	−.34	NS
	El.Ed.—A	NS	NS	NS	NS	NS	NS	NS	NS
	Clergy—RC	25.	.22	.22	.28	.32	.19	.30	NS
	Manual	−.41	−.49	−.34	−.22	−.27	−.28	−.30	−.41
	R²	.48	.42	.49	.45	.41	.31	.55	.48
E2	Clergy—Non	−.49	NS	−.40	−.55	NS	−.46	−.52	−.46
	El.Ed.—A	NS	NS	NS	NS	NS	NS	NS	NS
	Clergy—RC	.30	.29	.26	.30	.35	.23	.33	.29
	Industrial	−.38	−.43	−.34	−.23	−.24	−.42	−.50	−.52
	R²	.45	.38	.48	.45	.39	.37	.65	.52
E3	Clergy—Non	−.41	NS	NS	−.55	NS	NS	−.38	NS
	El.Ed.—A	NS	NS	NS	NS	NS	NS	NS	NS

Clergy—RC	.32	.31	.28	.31	.37	.25	.35	.32
Unionization	−.41	−.36	−.38	−.35	−.38	−.41	−.46	−.47
R^2	.47	.35	.52	.51	.46	.37	.64	.50
N =	(96)	(89)	(96)	(92)	(88)	(96)	(97)	(92)
F1								
Clergy—Non	−.57	−.51	−.46	−.60	NS	−.54	−.54	−.50
Clergy—A	NS	.23	NS	NS	NS	.35	.33	.26
Clergy—RC	.26	.23	.22	.27	.32	.20	.30	.23
Manual	−.38	−.46	−.32	−.21	−.27	−.24	−.26	−.37
R^2	.48	.45	.50	.46	.41	.38	.61	.52
F2								
Clergy—Non	−.48	NS	NS	−.57	NS	−.51	−.55	−.48
Clergy—A	NS	NS	NS	NS	−.31	NS	NS	NS
Clergy—RC	.30	.28	.25	.29	.35	.22	.32	.28
Industrial	−.41	−.41	−.37	NS	−.40	−.31	−.44	−.50
R^2	.45	.37	.48	.45	.42	.38	.64	.51
F3								
Clergy—Non	−.43	NS	−.34	−.57	NS	−.50	−.49	−.41
Clergy—A	NS	NS	NS	NS	NS	.25	.19	NS
Clergy—RC	.32	.30	.28	.31	.38	.24	.34	.31
Unionization	−.39	−.31	−.38	−.35	−.46	−.33	−.40	−.41
R^2	.47	.36	.52	.51	.48	.40	.66	.51

The dependent variable is the Unionist share of the parliamentary vote.
Entries are the *standardized* coefficients from nonstepwise regression equations. The R^2 figures are unadjusted.
The equations included dummy variables for "peripheral England," Wales, and Scotland. The value of the coefficients are reported elsewhere.
See Table 6.9 for abbreviations.

TABLE 6.11. Best-fitting Basic Equations, 1885–1910

Election	Nonconformity	Anglicanism	Roman Catholicism	Working Class	Multiple R^2
1885	−.49 (worship)	NS (day school)	.23 (clergy)	−.30 (manual)	.52
1886	−.38 (Sunday School)	NS (clergy)	.24 (clergy)	−.36 (manual)	.46
1892	−.35 (worship)	NS (day school)	.24 (clergy)	−.31 (unionization)	.54
1895	−.52 (worship)	NS (day school)	.27 (clergy)	−.23 (unionization)	.55
1900	NS (worship)	NS (clergy)	.36 (clergy)	−.42 (unionization)	.50
1906	−.50 (clergy)	.25 (clergy)	.24 (clergy)	−.33 (unionization)	.40
1910, Jan.	−.47 (Sunday School)	NS (clergy)	.32 (clergy)	−.28 (unionization)	.69
1910, Dec.	−.27 (worship)	NS (clergy)	.26 (clergy)	−.45 (unionization)	.54

the best equation for each election (see Table 6.11), the equation explaining the greatest proportion of the variance in the vote, the same conclusion emerges. For six of the eight questions listed in Table 6.11, a religious predictor was the strongest variable in the equation.

These results, particularly those for the class measures, underline the point made above about the importance of conceptualization in electoral research. The level of class-based voting depends very much on which class indicator is brought into the equation. The two measures of unskilled workers washed out very early in the analysis. The proportion of manual workers in the occupied population was negatively associated with Unionist voting and significantly so in most equations, yet it was less powerful than one of the religious predictors in forty of forty-four tests. Equating the working class with the industrial sector improved the relative performance of the class interpretation, but a religious variable was still more powerful in all but nine of the equations. The best predictor of class voting, the estimate of trade union strength, had a coefficient larger than the most powerful religious predictor in only sixteen of forty-four trials.

The differential performance of the class measures shows that defining social aggregates by different rules is likely to affect the results of empirical analysis. What we found, to summarize very roughly the performance of the various measures, was that narrowing the scope of class analysis yielded substantial payoffs in the explanation of political behavior. The measure based on trade unionism was so powerful precisely because it was grounded in a theory that linked conditions of work to political consciousness. The alternatives were essentially nominal definitions, useful for social analysis but not necessarily relevant to political behavior. This finding suggests the wisdom of Kornhauser's admonition that research on class-based voting be conducted "within a structure of explicit theory about class relations as dynamic functioning processes."[24]

The relative strength of the trade union measure cannot really be taken as support for the class interpretation of politics under the Third Reform Act. Based on the results of the regression analysis, we cannot sustain broad claims about the electoral significance of class divisions. The measures based on conventional definitions of the working class demonstrated minor or counterintuitive relationships to voting patterns. Class politics were evident in the more limited sense of high levels of class-distinctive voting by the organized section of the industrial workforce. Since that population constituted only a small fragment of the total electorate, the measure cannot account for variations in the vote among the much larger section of the electorate outside the classification. For that, we will have to examine the other variables commonly invoked in electoral sociology.

Religion was of course the main alternative to class in this study, and the results of the analysis show strong religious effects which did not vary much despite multiple measures. Whether defined in organizational, communal or philosophical terms, Nonconformity was a strong, significant, negative predictor of Conservatism. Based on a comparison of standardized coefficients, Nonconformity was in fact the most potent variable in structuring the mass vote. Surprisingly, Anglicanism failed to attain significance as a predictor of Conservative voting. The inclusion of regional variables appears to have eliminated any independent Anglican effect upon the vote. Much more surprising was the consistently positive relationship between the distribution of Catholicism and Conservative-Unionist electoral support, a finding that also emerged from the correlation analysis earlier in this chapter. Rather than interpret the coefficients to mean that Catholic voters favored Conservative candidates—a most unlikely explanation—it makes

[24] Arthur Kornhauser, "Public Opinion and Social Class," *American Journal of Sociology* 55 (January 1950), 339.

sense to treat the coefficients as areal correlations which lead to false inferences about the behavior of individuals. Their status as relatively recent migrants from rural Ireland had allowed few British Catholics to achieve the economic security necessary for enfranchisement or voter registration; their geographical concentration nevertheless frequently sparked an anti-Irish backlash among Protestants who regarded the immigrants as competitors for scarce employment. Because the Liberals were regarded as especially sympathetic to Irish aspirations, this backlash took the form of voting against Liberal candidates. The positive coefficients might then represent the Conservative gain from the anti-Catholic sentiment expressed at the polls. The historical enmity between the Catholic Church and the Church of England makes it likely that the bulk of these votes came from Anglicans. This might also explain the absence of direct Anglican effects on the vote.[25]

If the data do not show a "modern" party system in which class rather than religion structures the party coalitions, is there any evidence that class effects grew over time at the expense of religious forces? Some of the more carefully worded statements about class effects before World War I have emphasized the growing importance of class cleavages over time, not the predominance of class conflict over traditional religious divisions. But even this modified version of the class interpretation was contradicted by the data. Simply put, there was no linear decrease in religious effect and no corresponding linear increase in class-voting from 1885 to 1910. This can be seen most clearly by abstracting from Table 6.10 the standardized coefficients for the Nonconformist variables, generally the most potent of the religious measures, and the coefficients for the three class measures. Coefficients lacking significance are represented in Tables 6.12 and 6.13 by parentheses around the actual value.

[25] See Miller and Raab, "Religious Alignment," p. 250. The same argument has been advanced by Kinnear, *British Voter*, p. 14.

Neither table suggests any linear trends or cleavage shifts. The coefficients for Nonconformity (Table 6.12) did bob up and down but there was no linear decrement over time. In fact, the only invariant tendency was a decline in the magnitude of the Nonconformist coefficients for 1900, but this seems not to have had any long-term effects. It is equally difficult to read any long-term trend into the class coefficients in Table 6.13. The coefficients were not markedly higher at the end of the period than they had been at the beginning. Two of the class measures did fall below significance in most of the equations for 1895, but this was not true for the trade union measure and, in any case, the coefficients returned to higher levels in 1900.

The stability of the cleavage structure also emerges from

TABLE 6.12. Standardized Coefficients for Nonconformist Effect Upon the Unionist Vote, 1885–1910

Form	1885	1886	1892	1895	1900	1906	Jan. 1910	Dec. 1910
Sunday School attendance, 1851								
A1	−.34	−.37	−.41	−.45	(−.20)	−.37	−.55	−.33
A2	−.30	−.35	−.39	−.45	(−.15)	−.37	−.50	−.32
A3	(−.27)	−.35	−.35	−.38	(−.10)	−.34	−.47	−.31
B1	−.35	−.39	−.42	−.43	(−.18)	−.45	−.59	−.36
B2	−.30	−.34	−.38	−.43	(−.15)	−.37	−.48	−.29
B3	(−.27)	−.35	−.34	−.35	(−.08)	−.34	−.48	−.31
Worship attendance, 1851								
C1	−.49	−.29	−.38	−.55	−.28	−.34	−.30	(−.24)
C2	−.52	−.42	−.41	−.56	−.31	−.35	−.31	−.28
C3	−.47	−.38	−.35	−.52	(−.25)	−.31	−.25	(−.23)
D1	−.39	−.36	−.36	−.48	(−.24)	−.30	−.29	−.24
D2	−.41	−.39	−.37	−.49	−.25	−.31	−.30	−.27
D3	−.36	−.36	−.32	−.44	(−.19)	−.27	−.25	−.22
Clergy, 1891								
E1	−.50	(−.39)	(−.38)	−.50	(−.12)	(−.32)	−.34	(−.31)
E2	−.49	(−.34)	−.40	−.55	(−.12)	−.46	−.52	−.46
E3	−.41	(−.18)	−.33	−.55	(−.14)	(−.36)	−.38	−.38
F1	−.57	−.51	−.46	−.60	(−.06)	−.54	−.54	−.50
F2	−.48	(−.35)	(−.38)	−.57	(−.01)	−.51	−.55	−.48
F3	−.43	(−.28)	−.34	−.57	(−.02)	−.50	−.49	−.41

"Form" refers to the basic equation form indicated in Table 6.9.
Nonsignificant coefficients are in parentheses.

TABLE 6.13. Standardized Coefficients for Class Effects
Upon the Unionist Vote, 1885–1910

Form	1885	1886	1892	1895	1900	1906	Jan. 1910	Dec. 1910
Manual workers, 1891								
A	−.29	−.36	−.24	(−.13)	−.25	(−.14)	−.15	−.28
B	−.30	−.38	−.24	(−.12)	−.23	−.20	−.22	−.35
C	−.30	−.39	−.25	(−.09)	−.24	(−.15)	−.18	−.31
D	−.19	−.32	−.22	(−.08)	−.27	−.24	−.26	−.37
E	−.41	−.49	−.34	−.22	−.23	(−.18)	−.18	−.30
F	−.38	−.46	−.32	−.21	−.27	−.28	−.29	−.41
Industrial workers, 1891								
A	−.29	−.31	−.25	(−.08)	−.36	(−.16)	−.27	−.35
B	−.22	−.31	−.18	(−.04)	−.21	−.32	−.39	−.43
C	−.28	−.34	−.25	(−.11)	−.39	−.30	−.38	−.45
D	−.28	−.34	−.34	(−.17)	−.40	−.31	−.44	−.50
E	−.38	−.43	−.34	−.23	(−.18)	−.24	−.29	−.34
F	−.41	−.41	−.37	(−.22)	−.24	−.42	−.50	−.52
Unionized workers, 1891								
A	−.32	−.24	−.30	−.26	−.44	−.22	−.28	−.32
B	−.30	−.27	−.27	−.21	−.34	−.32	−.39	−.41
C	−.31	−.29	−.31	−.23	−.42	−.25	−.31	−.37
D	−.29	−.24	−.32	−.25	−.46	−.33	−.40	−.41
E	−.41	−.36	−.38	−.35	−.35	−.28	−.32	−.34
F	−.39	−.31	−.38	−.35	−.38	−.41	−.46	−.47

See Table 6.12.

the best equations which were displayed in Table 6.11. If the vote had moved from a religious to a class basis during the period, we might expect some consistent pattern of change in the predictive capacity of the equations. A quick look at the values of R^2 in Table 6.11 reveals no such pattern. For most elections, the best equation accounted for slightly more than half the variance in Unionist voting. The pronounced deviations from that value are explicable in terms of particular election circumstances. The decline in predictive capacity for 1886 was probably due to the confusion caused by the schism within Liberalism which temporarily altered the traditional Conservative support pattern. The pronounced anti-Conservative backlash in 1906 was so widespread that it temporarily obscured the social distinctiveness of the party coalitions. The surge in predictive capacity in January 1910 is no surprise considering how well-defined the issues in the campaign were along both class and religious lines. These temporal shifts should be regarded as short-term fluctuations rather than as evidence of any fundamental realignment of electoral forces.

The dummy variables were entered to determine if the vote varied by region in a manner not explainable solely by the differential class or religious composition. The coefficients for the three regional variables, listed in Tables 6.14 to 6.16, indicate that regionalism was a significant political factor in several elections. A common pattern of negative coefficients testifies to the existence of anti-Conservative sentiment in areas outside central England. The variations among the three regional dummies suggest that the impact of regional forces depended greatly on the issues in each election. Thus, Wales registered notably high rates of anti-Conservative sentiment in 1892, probably in response to Liberal support for Welsh disestablishment; in 1900, during its opposition to the Boer War; and in the election of January 1910, when Lloyd George attained the status of a Welsh folk hero for his attacks on the aristocracy. The stable anti-Unionist vote in Scotland probably represents the strong Liberal tradition that characterized Scottish politics until the First World War.[26] The most intriguing pattern of all is revealed by the variable representing peripheral English counties. The measure was not significant to any consistent degree for 1885 to 1900, but it was an important predictor of anti-Unionist voting in all three elections at the end of the period. As the bulk of units in this category were in Lancashire, the change probably represents the growth of the "New Liberal" or "Progressive" movement which Clarke has documented in his research.[27] Whatever the differences in regional patterns from one

[26] Ian Budge and D. W. Urwin, *Scottish Political Behavior* (New York: Barnes and Noble, 1966), pp. 4–12.
[27] Clarke, *Lancashire.*

Table 6.14. Standardized Coefficients for Scottish Effects Upon the Unionist Vote, 1885–1910

Form	1885	1886	1892	1895	1900	1906	Jan. 1910	Dec. 1910
A1	−.55	−.40	−.37	−.43	−.40	−.23	−.30	−.39
A2	−.63	−.47	−.44	−.45	−.51	−.27	−.47	−.49
A3	−.53	−.36	−.36	−.43	−.40	−.22	−.38	−.37
B1	−.53	−.42	−.35	−.42	−.34	−.31	−.45	−.44
B2	−.58	−.51	−.39	−.44	−.38	−.36	−.51	−.51
B3	−.51	−.42	−.33	−.41	−.31	−.29	−.42	−.41
C1	−.36	(.21)	(.19)	−.24	(−.22)	(−.14)	−.28	−.31
C2	−.42	−.33	−.25	−.27	−.27	−.22	−.38	−.40
C3	−.35	(−.22)	(−.19)	−.24	−.22	(−.14)	−.28	−.30
D1	−.43	−.24	−.31	−.31	−.34	(−.20)	−.30	−.37
D2	−.50	−.33	−.41	−.36	−.45	−.29	−.41	−.47
D3	−.44	(−.23)	−.33	−.34	−.37	−.21	−.32	−.36
E1	(−.26)	(−.14)	(−.11)	(−.15)	(−.24)	(−.08)	(−.20)	(−.22)
E2	−.35	−.32	(−.19)	(−.20)	(−.31)	(−.11)	−.24	(−.26)
E3	−.28	(−.26)	(−.12)	(−.12)	(−.22)	(−.04)	(−.17)	(−.21)
F1	(−.20)	(−.40)	(−.04)	(−.05)	(−.32)	(−.15)	(−.01)	(−.03)
F2	(−.25)	(−.21)	(−.21)	(−.15)	.49	(−.04)	(−.14)	(−.19)
F3	−.26	(−.14)	(−.11)	(−.09)	−.38	(.13)	(−.02)	(−.06)

The letter in "Form" refers to Table 6.9.

TABLE 6.15. Standardized Coefficients for Welsh Effects
Upon the Unionist Vote, 1885–1910

Form	1885	1886	1892	1895	1900	1906	Jan. 1910	Dec. 1910
A1	(−.15)	(−.19)	−.35	(−.20)	−.37	(−.16)	−.23	−.28
A2	(−.06)	(−.08)	−.27	(−.16)	−.31	(−.12)	−.20	
A3	(−.02)	(−.003)	−.20	(−.11)	−.21	(−.07)	(−.13)	(−.11)
B1	(−.12)	(−.16)	−.34	(−.12)	−.38	(−.10)	(−.18)	(−.25)
B2	(−.08)	(−.12)	−.31	(−.04)	−.35	(−.13)	−.23	(−.25)
B3	(−.01)	(−.005)	−.24	(−.18)	−.29	(−.03)	(−.11)	(−.11)
C1	(.008)	(−.15)	−.36	(−.13)	−.31	(−.18)	−.42	−.34
C2	(.10)	(−.05)	−.28	(−.09)	−.24	(−.13)	−.36	−.25
C3	(.19)	(.05)	(−.20)	(−.04)	(−.16)	(−.05)	−.26	(−.14)
D1	(.03)	(−.17)	−.35	(−.12)	−.32	(−.19)	−.41	−.33
D2	(−.07)	(−.03)	−.24	(−.07)	(−.22)	(−.12)	−.32	(−.20)
D3	(−.12)	(.02)	(−.18)	(−.02)	(−.14)	(−.07)	−.26	(−.13)
E1	(.02)	(−.14)	(−.35)	(−.16)	−.42	(−.19)	−.37	(−.27)
E2	(.11)	(−.09)	(−.26)	(0.06)	(−.36)	(−.01)	(−.15)	(−.07)
E3	(.20)	(−.08)	(−.17)	(.09)	(−.22)	(−.05)	(−.09)	(−.05)
F1	(−.05)	(−.07)	(−.31)	(−.07)	−.48	(−.04)	(−.22)	(−.13)
F2	(.12)	(−.04)	(−.24)	(−.01)	−.42	(.04)	(−.10)	(−.01)
F3	(.21)	(−.01)	(−.15)	(.13)	(−.30)	(.13)	(−.02)	(−.04)

The letter in "Form" refers to Table 6.9.

election to the next, the coefficients for the regional variables confirm the political distinctiveness of the "Celtic fringe" in the period before the First World War.[28]

The results discussed so far were based on analysis of the complete British data set. Because the aggregation procedure gives somewhat disproportionate weight to the sparsely populated, traditionally religious counties of Wales and Scotland, the results might conceivably overrepresent the role of religion and understate class effects on the vote. To determine if the results were so affected, the analysis was replicated using only the English units. Table 6.17 presents data on the best equation for each election using only the English cases.

Although the reanalysis does result in somewhat stronger class effects, the data in Table 6.17 generally conform to

[28] Hechter, *Internal Colonialism.*

TABLE 6.16. Standardized Coefficients for the "Peripheral England"
Effects Upon the Unionist Vote, 1885–1910

Form	1885	1886	1892	1895	1900	1906	Jan. 1910	Dec. 1910
A1	(−.02)	(−.07)	(−.10)	(−.15)	(−.13)	−.23	−.26	−.20
A2	(−.02)	(−.08)	(−.13)	(−.16)	(−.12)	−.23	−.24	−.20
A3	(.01)	(−.07)	(−.10)	(−.12)	(−.08)	−.20	−.22	−.18
B1	(−.01)	(−.07)	(−.12)	(−.15)	(−.11)	−.25	−.28	−.22
B2	(−.02)	(−.09)	(−.13)	(−.16)	(−.12)	−.24	−.25	−.21
B3	(.01)	(−.08)	(−.10)	(−.12)	(−.07)	−.22	−.23	−.20
C1	(−.06)	(−.12)	−.19	−.22	(−.15)	−.33	−.37	−.27
C2	(−.04)	(−.12)	(−.16)	−.21	(−.14)	−.28	−.31	−.24
C3	(−.02)	(−.11)	(−.14)	(−.16)	(−.08)	−.26	−.29	−.23
D1	(−.06)	(−.11)	−.17	−.20	(−.16)	−.27	−.33	−.25
D2	(−.04)	(−.11)	(−.15)	−.19	(−.14)	−.25	−.30	−.24
D3	(−.02)	(−.10)	(−.13)	−.15	(−.10)	−.23	−.27	−.22
E1	(−.03)	(−.09)	(−.17)	−.19	(−.14)	−.31	−.36	−.25
E2	(−.01)	(−.10)	(−.14)	(−.17)	(−.13)	−.24	−.27	−.20
E3	(.01)	(−.10)	(−.11)	(−.12)	(−.07)	−.23	−.26	−.21
F1	(−.02)	(−.07)	(−.15)	(−.16)	(−.16)	−.24	−.28	−.20
F2	(−.01)	(−.09)	(−.14)	(−.15)	(−.14)	−.22	−.25	−.19
F3	(−.02)	(−.08)	(−.11)	(−.10)	(−.09)	(−.19)	−.23	(−.18)

The letter in "Form" refers to Table 6.9.

the results obtained for all British units in Table 6.11 above.
It remains the case for six of the eight elections that a
religious variable was more powerful than a class measure.
There is no evidence from the English cases, as there was
none for Britain as a whole, that class displaced religion as
the major line of electoral cleavage by the end of the period.
In fact, in the last election before World War I, the value
of the Nonconformist coefficient reached its maximum,
and the disparity between it and the strongest class measure
reached a level surpassed only in one other election. A
measure of Nonconformity was generally the most potent
predictor of the vote, and the trade union measure was the
most powerful class indicator in both sets of data. Likewise,
the direction of the coefficients, excepting the peculiar Anglican measure in 1900, followed the same pattern that was
observed in the British analysis.

The best that can be said for the revisionist view based

Table 6.17. Best-fitting Equation, English Units Only, 1885–1910

Election	Nonconformity	Anglicanism	Roman Catholicism	Working Class	Multiple R^2
1885	−.41 (worship)	NS	.28 (clergy)	−.34 (unionization)	.44
1886	NS (worship)	.21 (day school)	NS (clergy)	−.38 (manual)	.39
1892	−.30 (worship)	NS (clergy)	NS (clergy)	−.37 (unionization)	.30
1895	−.32 (worship)	NS (clergy)	.30 (clergy)	−.32 (unionization)	.34
1900	−.30 (Sunday School)	−.37 (clergy)	.43 (clergy)	−.39 (unionization)	.46
1906	−.39 (Sunday School)	NS (clergy)	NS (clergy)	NS (unionization)	.35
1910, Jan.	−.37 (Sunday School)	NS (clergy)	.31 (clergy)	−.36 (unionization)	.56
1910, Dec.	−.43 (Sunday School)	NS (day school)	.23 (clergy)	−.31 (industrialization)	.45

on Table 6.17 is that class had achieved a rough parity with religion before World War I. Even that statement requires that we ignore the real difficulties of measuring religion, especially in comparison to the close correspondence between conceptualizations of the class structure and the occupational data provided by the census. The essentially premodern character of the prewar alignment, even in England, becomes more evident when the results of Table 6.17 are compared with comparable analysis of Conservative electoral support after 1918.[29] Data for such a comparison are presented in Table 6.18. In all five elections held between 1918 and 1929, Miller's class measure exceeded all of the religious variables in its effect on Conservative vote fortunes. The magnitude of class effects was considerably greater with a standardized regression coef-

TABLE 6.18. Best-fitting Equations, English Units Only, 1885–1929

Election	Class	Anglicanism	Catholicism	Non-conformity	Multiple R^2
1885	− .34	.09	.28	− .41	.44
1886	− .38	.21	.21	− .22	.39
1892	− .37	.01	.21	− .30	.30
1895	− .32	− .02	.30	− .32	.34
1900	− .39	− .37	.43	− .30	.46
1906	− .16	.12	.15	− .39	.35
1910, Jan.	− .36	.08	.31	− .37	.56
1910, Dec.	− .31	− .14	.23	− .43	.45
1918	.65	.47	.03	− .28	.43
1922	.70	.32	.07	− .40	.46
1923	.67	.40	.07	− .33	.53
1924	.66	.34	.10	− .30	.49
1929	.68	.52	.11	− .29	.58

See note 29 in the text.

[29] The data for 1918 to 1929 are taken from Miller and Raab, "Religious Alignment," p. 249. Miller's class measure is the proportion of employers and managers in the workforce and thus represents the middle class. The measures of class for the 1885 to 1910 elections represent the working class. This explains why the sign changes between 1910 and 1918. Miller's equations also included an indicator of rurality which we have not replicated.

ficient of about 0.65 (compared to a maximum value of 0.39 in the earlier period), and the class measure was usually double the value of the corresponding coefficient for Nonconformity. No doubt some of the differences between prewar and postwar analysis should be attributed to the closer fit between electoral and census units after 1911, the closer postwar correspondence between census population and electorate, and improvements in occupational coding that permitted finer discrimination of the class structure in postwar census tabulations. However, these improvements add only marginally to the capacity to explain electoral behavior (average r^2 of 0.41 for prewar, 0.50 for 1918 to 1929) and probably did not account for the dramatic differences in the relative power of the variables. Rather, the trend in the coefficients in Table 6.18 testifies to a marked shift in electoral cleavage patterns between 1910 and 1918— a change from a predominantly religious to a predominantly class alignment in voting.[30]

One last point should be made about the findings from the regression analysis. By the normal standards for historical election analysis, these are quite powerful results. The coefficients are sizable and account for a high degree of variation in the direction of the vote. Such findings are all the more impressive considering the problems of boundary matching and data gathering that combine to introduce a significant possibility of measurement error. The remaining variance is probably due to measurement error and to the importance of "local" factors in an age when the local community sharply bounded the lives and perspectives of many voters.

SUMMARY

What emerges from the analysis is a series of eight elections which were pretty much of a common piece. Conser-

[30] An exact replication of Miller and Raab appears in Table 8.3, Chapter 8.

vative fortunes varied with the concentration of Nonconformists and Roman Catholics and, to a lesser extent, with
the working-class concentration. Voting patterns also showed
regional effects and, to judge from the unexplained variance, were responsive to local factors and traditions.

The results leave little doubt that religion was the major
electoral factor in elections from 1885 to 1910. Class played
an important role but was secondary to religion in its capacity to structure the vote. The next chapter attempts to
penetrate the nature of religious influence by examining
the world-views disseminated by the major denominations.

CHAPTER 7

Religious Beliefs and Political Behavior

By the side of every religion is to be found a political opinion, which is connected with it by affinity. If the human mind be left to follow its own bent, it will regulate the temporal and spiritual institutions of society in a uniform manner, and man will endeavor . . . to *harmonize* earth with heaven.[1] —*Alexis de Tocqueville*

The statistical analysis in Chapter 6 revealed a political system stratified principally along religious lines. The power of religious variables to explain the division of the vote persisted even in the face of controls for social class and regionalism. This chapter attempts to examine the religious factor more thoroughly by presenting a qualitative portrait of the political culture embedded in the major British religious traditions. Like the rest of the monograph, the chapter employs quantitative analysis to sustain parts of the argument.

THE ROLE OF RELIGION

Several reasons for the pervasive linkage between religion and partisanship were first discussed in Chapter 5. It was noted there that denominations may function as interest groups, organized collectivities pursuing goals which necessitate their direct involvement in the policy-making

[1] Alexis de Tocqueville, *Democracy in America*, ed. Phillips Bradley (New York: Vintage Books, 1945), I, 310.

process. Religion may also constitute the basis for a sub-community in which political goals become part of group culture. We considered another possibility—that religion might be one of the elements characterizing or even defining a socially disadvantaged group. In that case, the common political orientation of the disadvantaged group probably owes more to social status that any religious effects as such. The ecological analysis of elections provided some support for the first two approaches, but the robustness of the religious coefficients after controls for class and region prompted us to dismiss the notion that religion was a mere surrogate for social disadvantage.

Another thesis about religious effects also found tentative support from the data analysis of British elections. Following Weber, we noted the possibility that religious groups may transmit distinctive political orientations which affect the behavior of their adherents in secular situations. This thesis was tested by observing correlations between the educational facilities maintained by denominations at midcentury and the partisan distribution of the vote from 1885 to 1910. Notwithstanding the enormous time lag in the data set, regression analysis showed remarkably strong statistical relationships, especially between Nonconformity and support for Liberal and Labour candidates. These results were interpreted as evidence that exposure to a religiopolitical creed early in life had behavioral repercussions many years later.

Such analysis runs against the grain of traditional social scientific research on the political consequences of religion. Suspicious of theories which assign independent causal power to ideas or cultural norms, scholars have been reluctant to accept models that posit a direct link between religion and political values.[2] Even when a demonstrable congruence between religious attitudes and particular patterns of political behavior is apparent, there is a suspicion that reli-

[2] For a typical caution, see Gerhard Lenski, *The Religious Factor*, rev. ed. (Garden City, New York: Doubleday-Anchor, 1963), p. 184.

gious ideas are no more than post-hoc rationalizations employed to legitimate behavior whose origins are likely to have a material basis. Though certainly not as prevalent as was once the case, this skepticism has limited the explanatory role of religion in theories of political action.

This study joins a growing list of works that regard the role of values, particularly those inspired by religion, as important politically influential variables. This phenomenological approach to religion discounts the institutional aspect of religion in favor of relatively greater emphasis upon religion as a form of human endeavor and activity.[3] Religion is that sphere of activity in which men attempt to find some meaning for their existence and which they use to impress a degree of order on the universe. Because of the uniquely human capacity for thought and speculation, men find a need for transcendence. As Kleppner wrote,

Daily, the human actor is faced with an array of situations and events that require interpretation. To understand his world he must make these personally relevant. If the human mind were a *tabula rasa*, that would constitute a formidable cognitive task. Fortunately, the mind does not function in an atomistic way; it does not merely pile up shapeless experiences. Instead the human actor views "new" experiences through an interpretive framework deriving from the sum of his past experiences and value orientations. This framework, or perspective, constitutes the matrix through which he perceives his environment. Through it, the human actor imparts structure and meaning to the "great blooming, buzzing confusion" in the world about him.[4]

[3] Michael Banton, ed., *Anthropological Approaches to the Study of Religion* (New York: Frederick A. Praeger, 1966); Peter Berger, *The Sacred Canopy* (Garden City, New York: Doubleday-Anchor, 1967); Peter Berger and Thomas Luckmann, *The Social Construction of Reality* (Garden City, New York: Doubleday-Anchor, 1966); Robert W. Doherty, "Sociology, Religion and the Historians," *Historical Methods Newsletter* 6 (1973), 16; David Martin, *The Religious and the Secular* (New York: Schocken, 1969); Roland Robertson, *The Sociological Interpretation of Religion* (Oxford: Basil Blackwell, 1970); Bryan R. Wilson, *Religion in Secular Society* (London: C. A. Watts, 1966).

[4] Kleppner, *Cross of Culture*, p. 72.

Religion, "the construction of objective, morally-binding, all-embracing universes of meaning," provides the matrix for satisfying the need for transcendence.[5]

The religious framework may provide clues for behavior in nonreligious settings. Weber noted an "elective affinity" between a particular religious impulse, Puritanism, and a type of economic activity, capitalism. It was not that Puritanism *caused* capitalism but rather, as Laitin has emphasized, that Puritanism endorsed a code of conduct conducive to success in a capitalist economy.[6] Weber hinted that the same process might be at work in politics.[7] Consider the individual whose religion teaches that man is inherently evil, such evil is not offset by good works or right behavior, and the only way to avoid the ultimate penalty for evil is by an intense and private faith—"a lonely relationship between man and God" with church as arbiter. Such a person is not likely to see much point in political reform and will frown upon misguided attempts to change the world. He will even resent attempted changes as intrusions upon his free choice. But consider now his opposite number—the man who is not taught to think in terms of any fixed and immutable human nature. Such an individual believes that man has the capacity to guarantee his own salvation if he will act with rectitude and dignity, shunning the temptations of the world. Such a belief system disposes the individual to sympathize with political reforms which will remove temptations to evil and encourage men to act responsibly.[8]

---

[5] Berger, *Sacred Canopy*, p. 176.

[6] David Laitin, "Religion, Political Culture and the Weberian Tradition," *World Politics* 30 (July 1978), 563–592.

[7] Max Weber, *From Max Weber: Essays in Sociology*, ed. H. H. Gerth and C. Wright Mills (New York: Oxford University Press, 1946), pp. 333–340.

[8] "One's judgment of the practicability of political and social change depends ultimately on one's conception of human nature."—R. H. Tawney, *The British Labor Movement* (New Haven, Ct.: Yale University Press, 1925), p. 170. For an interesting elaboration on the role of ideas about human nature, see Lawrence S. Wrightsman, *Assumptions About Human Nature: A Social-Psychological Approach* (Monterey, Calif.: Brooks/Cole, 1974). The connection between religion, views of human nature, and social and

Under the proper conditions, a religious tradition may come to have more than incidental effects upon political assumptions. The religious tradition may in fact become the basis for assumptions about the very nature of political conduct, a package of ideas and perspectives that form what Hammond has labelled a *political ethos*. In his careful formulation, an ethos is

a system of political attitudes and beliefs held by a group which defines itself other than in political terms. [It is] received through socialization processes; accepted early in life and relatively without question rather than rooted in contemporary structural or political discrepancies and accepted by choice in maturity; relatively independent of variations in personality and position in the social structure; and [furnishes] a set of standards and values motivating politically relevant decisions.[9]

It is tempting to pose this ethos approach as a stark alternative to more conventional models of religion, but it is a matter of differing emphasis rather than a clear-cut choice. Unquestionably, traditional conceptualizations of religion, such as the interest group model, put relatively greater stress upon the organizational as opposed to what might be called the ideational aspect of religious experience. However, it must be recognized that an ethos has to be formed, transmitted, organized, and guided—the work of institutions such as congregations, interfaith coalitions, church schools, the clergy, and all the other concrete manifestations of the visible church. The ethos approach is most usefully deployed not as an opponent of traditional models but as a complementary approach that identifies the mech-

---

political thought has been explored by Jack O. Balswick, "Theology and Political Attitudes Among Clergymen," *Sociological Quarterly* 11 (Summer 1970), 397–404, and Leo Driedger, "Doctrinal Belief: A Major Factor in the Differential Perception of Social Issues," *Sociological Quarterly* 15 (Winter 1975), 67–68.

[9] Hammond, *Politics of Benevolence*, p. 6. For a similar approach, see Ronald P. Formisano, "Analyzing American Voting, 1830–1860: Methods," *Historical Methods Newsletter* 2 (March 1969), 4.

anisms through which the religious impulse is conveyed to secular environments.

With that understanding, we can make some attempt to penetrate the politically relevant dimensions of late Victorian religion. Why did Liberalism elicit such positive reactions from Nonconformists, especially when such an attachment may have contradicted class interest? What was the basis of Anglican attachment to the Conservative party? Without ignoring the factors that have been discussed by other scholars, this chapter concentrates upon the relatively neglected dimension of the politically relevant world-view of the major religious groups in Britain.

THE POLITICAL ORIENTATION OF LIBERALISM

The basic assumptions which undergirded the behavior of the British political parties in the period cannot be fully understood without a recognition of their religious basis. The ethos or spirit of each party owed much to religious conceptions. To quote an anonymous editorial writer for a Norwich newspaper: "Party differences are more than differences of opinion; they are differences existing in those qualities of human nature out of which opinions spring. They are differences in temperament, in frames of mind, in the way in which men habitually look at affairs."[10] This was certainly true for Liberalism.

The major orientation underlying Liberalism, its spirit, was Puritan.[11] When the Puritan surveyed the social order, he was deeply moved by its shortcomings—by the poverty, squalor, unemployment, and disease so prevalent in a rapidly industrializing society. His religion taught him that social vice was avoidable and not due to any inherent character defect in man. If, as he believed, "all men can be saved by a direct confrontation with Christ . . . through the

[10] *Eastern Daily Press*, March 25, 1907, p. 7.
[11] *Sussex Evening Times* (Brighton), October 8, 1896, p. 2, referred to the Liberals as the "Puritan Party."

conversion experience," then the existence of a vast sub-merged population was attributable directly to "the failure of the churches to convert the mass of the people to an active Christianity."[12] The political task of the Puritan was obvious: he had to help make his fellow men thrifty, sober, and industrious by removing all sources of temptation which were amenable to legislative treatment. He accordingly urged on the state the opportunity, duty, and obligation of passing laws which would compel men to act responsibly. Compulsion was regrettable but necessary because men degraded by sin were in no fit condition to receive the word of God.

This Puritan inheritance owed much to the doctrines of John Calvin and his Reformation-era disciples. The heart of the Puritan experience, as noted by virtually all commentators, was the experience of rebirth, the momentous conversion "which separates the Puritan from the mass of mankind and endows him with the privileges and duties of the elect."[13] As part of his salvation, the reborn sinner must strive to bring all of mankind within the pale of God's grace. That is the obligation which conversion confers. It was not for the Christian, Calvin wrote, "merely to seek and secure the salvation of his own soul."[14] Rather, he was obliged by rebirth to demonstrate a commitment to God through "a dedication to warfare against sin."[15] This entailed a decisive rejection of the other-worldly orientation that had hitherto characterized Western Christianity.

A particular vision of human nature is at the heart of this view.[16] On the one hand, Puritans accepted the premise

---

[12] Richard Jensen, *The Winning of the Midwest* (Chicago: University of Chicago Press, 1971), pp. 65–67; W. Ivor Jennings, *Party Politics* (Cambridge: Cambridge University Press, 1962), II, 116.

[13] Alan Simpson, *Puritanism in Old and New England* (Chicago: University of Chicago Press, 1955), p. 2.

[14] Quoted in Walzer, *Revolution of the Saints*, p. 54.

[15] Simpson, *Puritanism*, p. 2.

[16] Merle Curti, *Human Nature in American Historical Thought* (Columbia: University of Missouri Press, 1968), pp. 10–11.

of orthodox Christianity that men were inherently degraded and "would permit their baser passions to lead them astray again and again." On the other hand, men retained enough divine inspiration to make them capable of grasping the possibility of a better world. Under the guidance of the elect, the masses could be brought to improve their conduct and move closer to God's standard for them. The sense that men could act with more rectitude bespeaks a belief that humanity could change and grow. The task of the elect was to apply the pressure that would force humanity into a divinely inspired mold.

Men committed to spreading the glory of God treated the world not as a burden to be endured until the moment of heavenly reward but as a challenge to be met directly. If the earth was "the theater of God's glory," a commitment to Puritanism inescapably involved a commitment to change the world through any available means. As Walzer noted, the "saints" who had experienced rebirth approached political action as part of their mission:

The Puritan cleric insisted that political activity was a creative endeavor in which the saints were privileged as well as obliged to participate. The saints were responsible for the world—as medieval men were not—and responsible above all for its continual reformation. Their enthusiastic and purposive activity was part of their religious life, not something distinct and separate: they acted out their saintliness in debates, elections, administration and warfare.[17]

This commitment to secular action fostered a belief in liberty but not in the laissez faire tradition.

The Puritan favored liberty not in the abstract but as a means to an end.[18] When the Puritan was not free to pursue his mission because of human constraints, he used liberty as a rallying cry. As eager as he was to remove shackles

[17] Walzer, *Revolution of the Saints*, p. 12.
[18] J. B. Brebner, "*Laissez Faire* and State Intervention in Nineteenth-Century Britain," *Journal of Economic History* 8 (1948), supp. 8, 59–73.

that kept him from God's work, the Puritan did not hesitate to impose limits that bound other men to forms of conduct approved by his sense of rectitude. There is no contradiction in this simultaneous emphasis upon liberty and discipline if we keep in mind the instrumental orientation of Puritanism toward liberty, which was useful only if it freed men to act out the purpose of God. Where the Puritans were a persecuted minority, they advocated liberty in order to enlarge the scope of Puritan action. In environments where Puritanism was ascendant, whether in Britain, the Continent, or the New World, the Puritan had little compunction about the use of secular repression as a tool of moral regeneration.

Despite the long and tangled path between the ideas of John Calvin and the Liberal tradition of the late nineteenth century, the two were joined in spirit by a continuity of the Puritan impulse. In fact, the Puritan spirit explains many of the distinctive features of the Liberal party. Consider, for example, the insistence of Liberals on exploring the political relevance of religion. Liberals were contemptuous of those who would treat religion primarily as a "metaphysical subtlety of doctrine" or restrict it to a set series of formal observances.[19] To the Puritan, religion was not some otherworldly doctrine nor an activity which should fill Sunday mornings but a positive guide to human conduct—a set of rules which, if followed in daily life, would lead to the achievement of heaven on earth. Puritans read their Bible broadly as a "Social Gospel" and made the Liberal party a vehicle for fulfilling its commandments. Politics offered the Puritan an opportunity to bring heaven closer by removing institutional obstacles to rectitude. A good Christian, to the Puritan, was a person who used every means to further the cause of righteousness and who ap-

[19] "Religion and Politics," *Norfolk Review*, no. 3 (July 1895), 51. See also Charles Booth, *Life and Labour of the People in London*, 3rd ser. (London: MacMillan, 1903), VII, 119; Blewett, *Peers, Parties and People*, p. 344; John Kempster, *The Bible, The Teetotal Textbook* (London: Richard J. James, 1904), p. 4; Frederick Smith, *Simple Lessons for Young Abstainers* (London: United Kingdom Band of Hope Union, n.d.).

proached the ballot as "the sacrament of human brother-
hood."

A speaker at an eve of poll meeting in Norwich in January
1910 captured the Puritan political attitude when he told
his Nonconformist audience: "They were compelled by their
religious convictions to be a political people. It was impossible for them to escape from their political witness because
they were the followers of Jesus Christ and wanted to see
his kingdom set up on Earth."[20] At Brighton that same
year, Nonconformist electors were urged to support the
Liberals' Parliament bill because "the House of Lords had
stood in the way of the advancement of righteousness and
the Kingdom of God in the country."[21] The Puritan was
repeatedly admonished to regard his vote as a "sacred religious trust" to advance humanity along the path of righteousness. A Norwich Liberal wrote defiantly:

We want the fervor of high purpose in politics. We want our
public life to be the expression of our national hunger and thirst
after righteousness. . . . We want the religious men and women
of England to use their political power for the purpose of insisting
that the purpose of our national organization of life is not merely
to make money but to live justly; that the business of Parliament
and of every local authority is to act as the organized conscience
of the community.[22]

The man who thought otherwise was no Christian:

That gospel which does not concern itself with man's body, mind
and environment, as well as his soul, is a contradiction in terms,
a travesty of truth, a mockery of religion; it is no "good news"
and usurps a title to which it has no claim. If we cannot make

[20] *Eastern Daily Press*, January 15, 1910, p. 10. See also the issue of July
12, 1895, p. 6; *Bradford Observer*, October 17, 1885, p. 4; H. F. Lovell
Cocks, "The Nonconformist Conscience," *Hibbert Journal* 38 (1939–1940),
472; Horton Davies, *The English Free Churches*, 2nd ed. (London: Oxford
University Press, 1963), p. 187; John W. Grant, *Free Churchmanship in
England, 1870–1940* (London: Independent Press, n.d.), p. 88; Stephen
Mayor, "Some Congregational Relations with the Labour Movement,"
Transactions of the Congregational Historical Society 18 (1956), 31.
[21] *Brighton Gazette*, November 30, 1910, p. 2.
[22] "Religion and Politics," p. 52.

our politics part of our religion, we have no right to cast even a vote. If we cannot take our Christianity into even a Borough Council, we ourselves ought to remain outside. If the message we believe in does not rank us in eternal, vehement opposition against the sweater, the slum-landlord, the trafficker in human lives, we need not expect the masses to take seriously either it or us. . . . If we are not forever seeking to remove the shackles which fetter men's bodies, minds and spirits, we have yet to learn the alphabet of the programme of Christianity.[23]

The Liberals accordingly saw themselves as the "Kingdom of God political party."[24]

The Puritan spirit also explains the moral and evangelistic fervor in which the Liberals cloaked their proposals. More than one late Victorian carped at the noxious "holier than thou" attitude of the Liberals. Gladstone—to cite the famous taunt of a Radical MP—was always prone to discover that his newest reform proposal, each "ace up his sleeve," had been put there directly by God Almighty.[25] Lesser Liberals were prone to the same tendency. A rather modest temperance proposal was justified in these apocalyptic terms:

We cannot give life to the dead; but we can roll away the stone that seals them in darkness and the grave; and each one of us can do something in the home or in the school, the world or the church, in the polling-station, and at the throne of grace, to hasten the day when all our people shall be upon the side of Christ, and Satan beneath their feet. Then shall our voices mingle with the great "voices of heaven" in the gladsome shout—"The kingdom of the world is become the Kingdom of our Lord and of his Christ; and He shall reign for ever and ever."—AMEN![26]

[23] Richard Mudie-Smith, "Introduction," in *The Religious Life of London,* ed. Richard Mudie-Smith (London: Hodder and Stoughton, 1902), p. 13.

[24] Cocks, *The Nonconformist Conscience,* p. 85, cited in Grant, *Free Churchmanship,* p. 181.

[25] Cited in Hamilton Fyfe, *The British Liberal Party* (London: George Allen and Unwin, 1928), p. 104. See also Edgar Royston Pike, *Political Parties and Policies* (London: Sir Isaac Pitman, 1934), p. 34, and Trevor Lloyd, *The General Election of 1880* (London: Oxford University Press, 1968), p. 91.

[26] Kempster, *The Bible, the Teetotal Textbook,* p. 15.

Such fervor was the direct outcome of perceiving politics as an "exercise in morality."[27] If political questions were at base moral issues, and if, to cite a Norwich minister, political strife was "nothing more than debate between honest men as to the application of Christian truth to the relations of life," then one side had to be correct and the other side in error.[28] A Puritan does not easily compromise with fundamental error; the Liberals, following their Puritan conscience, never advocated and campaigned—they exhorted and crusaded.

The Puritan inheritance of Liberalism goes a long way to explain why the Liberals stressed certain issues throughout the period. The Liberals identified the institutions or practices that constituted temptations and led men astray to evil behavior. Whatever threatened the moral purity of the people was a fit object of attack. The Bradford Free Church Council told its followers to cast their votes for candidates pledged to "temperance, purity, education freed from clericalism, the just treatment of Labour and the moral health of the people."[29] In the cities, the Liberals attacked horse racing, Sunday opening of museums and libraries, and legalized betting. But the evil which most agitated the Puritans was drink, justifying Harcourt's observation that "temperance is the backbone of the Liberal party."[30]

The Liberal Puritan attacked drink because he thought it lay at the root of the "social question." John Burns, one of the organizers of the great London Dockers' Strike and the first working-class Cabinet minister, characterized alcohol as a social poison:

The tavern throughout the centuries has been the antechamber of the workhouse, the chapel-of-ease to the asylum, the recruiting

[27] D. G. Wright, "Politics and Opinion in Nineteenth Century Bradford, 1832–1880" (Ph.D. thesis, University of Leeds, 1966), I, v. See also Robert Blake, *The Conservative Party from Peel to Churchill* (London: Fontana, 1970), p. 119, and Moore, *Pit-men*, pp. 194–195.

[28] *Eastern Daily Press*, November 21, 1885, p. 3.

[29] *Bradford Observer Budget*, October 7, 1905, p. 8.

[30] Letter, Harcourt to Morley, 1888, cited in Michael Barker, *Gladstone and Radicalism* (Brighton, Eng.: Harvester Press, 1975), p. 209.

173

station for the hospital, the rendezvous of the gambler, and the gathering ground for the gaol. Alcohol pollutes whatever it touches. It enervates what it does not enslave. It destroys slowly that which it does not degrade quickly. For the individual it is a murrain, for the nation it has become a self-inflicted obstacle to all phases of progress, and it lies athwart the path of personal reformation, municipal progress, and state amelioration.[31]

A poor but conscientious worker on payday had to thread his way through streets lined with public houses, each beckoning him momentarily to forget his squalid surroundings through the warmth of the bottle. A select few, fortified by religion, escaped the temptation, but many more succumbed to the unbearable pressure.[32] Those who fell to the lure of the public house were in no fit condition to be good Christians, good workmen, or good citizens and family men. So it fell to the Christian to do all he could to remove the temptation from the worker. In the cities, Liberals fought to restrict the supply of liquor in the workhouse and at public festivities. Nationally, Liberalism was harnessed to measures such as Sunday closing of pubs, local option to deny liquor licenses, and heavy taxation of spirits, all of which would cut down the availability of the hated substance. The long-term goal, lest it be forgotten, was social reform. John Burns stated it directly:

The general summary of my life's experience amongst the working class of this and other countries—sharing their aims, voicing their ideals, championing their causes, leading their movements, a sentinel on the outworks of their social hopes—is that with many of them Drink is their bane, drunkenness their curse, and excessive drinking their greatest defect. From every aspect of their individual social and political condition, it is the worst and chief cause of many of the difficulties that beset and burden them as work-

[31] John Burns, *Labour and Drink* (London: Lees and Roper Memorial Trustees, 1904), p. 1. For a local expression of the same idea, see *Express and Star* (Wolverhampton), October 25, 1888, p. 2.

[32] On pub attendance, see Lady Florence Bell, *At the Works* (London: Edward Arnold, 1907), pp. 10, 132, and "Statistics of Attendance," *Nonconformist and Independent*, February 2, 1882, p. 3.

ingmen, husband, father, breadwinner and citizen. Karl Marx described the British workman as "the prize fighter in the international army of Labour." If that be true, as it certainly is, their physical, mental and moral fitness for their manifold responsibilities would be keener and more effective if they always displayed the abstinence from liquor by which alone athletic vigour can be secured.[33]

The Liberals would wear proudly the label of "social purity party" which cynical Conservatives pinned on them as an insult.

The Liberals were often denigrated for their rigidity. They were held to be overly attached to anachronistic palliatives and inclined to fight battles after the war had ended. In a widely distributed Fabian tract, Sydney Webb unkindly characterized the "19th Century Liberal":

> They have hung up temperance reform and educational reform for a quarter of a century because instead of seeking to enable the citizen to refresh himself without being poisoned or inebriated, and to get the children thoroughly taught, they have wanted primarily to revenge their outraged temperance principles on the publican and their outraged Nonconformist principles on the Church. Of such Liberals it may be said that the destructive revolutionary tradition is in their bones; they will reform nothing unless it can be done at the expense of their enemies. Moral superiority, virtuous indignation, are necessaries [sic] of political life to them; a Liberal reform is never simply a social means to a social end, but a campaign of Good against Evil.[34]

Reformers were particularly frustrated by the Liberal's apparent indifference to the "social question." The nostrums of the Liberals seemed irrelevant and beside the point in an age of increasing social consciousness—and so the Liberals were told by some working-class spokesmen.[35] But the Liberals would not abandon their cherished causes and

---

[33] Burns, *Labour and Drink*, p. 4.

[34] Sidney Webb, *Twentieth Century Politics: A Policy of National Efficiency,* "Fabian Tract #108," (London: Fabian Society, 1901), p. 4.

[35] *Brighton Gazette*, October 18, 1906, p. 5.

expressed frustration at the hostility of the people who should have been their allies in the cause of progress. To the Liberals, with their Puritan heritage, the drink question *was* the social question and their attacks on liquor were efforts at social betterment. If liquor was the cause of poverty, as the Puritans believed, attacks on poverty which did not restrict the flow of alcohol were themselves beside the point. It is not difficult to see how this attitude estranged the Liberals from their erstwhile left-wing allies.

When the establishment of permanent municipal relief committees was first proposed in Wolverhampton, the Liberal newspapers led the opposition to the scheme.[36] Individuals were poor, readers were told, because they took to drink. If the state stepped in with assistance for a poor man's family, that man would have no incentive to stay off the bottle. So the Wolverhampton Liberals opposed one of the basic building blocks of the welfare state because they saw some deterrent value in the threat of poverty. The well-meaning designs of secular reformers, to the Liberals, were plans that would merely exacerbate existing problems. John Burns reacted with scorn to those benighted reformers who sought to reduce poverty only by raising wages. "As the escape from poverty is in many cases celebrated by a series of drunken orgies," he said, "a rise in wages often poses more of a curse than a blessing."[37] T. P. Whittaker, a leading Liberal MP and temperance worker, followed the same reasoning when he opposed state action to improve working-class housing:

Go through those colliery villages, and you will see that many of the homes are clean and bright and comfortable, and the wives and children are cheerful, happy and well cared for. Others are neglected, dirty and miserable, and the women and children correspond. Make inquiry, and you will find, in practically every case, that the bright and happy home is a sober one and the neglected and miserable one is a drunken home. Does anyone with the

[36] *Evening Express and Star*, July 18, 1885, p. 2.
[37] Burns, *Labour and Drink*, p. 15.

slightest knowledge of the facts suppose that if the occupants of these homes were exchanged, and the bright, happy, and sober family were put into the dirty and poverty-stricken home, and the drunken and miserable family were put into the clean and well-kept cottage, the families would be transformed also? Not a bit of it. The houses would not transform the families, but the families would speedily transform the houses.[38]

Such utterances were well within the spirit of classic English Liberalism. Richard Cobden, one of the patron saints of nineteenth-century Liberalism, had set the same tone years earlier when he said:

Every day's experience tends more and more to confirm me in my opinion that the Temperance cause lies at the foundation of all social and political reform. It is in vain to seek, by the extension of the franchise, or by Free Trade, or by any other means, to elevate the labouring masses. In fact, their destiny is in their own hands, and they will, as a class, be elevated or depressed in the social scale, in proportion to the extent of their virtues or vices. They are, therefore, the truest friends of the working millions who are labouring in the cause of Temperance.[39]

No wonder the Liberal temperance reformers reacted with bland incomprehension when they were accused of indifference to social issues.

The argument that Liberalism was actuated by the Puritan spirit subsumes the traditional religious model which connected the "interests" of Nonconformists with the Liberal party. The ethos approach also connects the "ideas" of Nonconformity with the Liberal party. The two approaches are not wholly incompatible, as noted above, because the Puritan spirit was organized and disseminated by the Protestant Nonconformists, and Free Church leaders

[38] T. P. Whittaker, *The Economic Aspect of the Drink Question* (London: Lees and Roper Memorial Trustees, 1902), pp. 40, 45–46, 47. See also Alfred Illingworth, *Fifty Years of Politics* (Bradford: Bradford and District Newspaper Company, 1905), p. 46.

[39] Cited in George B. Wilson, ed., *Alliance Yearbook and Temperance Reformers Handbook for 1910* (Manchester: United Kingdom Alliance, 1910), p. 37.

worked diligently to defend both the ideas and the institutions associated with the ethos.

CONSERVATISM

The central tendency of Conservatism, by contrast, was distinctly non-Puritan. The Conservative who confronted social reality also saw the poverty, unemployment, malnutrition, and overcrowding which so moved the Puritan. He was, however, much less sanguine about the prospects for reform. The awful conditions of life on earth he ascribed to defects in human nature. Man, he averred, was born in a state of sin and would die in sin. Life was essentially "a faithful and resigned stewardship in an inscrutable world created by an unfathomable God."[40] If man was beyond redemption, there was little point in social engineering. To quote a recent Conservative theoretician: "Once you have accepted man for what he is, once you have replaced perfection by improvement, once you have learned to postpone the Kingdom of God to the timeless plane of the *Civitas Dei*, then the principles of Conservatism become clear."[41] A man's material condition was secondary and irrelevant to his spiritual condition. The rewards of afterlife for the righteous would more than make up for the privations of life on earth. A man's spiritual condition, in turn, was nobody's business but his own and his church's.

Much that is distinctive in Conservatism derives from the non-Puritan perspective. As adamantly as the Puritan stressed the link between religion and politics, the Conservative insisted on distinguishing between the sacred cosmos of religion and the profane world of political life. The theological underpinning to the separation of body and soul was

[40] Kleppner, *Cross of Culture*, p. 73.

[41] R. J. White, *The Conservative Tradition*, 2nd ed. (London: Adam and Charles Black, 1964), pp. 3–4. See also the *Norwich Diocesan Gazette* 11 (1905), 3, and 12 (1906), 3, and Kenneth Pickthorn, *Principles or Prejudices* (London: Signpost Press, 1944), p. 9.

expressed most clearly by a clergyman who fought against it:

Christianity, it is said, moves in a higher realm than that of hum-drum toil, and operates for far higher purposes than settling the disputes of capital and labour, and adjusting profit and loss, organizing production and distribution, fighting a dangerous plutocracy, and mediating peace between the masses of wage-earners and a narrowing number of wage-payers. It does not "preach a gospel of material blessedness." It ministers to a mind diseased by sin, banishes remorse and prepares for death and eternity. It is not concerned with this fleeting life . . . but with the infinite development of the human spirit through the eternity, and in the home, of God.[42]

If that were true, the person who dragged religion into politics was guilty of a dangerous materialism and did no good for his own soul. Of course, the good Christian was charged to keep an eye out for threats to his Church and stand fast in the face of danger. But aside from that defensive posture, the Church frowned upon attempts to buttress political causes with scriptural authority. The non-Puritan construed his Bible strictly. Anything mentioned favorably was to be respected for its divine origin; anything not prescribed or endorsed was to be a matter of individual conscience, something over which reasonable people could disagree.[43] So if the Bible did not explicitly endorse slum clearance, redistribution of income, and prohibition, then it was absurd to claim scriptural support for those causes, and good Christians were free to decide for themselves.

The tone of Conservatism was markedly different from Liberalism and that, too, can be explained by the religious orientation behind it. The non-Puritan supported a pro-

[42] John Clifford, *Socialism and the Teaching of Christ*, Fabian Tract #78 (London: Fabian Society, 1897), p. 2. Kenneth Inglis equates this notion with evangelicalism; see his "English Nonconformity and Social Reform, 1880–1900," *Past and Present*, no. 13 (1958), 83.

[43] Reverend Canon West, *The C.E.T.S. and Party Politics* (London: CETS Temperance Publication Depot, 1891), p. 2. See also J. Johnson Baker, *Three Aspects of Temperance* (London: CETS, n.d.), p. 2.

posal not because it was divinely ordained but because it promised concrete benefits. Persons should act with dignity not because they had to but because they chose to do so. "We believe," said the Dean of Rochester, "in conviction, and not in constraint; in the love of virtue rather than in the fear of sin; in Divine Guidance rather than in human laws."[44] The person who attempted to force his reading of the Bible and his conception of morality upon another was a great danger to society. Liberal crusades on behalf of principle were routinely denounced as unconscionable intrusions upon the rights of freeborn Englishmen.

Indeed, the constant theme underlying the speeches of Conservatives was laissez faire liberalism, a notion traditionally associated with the Liberals. Bradford electors were confronted in 1885 with a circular from "An Englishman" headed "Liberty Against Tyranny":

ELECTORS,

You are told by the Teetotalers ONLY TO VOTE FOR CANDIDATES WHO WILL FORBID YOU TO DRINK BEER!

VOTE HOW YOU PLEASE!

Teetotalers are already trying to take your tobacco from you, as well as your beer. Soon they will want to stop your meat . . .

Remember the class of people you are giving yourselves up to if you join the Teetotalers. They are so anxious to find you out doing anything wrong, that THEY ARE OBLIGED TO EMPLOY SPIES TO ENTRAP YOU.

DON'T LET THEM HAVE IT ALL THEIR OWN WAY. You have a right to SOME enjoyment in life as well as the rich, and you have a right to expect that Teetotalers should pay their fair share of the Country's Taxes.

THINK NO WORSE OF THE MAN WHO DECLINES TO ROB YOU OF YOUR BEER.[45]

---

[44] Quoted in John Kempster, *The Dean and the Drink* (London: Bowers Brothers, 1892), p. 13. See also Pickthorn, *Principles*, p. 20, and White, *Conservative Tradition*, pp. 4–5.

[45] The circular is in the elections file at the Bradford Central Library.

Two years later, when an avowed Prohibitionist sought re-election to a Bradford parliamentary seat, his constituents were informed by a handbill:

Bradford possesses as its parliamentary representative for the East division a professing Christian, who is an apostle of "prohibition" i.e., the total and immediate suppression of trade in alcoholic beverages by compulsory state prohibition, and hence compulsory total abstinence for individuals. . . . Are we sane to decree our own slavery, appointing meanwhile a few converted drunkards, old women, fanatics and fools to be our keepers? . . . above all return not fawning fanatics, canting humbugs and would be tyrants to represent us in Parliament.[46]

The same theme sounded in Brighton. Conservative newspapers insisted that the availability of liquor at public functions was a matter for individual conscience, not public policy.[47] When temperance forces persisted, the newspaper found it "inconceivable that fully grown men, citizens of a country which is ever boasting of its freedom, will tolerate this meddling with their personal affairs merely to satisfy the anti-drink and Sabbatarian fanatics."[48] The Conservative candidate for Norwich in 1906 declared that his party "would have nothing to do with the infringement of individual liberty," an undistorted echo of the Conservative MP for Reading who had earlier stated that, "so long as he had a seat in Parliament, he would resist any effort which might be made by the bigoted to interfere with any man's just rights."[49] To the non-Puritan, in sum, combining religion and politics would threaten the rights of the freeborn Englishman.

Even if the Conservatives agreed with the Liberals on

---

[46] The handbill is also in the elections file at the Bradford Central Library. See also *Bradford Observer*, July 16, 1895, p. 5.

[47] *Sussex Evening Times*, October 17, 1907, p. 5.

[48] *Brighton Gazette*, March 28, 1908, p. 5. A similar denunciation is in the *Sussex Evening Times*, October 25, 1893, p. 2.

[49] *Eastern Daily Press*, January 13, 1906, p. 9, and *Reading Observer*, March 12, 1887, p. 2.

the existence of a problem, they were usually compelled by their religious beliefs to advocate a different solution. The Liberals were generally eager to harness the power of government in attempts to remove temptation. The Conservatives, true to their non-Puritan orientation, were prone to trust to the soul of the individual the task of resisting temptation. For example, many non-Puritans agreed with Puritans that drink was a serious problem, and they would have liked to see alcohol consumption drop. Yet they invariably objected to the methods which the Liberal Puritans used. The director of the Church of England Temperance Society (CETS) declared flatly in Reading that "intemperance was a sin and could only be put down by reforming the people and winning their hearts for Jesus Christ."[50] In the same vein, the Archdeacon of Norwich counselled the Norwich branch of the CETS:

If . . . we believed, as we did earnestly believe, that this temperance question was at the root of it a religious question—and that men would never have real power over their surroundings or over their temptations unless they were sustained by the energy of the Christian faith and the sacraments, it should be the supreme duty of our lives to bring those people one by one under the influence of the cross of Christ.[51]

The solution to the problem of sin lay in the soul. Even if they thought liquor the source of great evil, non-Puritans expressed little faith in government action and opposed Sunday closing, local option, and heavy taxation. The education of public opinion was greatly to be preferred to legislative coercion. "Dealing with the problem by legislation," said the President of the Norwich CETS, "was only touching the fringe of the difficulty, because the evil lay in human nature itself, and human nature could only be purified by religious influence."[52] The Conservative non-Pu-

[50] *Reading Observer*, March 21, 1903, p. 2; *Norwich Diocesan Gazette* 10 (1904), 27–28; *Norfolk Chronicle*, October 17, 1896, p. 12.
[51] *Eastern Daily Press*, November 5, 1902, p. 8.
[52] *Ibid.*, and *Express and Star*, June 28, 1892, p. 3.

ritans, in sum, were reluctant to use government as an agency of salvation.

The Conservatives were as rigid as the Liberals in their attitude toward general social reform. They acknowledged the existence of conditions which were called, collectively, "the social problem," but they inclined to downplay it. Left-wing reform was often rejected as incompatible with the dictates of Christianity.[53] Most Socialist reforms, argued the non-Puritan, ignored the role of God, worship, personal conversion, and spiritual regeneration, and toyed instead with the material aspects of society. This approach over-looked a fundamental non-Puritan truth, which was stated by the dean of Norwich Cathedral:

When he heard so much about the beneficent results that were expected from the action of this Government or that Government in dealing with the liquor traffic, and when he found that so little progress was made by one Government or by another, he came to the conclusion that it was not of the least use in these days to expect over-much from the Government . . . he believed it to be an indisputable truth that no Government could do for a man half as much as every man could do for himself . . . [54]

With that perspective, broad-ranging social reform was not likely to get a sympathetic hearing.

Lest this presentation imply too mechanistic a view of the link between religion and political outlook, we must acknowledge the conditional nature of the relationship. Because nothing is automatic about the translation of social conflicts into partisan cleavages, religious orientations had to be organized and harnessed to political referents. A party will embody the political spirit of a religion only when political elites seek to make the party a spokesman for a religious impulse. The religious orientations described above

[53] Stanley A. Pierson, "Socialism and Religion: A Study of Their Inter-action in Great Britain, 1889–1911" (Ph.D. thesis, Harvard University, 1957), pp. 6, 244–245, 253.

[54] *Eastern Daily Press*, October 12, 1892, p. 5, and *Brighton Gazette*, October 20, 1904, p. 6.

are *dispositions*; it required positive action by party leaders to capitalize on those affinities and harness the latent sympathies of the denomination to the party.

The two architects of the Victorian party alignment consciously evoked certain sociopolitical values as a basis for party coalitions. Gladstone's penchant for moralizing political issues prompted his biographer to label his subject as a "Christian Statesman."[55] Though imbued with a High Church background, Gladstone came to embody the ideals of Nonconformity as applied to political questions, a development which cemented the alliance of Nonconformists with the Liberal party.[56] Disraeli, who rejected the approach to politics as a form of moral combat, adopted a series of positions with less evidence of consistency or commitment.[57] This pragmatism, a pronounced reluctance to endow political questions with moral qualities, reflected a style of politics still evident in the "empirical" orientation of modern Conservatism.[58] There were also party leaders whose orientations were not consonant with a party ethos. Lord Rosebery, to cite the most prominent case, lacked the confidence of the Nonconformist activists in the Liberal party partly because of his involvement with horse racing. Failing to maintain that essential basis of support, his tenure as Leader was short and stormy.

This aside is meant only to affirm that the link between religious groups and a political party required action by elites.

THE POLITICAL ORIENTATION OF RELIGIOUS GROUPS

Two opposing religious orientations, Puritan and non-Puritan, constituted the basis of party conflict during the

[55] Philip Magnus, *Gladstone, A Biography* (New York: Dutton, 1954).

[56] R. T. Shannon, *Gladstone and the Bulgarian Agitation* (London: Nelson, 1963).

[57] Blake, *Conservative Party*, p. 119.

[58] Ian Gilmour, *Inside Right: A Study of Conservatism* (London: Quartet Books, 1978).

period of the Third Reform Act. The disposition of the various denominations toward these contrasting orientations reflected the pull of tradition, patterns of historical development, and a commitment to a particular ethos. We first consider the nature of the two major groupings, Protestant Nonconformity and Anglicanism, and then deal with the two anomalous groups, Wesleyan Methodists and Roman Catholics.

Protestant Nonconformity. The Puritan movement began as an attempt to purify the Church of England and free it from Catholic influence. In the course of time, Puritanism developed its own distinctive theology and doctrines of church governance. Like most purification movements during the Reformation, it was greeted by the established Church with suspicion and outright hostility. The English Puritans eventually seceded from the state Church and established their own dissenting denominations. The groups known collectively as Protestant Nonconformity, principally the Congregationalists, Baptists, Unitarians, and Quakers, were direct descendants of the Puritans and inherited their religious fervor and political style. The mainline Protestant groups were the most strongly Puritan of all denominations and thus, we argue, gave their political support wholeheartedly to the Liberal party.

Most of the quotations which illustrate the Puritan political style are taken from spokesmen for Nonconformist bodies. We have also seen many statements which stress Nonconformist-Liberal identity. The affinity between doctrines of Puritanism and the Liberal party certainly explains the connection, but what is not self-evident is the reason for the virtual unanimity of what might be called traditional Nonconformity's support for Liberalism. On social grounds alone, the Protestant Nonconformists ought to have split internally. Though the various Protestant groups were not nearly as proletarian as spokesmen liked to claim, their congregations did comprise both skilled working-class and lower middle-class communicants. As time passed, these two groups began to split over questions of social reform.[59] This eventual split should not be allowed to overshadow the impressive degree of political unity maintained by the Nonconformists throughout our period. At the outbreak of World War I, the Liberals held sway and few would have predicted the eventual breach with Labour. Assuming that the Nonconformists were the backbone of Liberalism, how and why did they maintain such unity?

The answer probably lies in the organization of the Dissenters. In some important respects, the Nonconformist bodies resembled "sects." Weber, following Troeltsch and others, defined a sect as "a community of personal believers of the reborn."[60] The sect was a voluntary association of like-minded people who had to earn their way into an organization and maintain certain standards of conduct in order to retain membership. Sects demanded strict adherence to codes of conduct and might expel the individual who lapsed from the path of righteousness. Sects also undertook strenuous efforts to educate their young in the principles of their belief. Birth into a sect was not itself sufficient for membership; the prospective member had to demonstrate a "personal embrace" of the faith. For all these reasons, the sect was an extremely cohesive body. Even persons who left the sect formally were likely to retain the ideas associated with it.

The sect-like nature of Protestant Nonconformity accounts for its impressive political unity. In order to enter a denomination, a person had to exhibit attachment to the creed, behave in a manner consistent with it, and be expelled for lapsing if necessary. The children of members and nonmembers were educated to the faith in the Sunday schools and Church schools which played such a large role

[59] O. F. Christie, *The Transition to Democracy* (London: George Routledge, 1934), p. 242; Mayor, "Some Congregational Relations," pp. 25–27; Moore, *Pit-men*, p. 43.

[60] Weber, *Protestant Ethic*, p. 145.

in church life.[61] This religious cohesiveness explains the doctrinal unity of the Nonconformists and the unity spilled over into political activity. We should thus expect to find the various Protestant denominations to be cohesively pro-Liberal.

Church of England. If Puritanism was synonymous with Protestantism, then the Church of England ought to have been a Puritan body. Henry VIII severed the Church of England from the Catholic Church and converted it to Protestantism. The separation was maintained and the Church purged of Catholic tendencies under Henry's successors. So, at least, a literal reading of English history might have it.[62] But the model presented and tested here argues quite the reverse. The Anglican Church was a non-Puritan body and its center of gravity was in the Conservative party. Why?

The split between the Church of England and Rome was at first political, not ecclesiastical:

In the beginning Anglicanism was merely an expedient for passing the authority of the Church out of the hands of the Pope and into those of the King. All that was possible was retained from Catholicism—the Episcopal hierarchy, the apostolic transmission, and a large number of rites. For the greater security, a minimum of Calvinism was introduced, as a guarantee and safeguard against a return to Papistry. Anglicanism was, in the main, merely a more or less reasonable compromise, a religion of gentlemen and men of the world who required a certain luxury of collective ceremonies to fill the place of the individual faith so often absent, and who attached themselves to a liturgy in order to retain an illusion that they believed in something.[63]

[61] Booth, *Life and Labour*, 3rd ser., VII, 139, 188, 404.
[62] Arthur Bryant, *Protestant Island* (London: Collins, 1967), pp. 9–13.
[63] Emile Boutmy, *The English People*, trans. E. English (London: T. Fisher Unwin, 1904), pp. 81–82. See also George Santayana, *Soliloquies in England* (London: Constable, 1972), pp. 83–86.

Whatever its formal creed, its origin suggests that Anglicanism was "Catholicism minus the Pope."[64] It is reasonable to suppose that since mass religious attitudes change very slowly, many Anglicans continued to think as if they were Catholics. So Anglicans retained the Catholic, non-Puritan outlook that manifested itself as support for the Conservative party. The non-Puritan perspective is evident in many of the quotations cited above and in the credo published by a group of High Church clerics. Man owed:

To God—Christian Wisdom
To Men—Christian Justice
To Self—Christian Temperance
To the hindrances of environment—Christian fortitude.[65]

Because of its origin, Anglicanism was always forced to slip precariously between "the clashing rocks of Romanism and Puritanism," between a Catholic outlook, a heritage of the historic connection with Rome, and a Protestant outlook, foisted upon the faithful to settle a political dispute. The tension between competing poles accounts partly for the relative disunity of Anglicans in politics. Church leaders frequently broke into competing ecclesiastical parties in the centuries after the Reformation. Advocates of Anglo-Catholicism, who wanted the Church to retain its Romish heritage, fought continuously with those who resisted "Papist" tendencies. The division periodically spilled over into politics. Around the turn of the century, many influential Anglicans demanded that the Conservative Government appoint an independent commission to investigate the extent of Catholic "ritualizing" tendencies in the state Church and punish those priests guilty of infractions. The reluctance of the Government to intervene over the heads of bishops led to bitter disputes, particularly in Brighton, one of the

[64] Boutmy, *English People*, p. 261.
[65] *Lux Mundi*, cited in Helen Merrell Lynd, *England in the Eighteen-Eighties* (1945; reprint ed., London: Frank Cass, 1968), p. 316.

Anglo-Catholic centers in England.[66] The "Church Protestants," those Anglicans who feared the resurgence of Catholic practices, mobilized their political strength and actually opposed the official Conservative parliamentary nominees in 1900 and 1906.[67] This internal dispute reduced the political cohesion of the Church of England.

The political distinctiveness of Anglicanism was further reduced by the impact of the Evangelical movement in the nineteenth century. The great wave of revivalism that swept across Britain early in the century split off large segments of the Church but left a significant residue of Evangelicals within it. Though family tradition kept them within the Church and Tory nexus, these twice-born Anglicans subscribed to a view of the world hardly distinguishable from the Puritan orientation identified above.[68] The work of Evangelical Anglicans makes the same emphasis on rebirth through conversion and an insistence that inner salvation is not enough. To confirm his state of grace, the Christian must go beyond prayer, serving the Lord by extending God's mercy to his fellows. Leading a Christian life, for the Evangelical, meant active involvement in the secular world.

Considering the common premises uniting the two movements, it is hardly surprising to learn that Evangelical Anglicans followed the Puritan political style. Politics was an arena used by the Evangelicals to bring about the eradication of sin and "Parliament was for them a mighty instrument to right the wrongs of the nation and of all man-

[66] H. Hamilton Maugham, *Some Brighton Churches* (London: Faith Press, 1972), pp. iv–v; *Parliamentary Papers*, 1906, XXXIII, Cd. 3040, "First Report of the Royal Commission on Ecclesiastical Discipline," 19–21, 388–389, 398–399, 424.

[67] On the political consequences of ritualism, see *Yorkshire Daily Observer*, January 13, 1906, p. 1; *Brighton Gazette*, October 31, 1885, p. 5; February 4, 1899, p. 4; September 29, 1900, p. 5; October 4, 1900, p. 8; March 30, 1905, p. 8; April 1, 1905, p. 8; April 6, 1905, p. 4; January 13, 1906, p. 5; and October 5, 1907, p. 5; *Sussex Evening Times*, September 27, 1890, p. 3; *Reading Observer*, September 22, 1900, p. 8; October 27, 1900, p. 5.

[68] Ian Bradley, *The Call to Seriousness* (New York: Macmillan, 1967).

kind."[69] No effort was spared in the attack on practices that prompted men to degrade themselves, and Evangelicals led various movements for social reform. In these efforts, the Evangelicals often felt themselves estranged from their co-religionists and more comfortable with the Nonconformists who shared their affinity for earnest, moralistic politics.[70] This type of Anglican political style, though restricted to a minority of clergy and laymen, nevertheless diminished the consistency of political orientation in the Church of England.

In accounting for the relatively low degree of political cohesion among Anglicans, we must not overlook the importance of organization. Anglicanism, unlike Protestant Nonconformity, was not a sect religion. The Church of England was, in Weber's term, "a corporation which organizes grace and administers religious gifts of grace, like an endowed foundation. Affiliation with the church is, in principle, obligatory and hence proves nothing with regard to the Member's qualities."[71] Unlike a sect, Church membership is automatic, and very little affirmation is required of members. The Church makes some effort to impart its point of view to young people, but, since membership is more a matter of private faith than intellect, it is more concerned with transmitting loyalty to the institution than with any particular doctrines. It would thus accept converts without imposing entrance requirements. In fact, every person born in England was considered by the Church to be an Anglican. All these characteristics would lessen unity of outlook and produce a body of diverse orientations. The religious diversity would carry over into political life where

[69] *Ibid.*, p. 174.

[70] G. Kitson Clark, *Churchmen and the Condition of England* (London: Metheun, 1973); Donald O. Wagner, *The Church of England and Social Reform Since 1854* (New York: Columbia University Press, 1930).

[71] Max Weber, "The Protestant Sects and the Spirit of Capitalism," in *From Max Weber: Essays in Sociology*, ed. and trans. H. H. Gerth and C. Wright Mills (New York: Oxford University Press, 1958), pp. 305–306.

some Anglicans would be Puritan-type Liberals, but most would be non-Puritan-type Conservatives.

Wesleyan Methodism. The Wesleyan movement split off formally from the Church of England after the death of its founder. Though it took some time, standard accounts reveal, the Wesleyans eventually joined with the Protestant Nonconformists who had split earlier and became a part of "Political dissent," i.e., pro-Liberal. This account is based largely on an interest group definition of religion, however; it assumes that Wesleyan Methodism joined with old Nonconformity to fight the privileges of the Establishment and remove the disabilities of Dissenters. The ethos model, on the other hand, assumes that while the majority of Wesleyans were Puritan and associated themselves with the Puritan party, the Liberals, a healthy minority were more swayed by the non-Puritan Anglican tradition and voted Conservatively.

The origin of Wesleyan Methodism differs sharply from that of Protestant Nonconformity. Wesleyanism began as an effort to breathe new life and vigor into the Church of England—to bring the message of God to the field hands and to the depressed industrial population that hitherto lay out of the Church's grasp. Throughout his life, John Wesley thought of himself as an Anglican cleric and much regretted that his methods put him at odds with the Church.[72] Elie Halevy captured this side of Wesleyan Methodism when he referred to it as the "High Church of Nonconformity" and a "Nonconformist sect established by Anglican clergymen."[73] On the other hand, the spirit of Methodism was in many ways alien to Anglicanism, especially in its em-

[72] Robert L. Tucker, *Separation of the Methodists from the Church of England* (New York: Methodist Book Concern, 1918).

[73] Elie Halevy, *The Birth of Methodism in England,* trans. Bernard Semmel (Chicago: University of Chicago Press, 1971), p. 51.

phasis on the need for a joyous and active affirmation of religious belief.[74]

In many ways, just as Anglicanism was a compromise between Catholicism and Puritanism, Methodism lay between Anglicanism and Puritanism. Some of the doctrines of Methodism are Puritan: the emphasis on the possibility of salvation, the role of good works, the need for proper conduct in life. In other respects, Wesleyanism followed Anglicanism: the liturgy, the Episcopate, the importance of private faith. Methodists themselves seemed uncertain whether they should regard themselves as dissenters from the Church of England or merely as an offshoot. This indecision manifested itself in politics. Because of the stress on the possibility of salvation for all through good works, we argue, the Methodists were essentially Puritan and the majority followed that outlook with Liberalism. But there was a good bit of deviation. Among the non-Anglican denominations (excepting the Catholics who will be dealt with below), the Wesleyans were the least likely to support Liberal proposals for reform.[75] The Wesleyan position on liquor was a good deal more moderate than the Free Church position and in many ways resembled the position of the CETS. The Wesleyans were more tolerant of corrupting influences and less prone to treat nonreligious entertainment as evil.[76] They were also more inclined to favor public funding for denominational education and were the last of the Nonconformist bodies to turn over their schools to the

[74] On Methodist doctrine, see Rupert Davies, "The People Called Methodists—I. 'Our Doctrines,' " in *A History of the Methodist Church in Great Britain*, ed. Rupert Davies and Gordon Rupp (London: Epworth, 1965), I, 145–180; Maldwyn Edwards, *Methodism and England* (London: Epworth Press, 1943), p. 85; Moore, *Pit-men*, pp. 11, 54; E. R. Taylor, *Methodism and Politics, 1791–1851* (Cambridge: Cambridge University Press, 1935), p. 113; Wellman J. Warner, *The Wesleyan Movement in the Industrial Revolution* (1930; reprint ed., New York: Russell and Russell, 1967), pp. 65, 70.

[75] Blewett, *Peers, Parties and People*, pp. 347–349.
[76] Booth, *Life and Labour*, 3rd ser., VII, 132.

School Boards.[77] We should expect to find a divided Wesleyanism, with a majority as Puritan Liberals. The non-Wesleyan Methodists were likely to behave like the other Protestant Nonconformists.

Roman Catholicism. In the language of social research, Catholics constitute the persistent counterexample to the model. Insofar as doctrine promoted affinity, Catholics should have suported the Conservative party.[78] Puritanism, after all, was a response to Catholicism and came to stand for pretty much the opposite of Catholicism. The creed of the non-Puritan is essentially the Catholic catechism. Yet all signs indicate that the Catholic vote was Liberal. The anomaly is easy enough to explain. Catholic voters were subject to competing influences, one of which overcame the religious orientation. Most Catholic voters were Irish and the question of justice to Ireland, which for most Catholics meant the Liberal policy of Home Rule, was pressing. So the Catholic voted as an Irishman first and a Catholic second. Religion, in this instance, functioned both as interest group and surrogate for low social status.

Despite such deviant behavior, Catholics clearly exhibited the non-Puritan orientation. When confronted with evidence of social problems, Catholic doctrine counselled "patient acceptance of the limitations of life and of the inequalities of fortune."[79] Like the Anglican, the Catholic relied for progress not on social institutions and human laws but instead trusted "to correction of minds by true teaching and reforming hearts by instilling virtue."[80] Consequently,

---

[77] Elie Halevy, *Imperialism and the Rise of Labour*, trans. E. I. Watkins (London: Ernest Benn, 1951), p. 174; *Parliamentary Papers*, 1884–1885, XI, Return 275, "Report of the Select Committee on School Board Elections (Voting)," 121–122.

[78] Pierse Loftus, *The Conservative Party and the Future* (London: Stephen Swift, 1912), pp. 98–99.

[79] William J. Kerben, "The Roman Catholic Church and Social Reform," cited in Lynd, *England*, p. 300.

[80] *Ibid.*

Catholics were not inclined to undertake crusades for social betterment. Margaret McMillan, who tried to make the Bradford School Board an instrument of social progress, recorded that the Catholic members generally opposed her efforts. "Rome," she wrote,

> . . . never forgot the individual and was sensitive to every change in his condition or prospects. But she took little account of this perishing life, and her regard for the human body was very much that of the mediaeval ascetic or Jesuit priest. The soul alone persists and endures. The salvation of the soul is, then, the great end of life and all saviours. Nothing else matters. The people's children suffered and had suffered more cruelly during this century and the last, than ever before. No matter. The stake and the rack have a place in the scheme of salvation. The insanitary area may also cure heretics, may discipline fruitfully even the children of Mother Church.[81]

Catholics were adamantly opposed to most Liberal reform proposals. The Catholic attitude to temperance was indistinguishable from the Anglican. The emphasis, evident in the speech of the Canon of Wolverhampton at a dinner of licensed victuallers, was on individual freedom:

> With the earnest and sensible advocate of temperance, whether by reasonable legislation, or other legitimate means of total or partial abstinence, in order to prevent intoxication, I cordially agree. . . . But with your self-sufficient, rabid, domineering teetotaler, whose zeal entirely outruns his discretion, I, for one, have neither patience nor sympathy. . . . if we would succeed in repressing the horrible price of drunkenness, let us not depend upon "Local Option," which would be an intolerable tyranny upon every temperate man and woman that has an unalienable [sic] right to a glass of honest beer.[82]

Similarly, on education, the Catholics were most uncomfortable with Liberal nondenominationalism. "If we are

[81] Margaret McMillan, *The Life of Rachael McMillan* (London: J. M. Dent, 1927), p. 88.

[82] Wolverhampton and District, Inc., Licensed Victuallers' Friendly and Protective Society, *Jubilee Banquet, 1889* (Wolverhampton: Plimmer and Co., 1889), pp. 32–33.

constrained to choose between sacrificing what is essential to the preservation of our children's faith or what will place them on an equality in point of secular education with the other children of other faiths," said one priest, "we shall always prefer [to sacrifice] the latter alternative."[83] On several key Liberal positions, the Catholics were out of sympathy.

Whenever the issue was Home Rule, the Catholics followed the Liberals. When some other issue arose, however, the natural orientation of Catholics asserted itself and they supported the Conservative position. There is evidence of Catholic Conservatism in 1885, due both to Conservative flirtation with Home Rule and the Liberal stand on education.[84] In municipal elections, Catholics frequently deserted local Liberals who stood for nondenominational education and temperance.[85] Despite these aberrations, Home Rule drew the Catholics to the Liberal banner.

STATISTICAL ANALYSIS

Some of the argument about political orientations rests on impressions which cannot be tested, but other parts of the argument are susceptible to empirical confirmation. The analysis in Chapter 6, which showed stronger and more consistent Nonconformist than Anglican voting effects, validates the church/sect distinction advanced above. Two other data sets can be employed to test some of the predictions which grow out of the characterization of denominations as sources of politically relevant attitudes.

The relationships can be studied at the elite level by reviewing information about the religious and partisan affil-

[83] Reverend Sidney Smith, cited in Lynd, *England*, p. 304.

[84] C.H.D. Howard, "The Parnell Manifesto of 1885 and the Schools Question," *English Historical Review* 62 (1947), 42–51; see also Henry Pelling, *Social Geography of British Elections, 1885–1910*, p. 431.

[85] Catholic-Liberal tension on education is evident in these citations from the *Yorkshire Daily Observer*: November 3, 1902, p. 4; October 20, 1903, p. 3; October 26, 1903, p. 4; November 2, 1903, p. 5; November 8, 1907, p. 7; January 11, 1910, p. 9.

iations of candidates for Parliament. The best source for such information is the summary data on the political orientations of Nonconformist candidates in general elections between 1900 and December 1910.[86] In an age when the campaign and polling were privately financed, the candidacies in no way constituted a representative sample of the electorate or the population. Occupational analysis shows conclusively that candidates were concentrated disproportionately among men in business, industry, commerce and finance, agriculture, and the professions.[87] But this virtual exclusion of manual workers until the rise of Labour as a mass party does not render such data useless. In effect, the unrepresentativeness of candidates enables us to gauge the effects of religion on partisanship within a single broad category of the class structure—persons in nonmanual situations. Combined with other types of information, such an analysis provides insights about the religious dimension to political conflict.

Koss's data permit the computation of Liberal-Labour support among the major Nonconformist groups. By the use of several simplifying assumptions, these data can be extended to estimate the pro-Conservative leaning of Anglican candidates.[88] The relevant statistics appear in Table 7.1.

The table confirms the basic partisan alignments discussed throughout this book. In the four elections for which data are available, Anglicans were disproportionately affiliated with the Conservative cause, and Nonconformists stayed in the Liberal camp. Taking the four elections together, 64% of Anglican candidates fought under the Conservative

[86] Koss, *Nonconformity*, pp. 227–230.

[87] Blewett, *Peers, Parties and People*, p. 230.

[88] The crucial assumption is that all candidates not separately identified as Nonconformists were adherents of the Church of England. This permits the calculation of two variables: no. Anglican Conservatives = no. Conservative candidates − no. Nonconformist Conservative candidates; no. Anglican non-Conservatives = no. non-Conservative candidates − no. Nonconformist non-Conservative candidates. The Anglican propensity for Conservatism is then calculated as no. Anglican Conservatives/no. Anglican Conservatives + no. Anglican non-Conservatives.

TABLE 7.1. Partisanship Among Parliamentary Candidates by Denomination, 1900–1910

	1900		1906	
Denomination	N	P	N	P
Congregationalists	36	.94	92	.98
Baptists	8	1.00	21	1.00
Wesleyans	41	.83	42	.88
Other Methodists	13	.85	27	1.00
Unitarians	12	.67	8	.78
Friends	11	.91	8	1.00
Presbyterians	50	.58	6	.83
Total Nonconformist	171	.78	214	.94
Anglicans	780	.68	919	.60

	Jan. 1910		Dec. 1910		Total	
	N	P	N	P	N	P
Congregationalists	83	1.00	74	1.00	285	.99
Baptists	18	1.00	20	1.00	67	1.00
Wesleyans	39	.87	35	.92	160	.88
Other Methodists	23	1.00	26	.96	89	.97
Unitarians	17	.71	13	.77	60	.73
Friends	11	1.00	11	1.00	41	.98
Presbyterians	4	1.00	4	.75	64	.64
Total Nonconformist	195	.95	186	.96	766	.91
Anglicans	909	.64	885	.61	3493	.63

N represents total number of parliamentary candidates from the denomination. For the Nonconformists, P represents the proportion of the candidates seeking election as Liberal and/or Labour members. The P for Anglicans represents the proportion of Unionist candidates.

or Liberal Unionist banner. The figure ranged narrowly from 60% to 68% over time. To a much more pronounced degree, the Nonconformist candidates sought office as Liberals or Labour candidates. Even including the Presbyterians, whose status as Dissenters was questionable, more than 90% of the Nonconformist candidates ran under the auspices of the Liberal or Labour parties; when the Presbyterians are removed, the figure rises to 94%. The figure was at its lowest level in 1900, largely as a result of the split in Presbyterian ranks, and thereafter hovered around the 95% level. As predicted by discussion of the church/sect dichotomy, the partisan preferences were asymmetrical, the

197

Nonconformists exhibiting much higher cohesion than the Anglicans.

The utility of the ethos framework becomes clear when we look at finer denominational breakdowns. There are observable differences in the level of Liberal-Labour support among the eight varieties of Nonconformity listed in Table 7.1. At one extreme, the Congregationalists, Baptists, non-Wesleyan Methodists, and Quakers were unanimous or nearly so in their fidelity to anti-Unionism. Three remaining groups—Presbyterians, Unitarians, and Wesleyans—dropped below the 90% level. As noted above, the Presbyterians were uncertainly placed as Dissenters, and the Unitarian pattern owes much to the role of Joseph Chamberlain in the Conservative-Liberal Unionist alliance. The Wesleyans were also less loyal to Liberalism than the bulk of Nonconformists. The difference—4% if all non-Wesleyans are defined as Nonconformist and somewhat higher if the term excludes the Presbyterians—is consistent with our discussion of Wesleyan Methodism as the least Puritan of the Nonconformist denominations.

Limited in time and scope, the candidate data nevertheless provide suggestive evidence about the utility of the ethos approach to religious-based partisanship. The usefulness of the approach can further be gauged by turning once again to the ecological data base that has been used throughout the study. To analyze the variations in Liberal/Labour support among Nonconformity, the statistics of Sunday School attendance in 1851, the most powerful Nonconformist predictor, were broken down into three categories—Methodist, Baptist, and Congregationalist. These indicators are assumed to measure the exposure of the population to the political world-view associated with the denominations. As noted above, the Catholic educational facilities at the time of the religious census do not provide a particularly useful guide to the distribution of Catholicism in the latter part of the century. To measure the Anglican socialization effort, the best variable was based on the proportion of the population in Church of England day schools.

We include these two variables, Catholic and Anglican day school populations, only for the purpose of control and do not report the value of their coefficients.

The data in Table 7.2 are the regression coefficients for each of the three Nonconformist categories when used to predict the Unionist proportion of the vote. These coefficients were derived from equations which included for control purposes the regional dummies, the measure of the Catholic day school population, and the Anglican day school enrollment. The regression also included, in serial order, each of the three class measures which were useful predictors in the analysis reported in Chapter 6. The first coefficient was obtained from an equation which included the estimate of the population proportion engaged in manual labor, the second included the proportion of industrial workers, and the final entry included the trade union measure. Because of the high correlations among the three populations, each regression equation included only one of the three Nonconformist predictors.

The magnitude and significance of the coefficients sug-

TABLE 7.2. Nonconformist Denominational Effects Upon
the Unionist Vote, 1885–1910

Form	1885	1886	1892	1895	1900	1906	Jan. 1910	Dec. 1910
A. Methodist								
1	−.29	−.30	−.30	−.35	(−.05)	(−.20)	−.52	(−.18)
2	(−.24)	(−.25)	−.25	−.33	(.01)	(−.13)	−.34	(−.11)
3	(−.20)	(−.25)	(−.21)	−.28	(.09)	(−.11)	−.32	(−.10)
B. Congregationalist								
1	(−.16)	−.28	−.27	−.28	(−.16)	−.34	−.35	−.27
2	(−.10)	(−.21)	(−.22)	(−.25)	(−.10)	−.27	−.26	(−.19)
3	(−.14)	(−.26)	(−.25)	(−.24)	(−.14)	−.32	−.32	−.27
C. Baptist								
1	(−.22)	(−.18)	(−.23)	(−.20)	−.37	−.37	(−.23)	(−.22)
2	−.26	(−.23)	−.26	(−.21)	−.39	−.37	−.22	−.26
3	−.27	(−.26)	−.27	(−.27)	−.39	−.38	−.24	−.29

"Form" refers to class control: manual workers (1) or industrial workers (2) or unionized workers (3). Nonsignificant coefficients are in parentheses. Regressions also included three regional dummy variables.

gest inferences about patterns of denominational support over time. The most striking finding, aside from the familiar anti-Unionist orientation of the Nonconformists, is the election-specific nature of the relationship. None of the three denominational measures was strongly and consistently anti-Unionist in *all* elections; rather, substantial evidence suggests that the appeal of party leaders resonated differently for each group from one election to the next. The Baptists, who emerged from the candidate analysis as the most cohesive Liberal-Labour denomination, rallied especially strongly to the Liberal banner in 1885, 1892, and in all elections from 1900 to December 1910. The coefficients for the Baptists fell off in both 1886 and 1895. The Congregationalist coefficients were significant in 1892 and in the last three elections. The finding of very strong Liberal leanings in these two groups for the last elections of the period thus confirms the conclusions drawn from the candidate data. The Methodist commitment to Liberalism was most pronounced in 1892, 1895, and January 1910. There was a particularly striking difference in 1895, when the Methodists were much more pro-Liberal than the other two denominations, and in 1906 and December 1910, when the Methodist coefficients were small and insignificant and the other two denominations exhibited their strongest Liberal orientation. The differences in 1906 and December 1910 also are consistent with the analysis of candidate preferences.

Overall, the figures in Table 7.2 support the ordering of the denominations on a pro-Liberalism scale with the Methodists least cohesive (10 of 24 coefficients significant), the Congregationalists in the middle (12/24), and the Baptists the most cohesive (14/24). Finer distinctions amongst Methodists might well increase the difference between the Wesleyans and the other Nonconformist denominations. This gross analysis can profitably be supplemented by a consideration of the particular elections in which the denominations exhibited their strongest ties to Liberalism. Most observers of the period have argued that appeals to Nonconformity were most salient in the elections of 1885, 1906, January 1910, and December 1910. We have already noted the importance of disestablishment as an issue in 1885, the role of religious education in 1906, and the manner in which the challenge to the Lords in the contests of 1910 reflected Nonconformist hostility over past injustices. These elections most directly elicited the strongest response from the Baptists and Congregationalists, which further suggests that they were responding to religious appeals. The Wesleyans seemed intermittent in their Liberalism, just as the analysis of their belief structure suggested.

SUMMARY

A combination of qualitative and quantitative evidence supports the treatment of British religious groups as agencies transmitting politically relevant values to their adherents. These values, when manipulated skillfully by party elites, provided a basis for common political action by members of the denominations. The level of cohesion varied from one denomination to the next largely as a function of the extent to which the group attempted to influence the outlooks of its membership. The findings also direct our attention to the process of transmission and factors which apparently interrupted the process, culminating eventually in the decline of the religiously based Victorian party system.

CHAPTER 8

Transformation of the Party System

At some point early in the twentieth century, the British party system changed in two important ways. First, Labour replaced the Liberal party as the major party of the left. The Liberals, after three consecutive general election victories, split into competing wings during the First World War and were submerged in the first postwar election. Despite reunification and partial recovery in the 1920s, the party never again formed a government and has since participated only episodically in decision making. Labour became the second largest parliamentary party in 1918, when its popular vote exceeded the Liberal total, and was strong enough to form two shortlived minority governments in the twenties. After a period of drift in the 1930s, Labour emerged as the only credible alternative to the Conservatives, a position it continues to hold to this day.

The second important change involved the underlying social basis of the party system. The Victorian alignment was built on religion. The issues of the day had religious overtones and the parties were distinguished at base by the denominational affiliation of their adherents. At some time in the twentieth century, this ceased to be true. Class became the principal social factor distinguishing the parties and the major issues on the political agenda involved questions about the distribution of wealth and economic inequality.

This transformation of the British party system has not gone unnoticed and has in fact become *the* issue in research on British political development. What accounts for the massive shift in the status of the Liberal and Labour parties? To what extent was the change in the political landscape a function of changes in the group basis of partisanship? This chapter examines the most common answers scholars have given to these questions and suggests the need for supplementing existing accounts in several important respects.

The major argument of the chapter is that our understanding of the breakup and reformation of the British party system can be advanced by extending the ethos model discussed in the previous chapter. In particular, we suggest that an important factor in undermining the late Victorian alignment was a change in the method and agents of political socialization. This change reduced the role of religion in society, thereby undermining a party system built on a religious cleavage, and left the way open for social class to emerge as the major dividing line in politics. This interpretation does not fully explain the success of Labour at the expense of Liberalism, but it more accurately charts the process and explains some of the underlying social changes which facilitated the transformation. The interpretation is consistent with the statistical data that can be brought to bear on the problem.

THEORIES OF TRANSFORMATION

At some risk of oversimplification, we can place the scholars who have debated the transformation of the British party system into two camps, a traditional and a revisionist. As the use of a common terminology suggests, these groups overlap the two schools of thought about the nature of cleavage patterns under the Third Reform Act. The two camps differ on a number of fundamental points regarding both the nature and timing of the realignment which transformed the late Victorian party system and paved the way for the modern alignment.

The disagreement is sharpest on the question of *when*

the group basis of cleavage shifted from religion to class. The traditional view emphasizes a sharp discontinuity between the pre- and postwar basis of electoral cleavage. The prewar system, in which the voters were aligned in parties largely respecting denominational affiliation, is said to have given way rather quickly to a new system in which social class became the basis of partisan conflict. The traditional view attributes this change to a number of factors associated with World War I and suggests that such factors first affected the bulk of the electorate in 1918.[1] In the revisionist view of scholars like Clarke, Pelling, Blewett, and others, the transformation of the cleavage base of voting had largely been completed *before* the war. They point to several elections in the period from 1885 to 1910 as hastening the development of class consciousness and driving the bulk of the enfranchised workers to the Liberal banner. Long before 1918, they argue, British elections had become an arena for peaceful class conflict.[2]

The debate over timing leads straightforwardly to a further disagreement over the displacement of the Liberals by the Labour party. This process of change has traditionally been interpreted as a concomitant of the development of class awareness by the electors. Thus, G. M. Trevelyan, writing his *History of England*, contended that a change in the terms and focus of political conflict had rendered the Liberals obsolete and practically guaranteed Labour a ma-

[1] An example: "The explosion of class consciousness which took place immediately after the war, and the bitterness engendered by the depression which followed it, could hardly fail to have dramatic repercussions on the political system. It was they, rather than the split of 1916, which destroyed the old Liberal Party; and it was they which made it possible for Labour to replace it as the main progressive party in Britain." David Marquand, *Ramsay MacDonald* (London: Johnathan Cape, 1977), pp. 243–244.

[2] P. F. Clarke: "By 1910, the change to class politics was substantially complete. That from Liberalism to Labour had not really begun." In *Lancashire*, p. 406. The inclusion of Pelling in this group was based on the emphasis on class lines as sources of electoral cleavage in his *Social Geography*. His more recent comments suggest some doubts. See *Popular Politics*, 2nd ed., pp. ix–xi.

jor role in political life. "In our own day," he asserted in 1926, "the reassortment of the parties on the basis of industrial and social questions only, with no reference to religion, was the prime reason . . . [for] the disappearance of the Liberal and the advent of the Labour party in its place after the War."[3] The revisionists have challenged this interpretation directly, insisting that the cleavage shift from religion to class was a separate process from the displacement of the Liberals by Labour as the major anti-Conservative party. As already noted, revisionists argue that the social basis of voting had already shifted from denomination to class when the Liberals won three consecutive general elections between 1906 and 1910. Indeed, by recasting to meet the reality of working-class political consciousness, the Liberals had effectively promoted the new alignment and stood poised to capitalize upon it for continual electoral success. A series of mistakes at the elite level and plain bad luck are cited to explain why the Liberals collapsed and failed to follow up on their promise.[4] The revisionists thus dispute the air of inevitability with which some advocates of the traditional interpretation have cloaked the decline of the Liberals.

The debate over the timing of cleavage shift can be addressed with data at hand. Was there evidence of realignment before 1910, of a wholesale shift in the lines of electoral conflict from religion to class?[5] The most complete statement of the revisionist view in this matter can be found in Neal Blewett's work. Blewett has interpreted prewar elections in terms of critical election theory. According to such theory, election outcomes follow a cycle in which long pe-

---

[3] G. M. Trevelyan, *History of England*, vol. III (1926; reprint ed., Garden City, New York: Doubleday-Anchor, 1953), 255–256.

[4] These "internal" reasons are reviewed by Allen Sked, "The Liberal Tradition and the 'Lib-Lab' Pact," *West European Politics* (May 1978), 193–197.

[5] For a discussion of the appropriateness of the realignment model in British politics, see Kenneth D. Wald, "Realignment Theory and British Party Development."

riods of stability are punctuated by short and intense periods of electoral upheaval.[6] The stable phase, known variously as a "party system" or "sociopolitical period," is distinguished by a persistent policy agenda, a characteristic division of the vote with majority and minority parties, and a stable social basis for each mass coalition. The emergence of a new issue or set of issues that cannot be assimilated to existing patterns of party competition disrupts the standing coalitions, ushering in a short period of intense social conflict and electoral volatility. When the turmoil finally subsides, a new system emerges, with parties ranged on opposite sides of public issues and voters similarly reorganized on the basis of attitudes toward the issue that precipitated the disruption. The new system, with its own unique policy agenda, party configuration, and social identity for the electoral coalitions, persists until disturbed by the next period of realignment.

Blewett has characterized the general elections of 1886 and 1906 as particularly crucial choice points in the evolution of the modern British party system.[7] In his analysis, the general election of 1886 destroyed the Gladstonian alignment which had dominated party politics for forty years, replacing it with a new national majority committed to maintaining intact the union of Ireland and Britain. Three features of the 1886 election prompted Blewett to designate it as a critical realignment. First, the election produced a decisive change in the identity of the dominant party. The "motley and fragile" coalition forged in the mid-Victorian period gave way to the Unionist alliance which then enjoyed two decades of nearly absolute power. Sec-

---

[6] The major works on the concept are V. O. Key, "A Theory of Critical Elections," *Journal of Politics* 17 (February 1955), 3–18; Walter Dean Burnham, *Critical Elections and the Mainsprings of American Politics* (New York: W. W. Norton, 1970), and James L. Sundquist, *Dynamics of the Party System* (Washington, D.C.: Brookings Institution, 1973).

[7] Blewett, *Peers, Parties and People*, chs. 1–2. Blewett himself notes that these elections did not involve high levels of turnout but nevertheless uses the critical election model and terminology.

ond, the new Unionist hegemony was due to "fundamental changes in the patterns of partisan identification." The vote in 1886 showed evidence of new cleavages built around national, economic, and class differences, social bases which had not been readily apparent in earlier elections. Finally, the patterns forged by the election proved durable, persisting for the next three general elections despite the emergence of new issues and party conflicts. All of these features are consistent with the conception of a critical election as the catalyst in the destruction of an existing party system and the agent of a new political order.

The party system established in 1886 showed signs of decay by 1902 and was dealt a mortal blow by the results of the election of 1906. Like the election of 1886, the result in 1906 was a change in the identity of the dominant political coalition. The Liberals and their assorted allies (Irish Nationalist, Labour) won the first of three consecutive national elections. Though the severity of the Unionist defeat could be explained in part by a combination of transient causes, Blewett concludes that the results in 1906 suggested "fundamental and durable changes in the patterns of partisan identification." These changes, the sharpening of party conflict along class and regional lines, were ratified in the two elections of 1910. Had the First World War not intervened, Blewett argued, this new system might well have persisted for many years. By this account, the election of 1906 should be included in the class of critical elections in British political history.[8]

If this portrait is accurate, it would add considerable credence to the revisionist portrait of party change and force us to distinguish between the prewar social realignment of the electorate and the postwar rise of Labour.

[8] Based on a different type of data, Hugh Stephens has ratified Blewett's designation of 1886 and 1906 as critical elections. See his "The Changing Context of British Politics in the 1880s: The Reform Acts and the Formation of the Liberal Unionist Party," pp. 486–501, and also his "Some Effects of the 1903 Electoral Agreement between the Liberal Party and the Labor Representation Committee," unpublished ms.

Unfortunately, by looking only at changes in the composition of Parliament as a key to public opinion, Blewett has failed to prove his case about the rise of class-based voting before 1918. Though the elections of 1886 and 1906 produced alterations in the party balance in Parliament, changes in the identity of the majority party are neither necessary nor sufficient conditions for realignment. Changes in mass electoral patterns may occur without a change in the hegemony of a dominant party and the status of a dominant party might change without fundamental shifts in popular preference. In deciding on the appropriate criteria to define critical realignments, it is preferable to return to the original formulation of the concept by V. O. Key. Key's inspection of aggregate election results suggested to him the existence of a special class of elections "in which the depth and intensity of electoral involvement are high, in which more or less profound readjustments occur in the relations of power within the community, and in which new and durable electoral groupings are formed."[9] The concept has subsequently been refined, linked to changes in public policy, and extended for use in systems outside the United States. Definitions of realignment have not, however, strayed far from Key's emphasis on (1) high levels of mass participation; (2) marked instability in the electoral attachments of voters; and (3) the crystallization of party alignments on the basis of new social divisions.[10]

The prewar elections cited by Blewett and others as realignments do not seem to have exhibited any of these features. If critical elections are marked by high levels of public involvement, then the contests of 1886 and 1906 fail the test when we compare voter participation rates. Table 8.1 shows the difference between the observed and pre-

[9] Key, "Critical Elections," p. 4.

[10] The most recent work is summarized in Jerome M. Clubb, William H. Flanigan, and Nancy H. Zingale, *Partisan Realignment* (Beverly Hills, Calif.: Sage Publications, 1980), and Bruce Campbell and Richard Trilling, eds., *Realignment in American Politics: Towards a Theory* (Austin: University of Texas Press, 1980).

dicted rates of voter participation from 1885 to 1910 after adjusting for involuntary abstention due to the aging of the electoral register. Compiled annually in July of the preceding year, the register in force at a particular election included a large number of persons who had died or, more commonly, left the constituency in search of work elsewhere.[11] The regression of recorded turnout on the age of the register (in months) for each election of the period shows a strong (Pearson r = -0.56) and negative effect on turnout (b = -0.54%) for each additional month the register had been in force.[12] The equation can be used to generate a base line of "normal" turnout, the rate to be expected on the basis of the age of the register alone, and deviations from the prediction treated as a measure of public reaction to short-term forces in each election.

On the basis of the age of the register in force when the polling began, turnout in 1886 should have reached about 79%. The recorded participation rate of only 74% shows

TABLE 8.1. Observed and Predicted Turnout, 1885–1910

Election	Recorded Turnout (%)	Predicted Turnout (%)	Difference (%)
1885 (4)	81.2	83.1	− 1.9
1886 (11.5)	74.2	79.1	− 4.9
1892 (11.5)	77.4	79.1	− 1.7
1895 (12)	78.4	78.8	− 0.4
1900 (14.5)	75.1	77.5	− 2.4
1906 (6)	83.2	82.0	+ 1.2
1910, Jan. (6)	86.8	82.0	+ 4.8
1910, Dec. (16.5)	81.6	76.4	+ 5.2

The figures in parentheses indicate the age of the register in months.

[11] Blewett shows that the removal rate in working-class constituencies could reach as high as one-third of the register (*Peers, Parties and People*, pp. 357–362).

[12] All data for this analysis were obtained from Craig, *Parliamentary Election Results*, pp. 582–583. The analysis included Scottish constituencies even though the compilation of the register involved a slightly different schedule.

a substantially lower turnout than expected. This was in fact the lowest participation rate for all eight elections. Though turnout in 1906 was high, at 83%, this was only about 1% more than would be predicted on the basis of a relatively fresh register. This modest spurt of 1906 pales in comparison to the dramatic cases of electoral surge found four years later. Turnout in the elections of 1910 exceeded predictions by 4.8% (in January) and 5.2% (in December). There is nothing in Table 8.1 to justify assertions about high levels of turnout in either 1886 or 1906. After corrections for the age of the register, one of the elections identified as a critical realignment appears significant for the interest it did *not* generate, and the other produced a turnout rate barely above the expected level.

The same negative conclusion is appropriate when we look for evidence of disruption in traditional voting patterns, one of the hallmarks of a realigning election. Though Blewett performed no systematic analysis on this facet, Cornford followed the practice of American scholars who have attempted to detect realignment by calculating inter-election correlations based on party percentages of the vote in constituencies.[13] The onset of a realignment is signalled by a precipitous drop in the level of correlation between adjacent elections, and the crystallization of a new party system is inferred from a return to high levels of inter-election correlation. It follows that elections in different party systems produce very low correlations. Noting a sharp drop in correlations between Unionist percentages for both the 1885/1886 and 1900/1906 election pairs, Cornford concluded that 1886 and 1906 should be regarded as critical elections. The evidence does not justify that conclusion because the low correlations between the pairs might reflect only transient deviations due to the peculiar features of any one of the four elections.

The noncritical nature of 1886 and 1906 stands out from

[13] James Cornford, "Aggregate Election Data and British Party Alignments, 1885–1910," p. 111.

the correlation matrix for the entire election series, printed here as Table 8.2.[14] The last column of the table presents the mean correlation between each election and the other seven contests. Note that the elections correlating at the lowest level with all other elections were the contests of 1885 and 1900. The deviant nature of the results in those contests confirms the suspicions that the low correlations for the election pairs of 1885/1886 and 1900/1906 were due to the peculiar features of the first election in each pair. There is no basis for concluding from correlation analysis among adjacent election pairs that 1886 and 1906 were especially marked by high levels of volatility.

If realignments are critical junctures, marking off distinctive political eras, the elections of one period should bear little relationship to party profiles in another era. This is manifestly not an accurate statement based on the correlation matrix in Table 8.2. It is remarkable how some of the highest correlations link elections widely separated in time. The election of 1885, for instance, was supposedly separated from the election of January 1910 by two critical realignments, yet the two elections correlated at a level of +0.67, slightly higher than the correlation between the adjacent elections of 1885 and 1886. The election of 1886, which is said to have marked the birth of a new party system, correlated almost as highly with the results in January 1910 (+0.72) as with the contest of 1892 (+0.76). Similar anomalies raise doubts about the "fundamental" changes in voter alignments supposedly wrought by the realignment of 1906. How is it possible, to cite but one figure among many, that the first postrealignment election in the Unionist party system (the general election of 1892) correlated at +0.81 with the first election of the "new" party system initiated by the realignment of 1906? With

[14] The data for correlation consists of the constituency-level results in Craig. The slight difference between the correlations here and those reported by Cornford are probably due to the inclusion here of two-member constituencies and variations in candidate classification.

TABLE 8.2. Interelection Correlations, Unionist Shares of the Vote, 1885–1910

	1885	1886	1892	1895	1900	1906	Jan. 1910	Dec. 1910	Mean
1885	X	.66 (371)	.67 (475)	.58 (391)	.62 (350)	.57 (482)	.67 (503)	.66 (426)	.63
1886		X	.76 (375)	.69 (337)	.62 (306)	.63 (369)	.72 (386)	.68 (352)	.68
1892			X	.85 (399)	.68 (357)	.75 (467)	.81 (493)	.74 (418)	.75
1895				X	.74 (333)	.75 (385)	.78 (409)	.70 (365)	.73
1900					X	.60 (351)	.68 (368)	.60 (330)	.65
1906						X	.87 (500)	.83 (423)	.72
1910, Jan.							X	.95 (441)	.78
1910, Dec.								X	.74

The figures in parentheses indicate the number of constituencies contested in both elections.

these kinds of relationships, it is difficult to speak of any dramatic change in mass voting behavior.

The weakness of the revisionist case about class politics before the First World War is most evident when we search for evidence of durable shifts from religious to class-based voting in pre-1918 elections. "Realignment" refers to the process of regrouping and reshuffling of voting blocs, sudden and dramatic changes in the party allegiance of major social groups.[15] The ecological analysis in Chapter 6 detected no such reorientations among social groups between 1885 and 1910. Although the vote certainly moved more to a class basis in 1910, there was no corresponding diminution of religious influences which would indicate a full-scale transformation. Contrary to the revisionist arguments, such a realignment does seem to have occurred sometime between December 1910 and December 1918, the last election under the Third Reform Act and the first under the Fourth Reform Act.

The process is documented in Table 8.3, which traces cleavage patterns from 1885 through 1929. The table utilizes two data sets, the first collected for this study and the second constructed by Miller, analyzed by the same procedure.[16] In both data sets, the dependent variable is the Conservative-Unionist share of the parliamentary vote for English units only. The explanatory variables include a measure of rurality—the proportion of the male workforce employed in the agricultural sector—the per capita distribution of Anglican, Catholic, and other (Nonconformist) clergymen, and a measure of social class. The class measure is based on the proportion of the workforce in each unit which would have been put into Class II of the social grad-

---

[15] The development of new cleavage lines may be due to changes of mind among electors, a process of conversion, or the influx of new voters who divide along lines different from their predecessors. We return to this theme later in the chapter.

[16] The data for 1918 to 1929 are derived from Miller and Raab, "Religious Alignment," p. 249.

TABLE 8.3. Patterns of Voter Alignment, 1885–1929

	Anglican	Non-conformist	Catholic	% Agriculture	1951 Class	Multiple R²
1885	.31	−.27	.35	−.16	.23	.25
1886	.29	−.33	.21	−.18	.39	.21
1892	.24	−.36	.08	−.09	.10	.12
1895	.07	−.37	.22	.07	.15	.14
1900	−.03	−.02	.45	.04	−.04	.21
1906	.23	−.38	.10	.20	.09	.20
1910, Jan.	.26	−.49	.20	.20	.18	.30
1910, Dec.	.44	−.39	.22	−.05	.27	.32
1918	.47	−.28	.03	−.56	.65	.43
1922	.32	−.40	.07	−.17	.70	.46
1923	.49	−.33	.07	−.14	.67	.53
1924	.34	−.30	.10	−.15	.66	.49
1929	.52	−.29	.11	−.37	.68	.58

ing scheme adopted for the census of 1951.[17] We have followed Miller in using this measure to indicate the concentration of owners and managers. Of course, because of the greater precision of occupational coding after 1918, the measure can be regarded only as a rough approximation of class composition for the pre-1918 period.

Despite differences in data quality across electoral systems, it is clear that the traditional interpretation is accurate insofar as it draws a sharp line between pre- and postwar cleavage patterns. The longitudinal array of coefficients in Table 8.3 emphasizes the discontinuity between the first set of elections when religious factors were generally dominant, and the postwar set when class clearly gained ascendance in structuring the vote. The analysis sustains the traditional view of a dramatic alteration of cleavage bases between 1910 and 1918, a movement of the vote from a confessional to a class alignment. That finding leads inescapably to the conclusion that the rise of Labour and the decline of the Liberals are bound up in the same packet

[17] The attempt to construct Class II of the 1951 scheme using 1891 data depended on J. A. Banks, "The Social Structure of Nineteenth Century England as Seen Through the Census," in Richard Lawton, ed., *The Census and Social Structure* (London: Frank Cass, 1978), pp. 203–223.

with the substitution of class for religion as the major social division underlying the British party system.

EVALUATING THE TRADITIONAL MODEL

Though the traditional model of party transformation is more accurate than its revisionist rival on the matter of timing, the traditional interpretation fails to offer a complete explanation for the nature of the realignment. The weaknesses in the traditional account involve major assumptions about the decline of religion, the rise of class-awareness and the pivotal role of the franchise extension of 1918.

One central theme in the traditional literature is the decline of religion as a social and political force in Edwardian Britain. The Liberals of the late Victorian period are usually portrayed as a coalition of Nonconformists, united in opposition to the prerogatives of the Church of England and devoted to the removal of Nonconformist disabilities— a portrait largely affirmed by the statistical analysis in the last two chapters. The Nonconformist-Liberal linkage inspired a counterthrust by a Conservative coalition based, though less strongly, on an Anglican electorate. This religious alignment is said to have broken down as religion itself lost vitality and power, due to the product of modernizing factors such as the "new" Bible criticism, the rise of skepticism and faith in science, the spread of secular humanism, the availability of Sunday entertainment as an alternative to worship, the "suburban captivity of the churches," and, finally, the shattering impact of World War I on all faith and tradition. The consequence was a diminution in faith, the spread of indifference rather than heresy, and the removal of religion from the center of British life.[18]

This revolution in consciousness had a disastrous effect

[18] For a typical expression of this thesis, see R. K. Webb, *Modern England*, 2nd ed. (New York: Harper and Row, 1980), pp. 405–412.

on Nonconformity as a political force. The argument was expressed most forcefully in the classic account by John Glaser:

> On the eve of the war, Nonconformity, like official Liberalism, was politically exhausted and divided and hesitant as to the future. The issues in which Nonconformists were peculiarly interested, such as education and Welsh disestablishment, were only surface irritants outside of Wales. The old demand for disestablishment of the church of England had all but disappeared. Temperance and other moral reforms associated with the Nonconformist conscience were even less popular and less representative of English opinion than they had been twenty years earlier. The so-called "middle-class morality" was being challenged not only by Shavian wit but by social practice. Religion no longer held the primary place in the lives of most Englishmen. For religious people, the vital issue was not church vs. chapel, but Christianity vs. unbelief. Dissent no longer carried with it a significant burden of legal or social disability. This emancipation of Nonconformists was a triumph of Liberalism whose root was "respect for the dignity and worth of the individual." But when the iron went out of the soul of Nonconformity—when Dissent ceased to dissent—the robust vitality of traditional Liberalism was weakened.[19]

The few remaining Nonconformist grievances were not sufficient to form the basis for an effective electoral appeal and seemed trivial next to the demand for social reform. Yet the very success of Nonconformity in freeing itself from historic shackles had lowered the barriers between Dissent and the Church of England, so much so that the sons of leading Nonconformist families, the traditional source of Liberal leadership, could complete their social transformation by moving into the Church of England. Liberalism was sheared off at the base, when the organized working class demanded unacceptably broad social reform, and pruned at the top, as the Nonconformist elite migrated to the state Church and Conservative party. There remained

[19] John F. Glaser, "English Nonconformity and the Decline of Liberalism," p. 362.

only a small and vulnerable middle-class following. The Church of England suffered from a similar malaise and, in the absence of an organized challenge from Nonconformity, lessened its historic attachment to the Conservative party. Thus, the decline of religion undercut the traditional basis of group loyalties that had provided a structure to political coalitions.

The decline of religion as a social force was associated with increasing public consciousness of class differences, the second consistent theme in traditional accounts of party transformation.[20] The factors responsible for this sustained increase in class feeling are a matter of debate, but few would dispute the trend toward greater awareness of inequality or its growing political relevance.[21] The Labour party was the major beneficiary of this surge in class-consciousness as it came to embody the aspirations of the larger part of the working-class population. Persons worried about the threat to property posed by the demands of the emerging working-class movement fled en masse to the Conservative party. As the issue was joined between capital and labor, the Liberals lost their historic role as an agent of cross-class collaboration and were soon relegated to minor party status.

It was once thought that the rise of Labour was due principally to the conversion of Liberal workingmen, but recent electoral research casts doubt upon that interpretation, emphasizing instead the success of Labour in harnessing the sympathies of the electors who were enfranchised by the Fourth Reform Act in 1918. This reinterpretation is consistent with the trend among students of elections to recognize changes in the composition

[20] See Pelling, *Popular Politics*, 2nd ed., pp. 119–120; Ross McKibbin, *The Evolution of the Labour Party, 1910–1924*, p. 244. Of course, the classic account is George Dangerfield, *The Strange Death of Liberal England*.

[21] For one of the few explicit attempts to explain why the newly enfranchised were more aware of class than prewar voters, see Chris Chamberlain, "The Growth of Support for the Labour Party in Britain," pp. 474–489.

of the electorate as a major source of change in the aggregate distribution of partisan sentiments.[22] This was evident to Butler and Stokes whose cohort data indicated that "much the largest source of the increase in Labour strength reported between generations is due to recruitment of support among manual workers who could not associate a party allegiance with their father."[23] Labour's relative attractiveness to the previously nonpolitical workers was instrumental in the sudden growth of the party because the newly enfranchised dominated the postwar electorate.[24]

The transformation of the British party system is thus said to have involved three distinct trends which destroyed a party system that had seemed rooted in human nature itself. The first factor, *dealignment*, involved a loosening of party ties in the electorate, due principally to the decreasing salience of the religious controversy that had structured the Victorian alignment.[25] As parties became increasingly divorced from the reality of social conflict, which had now moved to a class basis, citizens increasingly resorted to nonelectoral avenues to promote political change.[26] The party system returned to equilibrium with the expansion of the electorate to include large numbers of new voters who were not attracted to a confessional style of politics but were highly susceptible instead to a Labour party which emphasized working-class interests. In response to this challenge, the Conservatives became more clearly than before an agent of middle-class interests. This second factor, *realignment*, synchronized the party system with the social structure. Finally, the new party system represented a *cleavage shift*

[22] Kristi Andersen, *The Creation of a Democratic Majority, 1928–1936* (Chicago: University of Chicago Press, 1979).

[23] Butler and Stokes, *Political Change*, 1st ed., p. 257.

[24] H.C.G. Matthews, R. I. McKibbin, and J. A. Kay, "The Franchise Factor in the Rise of the Labour Party," pp. 723–752. On the extension of the franchise in 1918, see Martin Pugh, *Electoral Reform in War and Peace, 1906–1918* (London: Routledge and Kegan Paul, 1978).

[25] Ronald Inglehart and Avram Hochstein, "Alignment and Dealignment of the Electorate in France and the United States," *Comparative Political Studies* 5 (October 1972), 343–372.

[26] Bob Holton, *British Syndicalism, 1900–1914* (London: Pluto Press, 1976).

which affected both the social basis of partisanship and the political agenda. The new system represented, albeit in muted form, conflicts between social classes—functional conflicts rooted in the process of industrial development. Voting moved from a religious and regional base to a class alignment, and the issues which dominated political debate had more to do with equality and distribution than with religious liberty or state-sanctioned morality.

The three assumptions about the decline of religion, the rise of class feeling, and the role of new voters as carriers of the realignment form the core of the traditional model of party transformation in Britain. Despite its plausibility and its superior predictive capacity, this model raises as many questions as it answers. Each of the core assumptions is problematic.

First, there is the problem of explaining the major social change said to have undermined party loyalties and promoted dealignment—the decline of religion. Religious indifference, concentrated in the social stratum which dominated the electorate after 1918, is the key independent variable, but its source remains a matter of mystery. The factors commonly cited to explain a breakdown of religion were certainly not limited to Britain. Throughout the Western world, new secular values challenged established religious thought, Sunday lost its religious character, and war challenged long-established beliefs. Yet only in Britain, it seems, was there a dramatic decline in religious feeling and a diminution in the level of confessional politics. Why did British religion prove so feeble, unable to resist the onward march of secular culture?

Then again, it is not self-evident that religion did actually decrease in importance as quickly as the party system underwent transformation. John Gay has reminded us that religious conversion is usually an individual phenomenon and that groups change their loyalties at a glacial pace.[27] This observation finds support in the studies of trends in

[27] John D. Gay, *The Geography of Religion in England* (London: Duckworth, 1971), pp. 42–43.

religious behavior and the frequent demonstration of the tenacious hold of religious values and customs upon large segments of the British people.[28] We need an explanation of dealignment consistent with evolutionary change in religious feeling, something not found in existing studies.

Explanations of dealignment are sensitive to another serious criticism: reflecting only the interest group model of political confessionalism, they assume that religion can be a significant electoral factor only if political conflicts involve overt religious controversies and if political parties openly seek adherents on denominational grounds. Research from other countries shows clearly that the decline of overt religious controversy need not automatically deconfessionalize party alignments. Religious issues have not for many years played a central role in Canadian political debate, yet religion, quite apart from class or ethnicity, continues to play a major role in structuring the vote.[29] The same has been said for Australia.[30] The American political agenda is largely bereft of overt Protestant-Catholic conflict, yet these groups continue to display divergent political tendencies that cannot be explained away by citing class or ethnic differences.[31] It is not only these countries, all of which originated as fragments of British society, that demonstrate

[28] K. S. Inglis, *Churches and the Working Classes in Victorian England* (London: Routledge and Kegan Paul, 1963), pp. 329–330; Andre Siegfried, *Post-War Britain*, trans. H. H. Hemming (New York: E. P. Dutton, 1924), p. 223. More generally, see Mass Observation, *Puzzled People* (London: Victor Gollancz, 1947).

[29] Grace M. Anderson, "Voting Behavior and the Ethnic-Religious Variable: A Study of a Federal Election in Hamilton, Ontario," *Canadian Journal of Economics and Political Science* 32 (February 1966), 27–37; John Meisel, "Religious Affiliation and Electoral Behavior: A Case Study," in John C. Courtney, ed., *Voting in Canada* (Scarborough, Ont.: Prentice-Hall of Canada, 1967), pp. 144–161, and also his "Bizarre Aspects of a Vanishing Act: The Religious Cleavage and Voting in Canada" (Paper presented to the Roundtable on Political Integration, International Political Science Association, Jerusalem, 1974).

[30] D. A. Kemp, *Society and Electoral Behaviour in Australia* (St. Lucia, Queensland: University of Queensland Press, 1978), ch. 6.

[31] David Knoke, "Religion, Stratification and Politics: America in the 1960s," *American Journal of Political Science* 18 (May 1974), 331–345.

the tenacity of religious values as precipitants of political blocs. Throughout the modern world, religion maintains its electoral significance despite the triumph of secular forms and the reluctance of parties to solicit support with overt denominational appeals. The decline of formal religious controversy need not presage a decline in the partisan relevance of denominational commitments and the consequent dealignment of religiously based party systems.

Second, if the decline of religion has not been adequately explained, neither is it clear why social class should have emerged as the major social cleavage and the principal line of partisan demarcation for the cohort entering the electorate in 1918. Other potential divisions could have replaced religion as the dominant source of electoral conflict. What has to be explained, to paraphrase Dangerfield, is how and why a sense of class feeling got into the air when it did. Why did the post-1918 cohort prove so much more amenable to class-voting than the cohort enfranchised in 1885?

Third, even more basically, the crucial assumption that partisan allegiance came to follow class lines is only partially correct. The Conservative party has persisted precisely because the class/party alignment is incomplete. In some respects, the most interesting aspect of the period after 1910 is the partial polarization of classes.[32] In a purely class-based party system, the numerical dominance of the working class would have reduced the Conservatives to a state of permanent opposition. The Conservatives have survived, even prospered, because their party has managed to retain the support of a significant fraction of the working class. The "working-class Tories," the subject of numerous studies, differ in major respects from working-class Labour voters, but it is not clear why some working-class voters are more

---

[32] W. L. Guttsman, "The British Political Elite and the Class Structure," in Philip Stanworth and Anthony Giddens, eds., *Elites and Power in British Society* (London: Cambridge University Press, 1974), p. 33.

prone than others to accept the attitudes and characteristics that predispose them to support the Conservative party.[33]

A catalogue of the weaknesses in existing theories of systemic change serves to indicate the requirements for a fuller explanation. A thorough explanation for the realignment which began in 1918 or thereabouts must include answers to these questions:

1. Why did religion lose its social force?
2. Why did class become the best predictor of partisanship?
3. Why did Labour gain the lion's share of the voters newly enfranchised in 1918 and an increasing share of each successive cohort?
4. Why did a significant share of the working class continue to support the Conservative party?

In the next section, we extend the ethos model to account for change after 1910. Following an exposition of the model, it is shown to provide answers for these four questions, and then it is tested for accuracy and insight.

INCORPORATING THE ETHOS MODEL

Though certainly not the only way to explain the links between religion and voting, the ethos approach calls attention to the significance of one factor, religious belief, as a source of politically relevant dispositions. Forgetting for the moment the series of caveats and qualifications that should accompany such an exposition, this approach may be extended to help explain some of the features of partisan change in Britain. Borrowing Weber's terminology, it has been argued above that a distinctive outlook, largely derived from religious belief, promoted an affinity between the voters and political parties of late Victorian-Edwardian Britain. Some voters, Puritan in spirit, believed the task of

[33] See, e.g., Robert McKenzie and Allen Silver, *Angels in Marble* (Chicago: University of Chicago Press, 1968); Eric Nordlinger, *The Working Class Tories* (London: MacGibbon and Kee, 1967).

the Christian was to help establish conditions which would bring earth much closer to heaven. Such Puritans used the Liberal party as a mechanism for removing institutional obstacles to upright conduct. Other voters were non-Puritans. Their belief in the inherent evil of man made them wary of attempts to build heaven on earth. The Conservative party was the vehicle used by non-Puritans to resist Liberal schemes that would deny them certain liberties.

According to the logic inherent in such an approach, the parties should have continued to prosper so long as the mass of voters were socialized to the outlook associated with them—Liberals to the Puritan ethos, Conservatives to the non-Puritan. This assumption is supported by a growing body of research which demonstrates that the persistence of traditional alignments is very much a function of early childhood socialization.[34] If one of the parties faltered, it stands to reason that something must have interfered with its method of transmitting political loyalty. Since political ideas derived in the first instance from religious perspectives taught in the home and school, there must have been a change in religious education, most probably in the school.

The bulk of voters in the electorate before 1910 had received their education in schools run by religious bodies. Prior to 1870, most schools were sponsored either by the Church of England or one of the Nonconformist bodies. Each school attempted to disseminate not only basic skills like literacy and numeracy but also the religious ideas associated with its sponsor. The National Society, the parent body of Anglican schools, made its intentions explicit:

Our work is to teach children the facts of our religion, the doctrines of our religion, the duties of our religion. We teach them the facts of our religion, that they may be intelligent Christians, not ignorant, as heathens; the doctrines, that they may not be

[34] William P. Irvine, "Explaining the Religious Basis of the Canadian Partisan Identity: Success on the Third Try," *Canadian Journal of Political Science* 7 (September 1974), 560–563.

Christians only, but Churchmen; the duties, that they may not be Churchmen only, but Communicants.[35]

The task of the rival Nonconformist societies was equally to turn out little Nonconformists.

These schools may not have done well in producing active communicants, but they could well have disseminated the basic religious outlooks of their denominations to their charges. Modern studies of religious education have concluded that young children are not sufficiently endowed with cognitive skills to appreciate the subtle theology taught by their churches; religious education seems instead to implant very broad and simplistic frameworks in the minds of students.[36] The religiopolitical orientations we have defined are precisely the kinds of broad and simple frameworks the religious training in the schools could transmit. When the student entered the electorate, he would follow his religious orientation to the political party associated with it. We assume that the students educated in Nonconformist schools picked up the Puritan outlook and followed that outlook to its logical conclusion in support for the Liberal party. A student from an Anglican school developed an outlook which disposed him to gravitate to the Conservative party. So long as most working-class children attended religious schools, they would divide politically along religious lines.

The value of these schools as agents of socialization was confirmed by an ecological analysis of the relationship be-

[35] James C. Greenough, *The Evolution of the Elementary Schools of Great Britain* (New York: D. Appleton, 1903), pp. 51–52. See also Henry Holman, *English National Education* (London: Blacker and Sons, 1898), p. 40; Henry James Burgess, *Enterprise in Education* (London: National Society, 1958); James Murphy, *Church, State and Schools in Britain, 1800–1970* (London: Routledge and Kegan Paul, 1971).

[36] Ralph Goldman, *Readiness for Religion* (New York: Seabury Press, 1965), and *Religious Thinking from Childhood to Adolescence* (London: Routledge and Kegan Paul, 1964); Robert O'Neill and Michael Donovan, *Children, Church and God* (New York: Corpus Books, 1970); Merton P. Strommen, *Research on Religious Development* (New York: Hawthorn Books, 1971).

tween denominational education and partisanship in the eight elections from 1885 to 1910. The analysis reported above in Chapter 6 showed strong links between 1851 religious education and voting under the Third Reform Act. The persistence of the relationship stands out in Table 8.4, which derived data on Catholic, Anglican, and Nonconformist elementary education from a government report on education at the turn of the century.[37] These measures, taken as usual over the total population, represent the tradition of religious socialization in the units; they serve as

TABLE 8.4. Effect of Denominational Education upon the Conservative-Unionist Vote, 1885–1910

	1885	1886	1892	1895	1900	1906	Jan. 1910	Dec. 1910
Anglican elementary schools, 1899	.21	(−.07)	(.09)	(.19)	(.05)	.33	.21	(.13)
Nonconformist elementary schools, 1899	−.63	(−.17)	−.47	−.52	−.65	−.59	−.47	−.40
Catholic elementary schools, 1899	.39	.27	.29	.41	.43	(.18)	(.16)	(.25)
Industrialization, 1891	−.26	−.39	(−.17)	(−.12)	(−.10)	(.10)	(−.14)	(−.11)
R²	.56	.35	.53	.54	.50	.39	.62	.39
N =	(79)	(71)	(79)	(74)	(69)	(74)	(77)	(72)

Nonsignificant coefficients are in parentheses.

[37] The data come from "Return . . . for each Public Elementary School Inspected in England and Wales," *Parliamentary Papers*, 1900, LXV, Cd. 315, pp. 12–19, and "Report of the Committee of Council on Education in Scotland for 1900–1901," *P. P.*, 1901, XXII, Cd. 585, 586, p. 46. The measures were derived from estimates of the number of children receiving elementary education in denominational schools. For each grouping, the number of schools was taken as a percentage of the total "voluntary" schools, and this fraction was then multiplied by the total number of students registered in the voluntary sector. Because of the need to measure growth patterns with data taken from various times within the period of the study, this chapter uses the set of surrogate constituencies with unchanging boundaries from 1885 to 1910. This required dropping the London units, which could not be held constant due to the thorough boundary revisions of 1894.

an estimate of the proportion of the population exposed to the ethos associated with the various denominations. Besides the three measures of religious education, the equations summarized in Table 8.4 included the measure of industrialization and the usual set of regional dummies. The relationships between education and partisanship followed expectations. The proportion of students in Nonconformist schools was a strong, negative predictor of Unionism, significant in all but one election. Anglicanism was positively associated with Unionism in seven of eight elections, significantly so in three cases. The table reveals the familiar Catholic-Unionist linkage which has previously been interpreted as a sign of the pro-Unionist backlash found in areas of Catholic concentration. It is again noteworthy that the coefficients for the denominational educational efforts generally dwarf the class measure. These data lend support to the argument about the role of religious schools as agents of political socialization.

What altered the alignment which had been reinforced by religious education? To judge by the changes associated with the passage of the Fourth Reform Act, the bulk of voters first enfranchised in 1918 seemed resistant to traditional political cleavages and open to new kinds of class-based political appeals. Their socialization must have been different enough to dispose a large share of the post-1918 cohort to support Labour, a political movement which had enjoyed little success in the late Victorian-Edwardian political system.

I want to suggest a role in this process for the system of elementary education. In looking for sources of partisan transformation, scholars have paid little attention to the religiously based system of elementary education, that, I have argued, played an important role in the content and direction of political socialization. Specifically, a case can be made that the transformation of the party system was facilitated by a major modification of the system of denominational education, a system which was revealed by the statistical analysis to be intimately associated with the confessional party system. The passage of the Education Act of 1870 had administered a severe shock to the old school system.[38] The publicly funded schools established by the new local boards posed a direct threat to the existing "voluntary" schools. The students in the "Board" schools were educated outside the bounds of the religious frameworks that had been transmitted to their parents. The new schools were nondenominational. Religious education was relegated to a minor role in the curriculum and a specified time of day. The lessons seem to have consisted of fairly vague and undogmatic Bible reading. Teachers were admonished not to promote particular dogmas and were forbidden to proselytize for any denomination.[39]

The religious training may have been sufficient to inculcate a generalized respect for religion, but it was nowhere near as concentrated as the education provided in the old sectarian schools. Persons educated in the new state schools failed to receive the cues that would have predisposed them to accept the outlook associated with the religious denominations. Without the appropriate cues, new voters would not be led so automatically to the parties which represented the particular religious outlooks. As persons educated in the board schools entered the electorate in increasing numbers, the party configuration would be susceptible to change.

The fact that voters no longer derived a political outlook from their religious perspectives does not itself explain why they should begin to derive political attitudes from class

---

[38] The standard works are Marjorie Cruickshank, *Church and State in English Education* (New York: St. Martins, 1963); Benjamin Sacks, *The Religious Issue in the State Schools of England and Wales, 1902–1914* (Albuquerque: University of New Mexico Press, 1965); Gillian Sutherland, *Policy-Making in Elementary Education, 1870–1895* (London: Oxford University Press, 1973).

[39] *Parliamentary Papers*, 1878–1879, LVII, Return 84, "Return of the Provision Made by Each School Board . . . Respecting Religious Teaching and Religious Observances . . . ".

affiliation. We may know how Britain got out of a religiously based party system; we still need to understand how it got into a system based on social class.

Each voter in a complex society belongs to several groups and could theoretically base his party loyalty on any one of them. How is it that some characteristics are more likely to form a basis for political cohesion than others? Why, when religion ceased to provide the crucial group link, did class take its place? The answer, first suggested by the work of Richard Rose, is that voters divide politically on the basis of the group characteristics most salient to them. Class seems to be the ultimate residual variable. Where citizens differ ethnically, religiously, or racially, political alignments follow ethnic, religious, or racial lines. Even in the United Kingdom, the standard model of a homogeneous society, such differences manifest themselves in political behavior. Where there are distinctive nationalities (Scotland and Wales) or religious groups (Northern Ireland) or races (the industrial Midlands), the differences impinge on politics. Class, it seems, is the basis on which persons divide politically only when all other differences are exhausted.[40]

If class became the fundamental dividing line in British politics, it must have been because the other differences that had previously cemented political blocs were absent. Clearly, the British electorate was racially and ethnically homogeneous. After the Education Act had worked its force on the school system, religious differences were moot. Class was thus the only major structural interest left to influence the political system. It became the dividing line in politics because none of the other potential cleavage sources were present in British society. It might not have become so

[40] Richard Rose, "Class and Party Divisions: Britain as a Test Case," pp. 129–162. See also Arend Lijphart, "Religious vs. Linguistic vs. Class Voting: The 'Crucial Experiment' of Comparing Belgium, Canada, South Africa and Switzerland," *American Political Science Review* 73 (June 1979), 453: "Social class is clearly no more than a secondary and subsidiary influence on party choice and can become a factor of importance only in the absence of potent rivals such as religion and language."

important if the old educational system had continued to socialize voters to a denominational tradition.

The educational changes should have affected the political parties in different ways. The Liberals were likely to lose the most from the change in socialization patterns. The Liberals had disproportionately recruited their votes from persons socialized to the Puritan ethos through the institution of Nonconformist schools. Although initially hostile to the Education Act, the Nonconformists soon came to see the School Boards as a vehicle for undercutting the Anglican schools and they surrendered control of the Nonconformist schools to the Boards.[41] As a result of the transfer, Nonconformists gave up the institution which had socialized sizeable portions of the electorate to the distinctive Puritan ethos. The voters who had been educated earlier in Nonconformist schools remained a potent force in the electorate and could be mobilized by an appeal to the Free Church tradition. But the Nonconformists, by giving up their schools, failed to reproduce themselves. The products of the board schools, disproportionately the children of Nonconformist parents, were less amenable to traditional appeals. Liberal leaders continued to justify their proposals on ethical grounds, but such appeals to righteousness were lost on voters who had not been sensitized to regard righteousness as a salient political goal.[42] The new voters, who came in time to dominate the electorate, were less and less receptive to the traditional Liberal appeals.

Labour was the main beneficiary from the change in socialization practices. Most of the new voters, especially the products of the board schools, were members of the working class. Had the old socialization system been main-

---

[41] This comes through repeatedly in the reports of the various royal commissions on education after 1870.

[42] Walter G. Inman, "The British Liberal Party, 1892–1939," pp. 151–152; Richard Price, *An Imperial War and the British Working Class* (London: Routledge and Kegan Paul, 1972), p. 72.

tained, they would have been socialized to a religious world-view and thus inclined to support the existing parties. Previous attempts to mobilize the working class had failed precisely because the workers thought of themselves as Anglicans, Nonconformists, or Catholics, not as workers.[43] If politics was to them a means for securing righteousness or defending the denomination, they could not be mobilized through class appeals. Labour succeeded when other working-class movements had failed because its potential constituency had been freed from a religious outlook through secular education. The graduates of the board schools were susceptible to political appeals couched in terms of class interests and could be mobilized on that basis. From such persons, Labour recruited its voters.

Not all workers were freed from their traditional religious outlooks, and therein lies the explanation for the success of the Conservative party in retaining the allegiance of some workers. The Church of England resisted the establishment of the School Boards and the hierarchy refused to let the "godless" board schools gain an educational monopoly.[44] The Church schools remained independent of the boards and continued to disseminate their non-Puritan

[43] Traditional explanations for the relative passivity of the British working class in the period before Labour have centered on institutional obstacles to working-class assertion. See, for example, H. F. Moorhouse, "The Political Incorporation of the British Working Class: An Interpretation," *Sociology* 7 (1973), 341–359. It is worth recalling that Engels thought the working class was already sufficiently well-represented before 1885 to rule England. See Frederick Engels, *The British Labour Movement* (London: Martin Lawrence, 1934), pp. 34–35. Borrowing from Gramsci's notion of hegemony, some recent writers have suggested that the workers voted for middle-class parties because they accepted the legitimacy of middle-class ideology. See Zgymunt Bauman, *Between Class and Elite: The Evolution of the British Labour Movement*, trans. Sheila Patterson (Manchester: Manchester University Press, 1972), and Robert Q. Gray, "Critical Note," *Sociology* 9 (1975), 101–104. I argue that workers accepted the middle class way of thinking about politics because it was transmitted to them through the agency of denominational education.

[44] Stephen G. Platten, "The Conflict Over the Control of Elementary Education, 1870–1902, and Its Effect Upon the Life and Influence of the Church," *British Journal of Educational Studies* 33 (1975), 276–302.

outlook to large numbers of young people. The Anglican schools were at a disadvantage in competing with the board schools but they kept their rate of loss considerably below the Nonconformists, who were only too happy to transfer their schools to board control. These changes are manifest in Table 8.5, which illustrates the changing patterns of education. The many working-class children still being educated in Anglican schools by 1885 were not freed from the traditional religious outlook associated with Conservatism. Working-class graduates of Anglican schools were socialized much as their parents had been and imbibed the same fundamental outlook. For them, class was not the relevant political divide and could not supplant religion as the key source of political cues. So long as the Church schools transmitted to working-class children the non-Puritan outlook, they contributed to the manufacture of working-class Conservatives.[45] As the Church schools gradually lost enrollment, they molded fewer and fewer workers to a Conservative outlook. We would then predict that the percentage of Conservative workers should decline in each succeeding generation.

Lest this argument be overstated, two points need to be clarified. We do not mean to suggest that the Education Act of 1870 was designed to transform the political system. If contemporaries had guessed the consequences of their actions, they would probably have killed the proposal. Thus qualified, the conditions attending the passage of the law take on ironic dimensions. The Liberals were responsible for pushing the bill through Parliament and claimed it proudly as one of their major contributions to British society. Yet the net effect of the act was to remove the props from under the Liberal party, making its eventual "death" even stranger than George Dangerfield suggested in his classic account. To add to the irony, the Labour party,

[45] This would seem to account for Birch's finding on the continuing importance of religion in Glossop politics. See Birch, *Small Town Politics* p. 112.

TABLE 8.5. Changes in Enrollment Percentages for Inspected
Elementary Day Schools in England, 1870–1910*

Year	Church of England (%)	Nonconformist and other** (%)	Board Schools (%)
1870	77.7	22.3	0.0
1871	75.6	23.0	0.0
1872	75.6	23.6	0.7
1873	73.0	22.0	5.0
1874	70.8	20.4	8.8
1875	67.9	19.0	13.1
1876	65.0	17.5	17.5
1877	62.6	16.3	21.0
1878	60.0	15.5	24.5
1879	58.0	14.8	27.2
1880	56.5	14.0	29.5
1881	55.0	13.4	31.6
1882	54.0	12.9	33.1
1883	52.7	12.6	34.7
1884	51.8	12.3	35.9
1885	51.0	11.9	37.1
1886	49.9	11.7	38.4
1887	49.2	11.4	39.4
1888	48.6	11.2	40.2
1889	48.1	11.1	40.8
1890	47.7	11.0	41.3
1891	47.2	10.8	42.0
1892	46.8	10.4	42.8
1893	46.5	10.0	43.5
1894	46.2	9.4	44.4
1895	45.2	8.9	45.9
1896	44.6	8.7	46.7
1897	44.0	8.4	47.6
1898	43.5	8.2	48.3
1899	43.1	8.1	48.8
1900	42.5	7.8	49.7
1901	42.0	7.6	50.4
1902	41.5	7.5	51.0
1903	41.2	7.4	51.4
1904	41.3	6.0	52.7
1905	40.4	5.1	54.5
1906	38.9	4.8	56.3
1907	38.0	4.2	57.8
1908	37.2	3.8	59.0
1909	36.3	3.3	60.4
1910	35.5	3.0	61.5

* Figures reflect average attendance.
** Comprises British and Foreign Schools Society and Wesleyan Methodist.
SOURCE:
Calculated from
    1870–1895—Gillian Sutherland, *Policy-Making in Elementary Education, 1870–1895* (London: Oxford University Press, 1973), Table 1.
    1896—*Parliamentary Papers*, 1896–1897, XX, p. 4.
    1897—*Ibid.*, 1898, XXII, p. 65.
    1898—*Ibid.*, 1899, XX, p. 49.
    1899—*Ibid.*, 1900, LXV, p. 93.
    1900—*Ibid.*, 1902, LXXVIII, p. 659.
    1902—*Ibid.*, 1910–1911, LIX, p. 9.

which gained most from the establishment of the board schools, never seemed to recognize the contribution of these schools to its movement. Although Labour candidates took an interest in the school boards, the evidence shows they were interested in the local boards mostly as large employers of labor.[46]

As a corollary, we must state emphatically that the rise of Labour had little to do with the ideas transmitted in the board schools.[47] The framers of the Education Code did not view the schools as agents of radical social reconstruction and would have been aghast had they been aware that the curriculum served that purpose. The new schools were important because of what they did *not* do; in contrast to denominational schools, they did not disseminate the kind of religious outlook which led to support for the existing parties.[48] The role of the board schools was passive; they

[46] *Bradford and District Trade and Labour Council Yearbook* (Bradford: J. S. Toothill, 1901), p. 20. A full discussion of education policies is found in Rodney Barker, *Education and Politics, 1900–1951* (Oxford: Oxford University Press, 1972), and Brian Simon, *Education and the Labour Movement, 1870–1920* (London: Lawrence and Wishart, 1965).

[47] But see Richard Shannon, *The Crisis of Imperialism, 1865–1915* (St. Albans, Hertfordshire: Paladin, 1976), p. 222, who argues that board schools became the nucleus for a collective working-class consciousness. For a general discussion of elementary education and class, see J. S. Hurt, *Elementary Schooling and the Working Classes, 1860–1918* (London: Routledge and Kegan Paul, 1979).

[48] This argument is based on a theory of political socialization which takes its assumptions from learning theory. An individual's behavior is said to follow from the cues which he is supplied by his environment.

essentially freed the worker from traditional religious outlooks, allowing him to form a party allegiance on the basis
of class interests.

EVALUATING THE MODEL

In outlining the deficiencies of existing theories of party
change after 1910, we established criteria which should be
applied to any new theories. The extended version based
on the ethos approach seems to satisfy those specifications.

First, the scenario calls attention to the force which brought
about the decline of religion and thus made a party realignment possible. A new system of education was the causal
agent. Second, it also explains why social class took the place
of religion as a source of party cohesion. After the religious
differences had ceased to be relevant, class was the only
remaining group characteristic that required a defense in
the political system. Third, the model, if we may use that
term, also accounts for the success of Labour in recruiting
new voters and its relative inability to convert former Liberals or the children of Liberals. The students who attended
the board schools came from working-class homes. In most
of those homes, the father was not enfranchised. A young
person raised in such a home would not receive partisan
cues and would thus be free to choose among parties when

The likelihood that a person will behave in a certain manner is a function
of the strength and consistency of the cues disposing him to that manner
of behavior. We argue that the likelihood of a worker supporting Labour
varies with the extent to which his environment, the home and the school,
transmits pro-Labour cues. Contradictory or inconsistent cues will lessen
the probability of the individual voting Labour. For application of such
contextual theories to partisanship, see Herbert McCloskey and Harold
E. Dahlgren, "Primary Group Influence on Party Loyalty," *American Political Science Review* 53 (1959), 757–776, and David R. Segal and Marshall
W. Meyer, "The Social Context of Political Partisanship," in *Social Ecology*,
ed. Dogan and Rokkan, pp. 217–232. Charles Booth seems to have recognized the importance of contextual reinforcement when he compared
the behavior of young Nonconformists raised in Nonconformist homes
with the behavior of young Anglicans who received religious education
solely from the schools: Charles Booth, *Life and Labour of the People of
London*, 3rd ser. (London: MacMillan, 1903), VII, 404.

first called upon to declare an allegiance. Most such voters would gravitate to the party associated with their class, which meant Labour in most cases. Lifelong Liberals would resist the new party and the children of those Liberals would prove somewhat intractable. Lastly, the model renders the phenomenon of working-class Conservatism more explicable. Workers socialized to the non-Puritan outlook through the Anglican schools would gravitate to the Conservative party.

Though this interpretation may be plausible, it presents enormous difficulties of proof simply because of the limited availability of data. Historically oriented survey researchers, who might have been expected to provide some material for empirical testing, have not paid much attention to the education factor and have not collected the kind of educational background data necessary for analysis. Though various government agencies provided some educational data for geographical areas, the reporting was sporadic and the coverage spotty. Even if better educational data were available, it would be difficult to link the information to partisan change because of wholesale constituency boundary revisions between 1910 and 1918. Because of these problems, the best that can be done with the available data is to demonstrate that some relationships predicated in the interpretation are not contradicted by the data.

The interpretation presented above posits certain relationships between the electoral, educational, and class systems. The growth of nondenominational education is said to have affected the workers who were first enfranchised by the 1918 Reform Act. If this was so, then the distribution of the working class ought to be associated with a low level of enfranchisement before the war and the spread of nondenominational education after 1870. The data set used throughout the study can supply some very rough indicators to check these predictions.[49] The concentration of the working class will be equated with the distribution of

[49] As indicated above, the data for this analysis have been aggregated for the constant units rather than the units matched to the 1891 census.

industrial workers, measured as described in Chapter 5. The level of franchise exclusion has been calculated by subtracting from 1.00 a proportion equal to the ratio of persons on the electoral register in 1910 to the estimated male population in the same year.[50] For all units used in the analysis, the mean value of disenfranchisement was 33.5%, which agrees with the best available estimates about the exclusiveness of the electoral system in prewar Britain.[51] Estimating the growth of nonsectarian education involved making a series of assumptions about data of very uncertain quality. Using the 1851 religious census, the number of students registered in schools under the aegis of the British and Foreign Schools Society was taken as a proportion of one-sixth of the unit population, the latter fraction being the common estimate for the school-age population.[52] This figure was meant to indicate the proportion of young persons exposed to a predominantly secular ethos at midcentury. To gauge the corresponding figure at the end of the century, the number of students registered in board schools was similarly taken as a proportion of one-sixth of the population in 1901. The measure of the growth of secular education was created by taking the difference between the 1899 and 1851 figures over a denominator of 1.00 minus the 1851 proportion. This denominator corrects for distortions due to the proportionality of gain scores to the base.[53] We must strongly emphasize that the educational

[50] The number of eligible voters was derived from Craig and, following Matthew, McKibbin, and Kay in "Franchise Factor," the potential electorate was calculated by multiplying the 1911 male population by 0.56. This is a measure of exclusion which indicates the proportion of male adults who were not registered to vote due to franchise restrictions or registration provisions.

[51] Blewett (in *Peers, Parties and People*, p. 359) estimates that only 60% to 65% of the adult males were on the register.

[52] This was the estimate of school-age population in England and Wales, but the Scottish authorities reported figures which indicated that the fraction of one-fifth was more appropriate and it was used for the Scottish units.

[53] Carl I. Hovland, Arthur A. Lumsdaine, and Fred D. Sheffield, "A Baseline for Measurement of Percentage Change," in Paul F. Lazarsfeld

data contain many errors, and the process of constructing the measure relied on assumptions which may not be accurate, so the measure of growth in secular education should be taken as no more than a rough, notional indicator of real growth patterns.

Correlating these three figures indicates that the prewar franchise limitations and the spread of secular education were positively associated with each other (r = 0.14) and that both were positively related to the concentration of industry (r of 0.10 for the growth of secular education and industrialization, r of 0.49 for disfranchisement and industry). These are not overwhelming relationships but they do not contradict the interpretation.

The plausibility of this account of partisan transformation may be further strengthened by a resort to simulation with some descriptive mathematical equations of voter change. The values for the parameters in the simulation are not exactly taken out of thin air but they are only rough estimates or, in a few instances, little more than guesswork. Rather than use these data to prove the correctness of the hypothesis, the simulation is intended only to illustrate the suggested mechanism of partisan change. It will achieve its purpose if the simulation clarifies the process by which changes in religious education may have helped to bring about far-reaching changes in the electoral universe.

The model will be formalized in terms of three age cohorts, entering the electorate at twenty-year intervals—1870 = t_1, 1890 = t_2, and 1910 = t_3. These cutting points are arbitrary but not unreasonable. Although it will prove convenient to speak of each cohort as if its members were the children of the preceding cohort, no direct biological relationship is asserted. We assume only that the families

and Morris Rosenberg, eds., *The Language of Social Research* (New York: Free Press, 1955), pp. 77–82. Because of the low correlation between "secular"—i.e., British schools—education in 1851 and board schools in 1899, there was no reason to use a more sophisticated measure of change.

from which each new cohort derived divide their party loyalties in the same manner as the preceding cohort.

The model begins with a simple electoral universe composed entirely of voters socialized either to a world-view as Anglicans (A) or non-Anglicans (N):

(1) Electorate (t_0) = A + N

In the first generation, a person's partisanship was simply derived from his religious education, which was consistent with his training at home.[54] A student educated in an Anglican school, reinforced by an Anglican home, will become a non-Puritan and support the Conservative party wholeheartedly:

(2) Conservative vote (t_0) = (1.00)A

By contrast, the voter educated to Puritanism in non-Anglican schools, also reinforced by his non-Anglican home, will give his loyalty to the Liberal party. So

(3) Liberal vote (t_0) = (1.00)N

So things stood up to the establishment of the board schools in 1870. For the generation of voters coming of age in 1870 (t_1), we shall arbitrarily select a value of 0.60 for A and 0.40 for N.[55] When inserted in equations (2) and (3), the values yield a vote division of

(4) Conservative vote (t_1) = (1.00)(0.60) = 0.60
(5) Liberal vote $\quad\quad (t_1)$ = (1.00)(0.40) = 0.40.

Twenty years later $(t_2 = 1890)$, a new group of voters enters the electorate, differing from its predecessors in one important respect. Some of its members have been social-

[54] There is evidence that some parents sent their children to schools sponsored by denominations other than their own: A. W. Newton, *The English Elementary School* (London: Longmans, Green, 1919), p. 49.

[55] These figures suggest base partisan loyalty in the population, not the actual vote. For a whole host of reasons, the two were not the same. The actual starting point is of little consequence for the rate of decline is governed by the change rates from the educational statistics.

ized to a secular outlook inconsistent with the religious tradition of their family. The passage of the Education Act in 1870 led to the establishment of state-supported schools which taught no religious doctrine and freed the student from a religious outlook. We have reasoned that graduates of state schools were inclined to look upon politics from the perspective of their class membership, not their religious affiliation. Since most of them were working class, they would support the Labour party. Both the Liberals and Conservatives should lose support in this new generation. The exact rate of decay will vary with the rate at which schools sponsored by the different denominations lost enrollment to the board schools.

To represent this change, we need to define some additional terms. Children from Anglican homes who attended Anglican schools will be known as "AA"; the children of Anglicans who graduated from the board schools will be called "AB"; the graduates of Nonconformist schools from Nonconformist homes are "NN"; and the children from Nonconformist homes who went to the board schools are "NB." The voters entering the electorate at t_2 are divided into four groups:

(6) Electorate (t_2) = AA + AB + NN + NB.

In order to estimate the values for these terms, we can use the admittedly imperfect government statistics of enrollment in certified schools, reported in Table 8.5. Between 1870 and 1890 enrollment in Anglican schools declined by 40% and in non-Anglican schools by 50%.[56] The change rates will be applied to the estimates of religious loyalty from the parental generation; they are reflected in the values at t_1. The Anglican generation (A = 0.60 for the entire electorate) divides into two groups, with 60% remaining in

---

[56] We represent the change by taking the Anglican share of children in certified schools in 1890 over the equivalent figure for 1870. This comes out to 47.7/77.7 or 0.6138. I have rounded to 0.60, and hence a loss of 0.40, to avoid the impression of spurious precision.

Anglican schools (so AA = 0.60 x 0.60 = 0.36) and 40% attending board schools (so AB = 0.60 x 0.40 = 0.24). The non-Anglicans (0.40 of the electorate at t_1) split evenly in two. Half attend non-Anglican religious schools (NN = 0.40 x 0.50 = 0.20) and the same fraction attend the board schools (NB = 0.40 x 0.50 = 0.20). The values for the four groups in the new political generation are summarized as follows:

(7) AA = 0.36
(8) AB = 0.24
(9) NN = 0.20
(10) NB = 0.20
              1.00

We can estimate the political loyalties of the generation coming of age at t_2 once we have estimated the partisan loyalty of each of the four groups. Those children socialized consistently, raised in a religious home and educated in a religious school, will support their "natural" party. So all members of group AA will vote Conservative and all from NN will support the Liberals. But we also have to deal with the two new groups which enter the electorate for the first time, the mixed groups, AB and NB. It would be naive to suppose that all children educated in board schools were free to divide politically on class lines. Given what we know about the process of political socialization, it seems evident that these first-generation graduates of the board schools would bear the imprint of the religious upbringing they got at home. We shall assume that young persons who receive inconsistent socialization—religious cues from the family, secular cues from the school—will behave inconsistently. Half will identify with the party of their parents and half will follow their class affiliation in political loyalty. This means the persons from AB and from NB go equally to the Liberals and Labour. Labour gets support only from the products of inconsistent socialization.

The overall partisanship of the generation at t_2 can be

calculated simply. The Conservative vote is the sum of the votes from all members of AA and half the members of the AB group or

(11) Conservative vote (t_2) = (1.00)(AA) + (0.50)(AB)
= (1.00)(0.36) + (0.50)(0.24)
= 0.36 + 0.12 = 0.48

The Liberal share is calculated by summing all of the NN group with 50% of the NBs:

(12) Liberal vote (t_2) = (1.00)(NN) + (0.50)(NB)
= (1.00)(0.20) + (0.50)(0.20)
= 0.20 + 0.10 = 0.30

Labour recruits only from the board-educated students and gets half of them:

(13) Labour vote (t_2) = (0.50)(AB) + (0.50)(NB)
= (0.50)(0.24) + (0.50)(0.20)
= 0.12 + 0.10 = 0.22

So the model predicts that the new voters entering the electorate in 1890 will be 48% Conservative, 30% Liberals, and 22% Labour.

The simulation predicts significant changes in the partisanship of the new cohort on the basis of changes in educational practice. The Conservatives will lose 20% over their support level from the preceding generation at t_1. The Liberals suffer somewhat more deeply, their support going down by 25% from one generation to the next, and Labour comes out of nowhere to challenge the Liberals as a major party of state.

The effect is muted if we account for the extent to which the overall electoral results will still be influenced by the first cohort. Let us estimate the overall effect of the differences in the partisan makeup of this new cohort by assuming that it displaces one-third of the electorate which entered at t_1. The size of the six groups in the electorate at t_2 is determined by multiplying each group's share of its cohort times the weight assigned to the cohort (0.67 to groups A and N; 0.33 to the four groups which entered at t_2). The result is the transition matrix in Table 8.6 which, when the appropriate multiplication and addition are conducted, yields an overall vote division of 57% for the Conservatives, 37% for the Liberals and 7% for Labour.

By the time of the next generation at t_3 (1910), the board schools had become the training ground for a clear majority of the young people, but their overall rate of growth had slowed considerably. The Anglican schools dropped only 25% of their remaining enrollment between 1890 and 1910 but the Nonconformist schools plummeted by another 75%. In the third generation, we have six distinct groups: third-generation Anglicans from Anglican schools (AAA); third-generation Anglicans from board schools (AAB); and third-generation "quasi Anglicans," board-educated and once-removed from their Anglican tradition (ABB). On the same principles, the descendants of the NN and NB groups are either NNN, NNB, or NBB. The electorate now consists of

(14) Electorate (t_3) = AAA + AAB + ABB + NNN + NNB + NBB.

The defection rates described above will enable us to give values to four of the terms. Applying the decline of 25%

TABLE 8.6. Transition Matrix for Electorate at t_2

Group		Degree of Support for		
		Conservative	Liberal	Labour
A	.402	1.00	0	0
N	.268	0	1.00	0
AA	.119	1.00	0	0
AB	.079	.50	0	.50
NN	.066	0	1.00	0
NB	.066	0	.50	.50

in Anglican enrollment to the children of the AB group (who were 0.36 of the cohort at t_2) produces:

(15) AAA = (0.75)(0.36) = 0.27
(16) AAB = (0.25)(0.36) = 0.09

and the decrement of 75% in non-Anglican religious schools translates into

(17) NNN = (0.25)(0.20) = 0.05
(18) NNB = (0.75)(0.20) = 0.15

The remaining two terms can be estimated if we assume that all the children of board-educated parents attended board schools, regardless of the religion of their parents. So

(19) ABB = (1.00)(0.24) = 0.24
(20) NBB = (1.00)(0.20) = 0.20

Following the logic established above, all consistent Anglicans (AAA) will vote for the Conservative party and so will half the "third generation" defectors to board schools (AAB). What of the "quasi Anglicans" (ABB)—those students from board schools and homes where the parents, though board-educated, came themselves from Anglican homes? Here is a major recruiting ground for Labour. The only factor which will prevent all the members of group ABB from supporting Labour would be the "lag factor" associated with generational change. The parents of members of group ABB, raised in Anglican homes, probably transmitted that tradition to some of the children. An Anglican ethos transmitted so tenuously will be a less potent influence than one transmitted directly; if so, the children of AB parents should be less Conservative than the children of AA parents, though both sets have Anglican grandparents. We assign a partisan propensity which takes account of the lag. Two-thirds of the quasi Anglicans would defect to Labour (0.67) and the remaining one-third (0.33) would support the Conservative party. The same principle would apply to the non-Anglican children, so we assign Liberal propensities of 1.00 to members of NNN, 0.50 to members of NNB, and 0.33 to the quasi non-Anglicans, NBB. Labour should get the support of all the non-Anglican children who do not support the Liberals.

In formal terms, the Conservatives would receive the following share of the total vote:

$$
\begin{aligned}
\text{(21) Conservative vote } (t_3) &= (1.00)(\text{AAA}) + (0.50)(\text{AAB}) \\
&\quad + (0.33)(\text{ABB}) \\
&= (1.00)(0.27) + (0.50)(0.09) \\
&\quad + (0.33)(0.24) \\
&= 0.27 + 0.045 + 0.079 \\
&= 0.394
\end{aligned}
$$

The Liberals would receive this share:

$$
\begin{aligned}
\text{(22) Liberal vote } (t_3) &= (1.00)(\text{NNN}) + (0.50)(\text{NNB}) + \\
&\quad (0.33)(\text{NBB}) \\
&= (1.00)(0.50) + (0.50)(0.15) + \\
&\quad (0.33)(0.20) \\
&= 0.050 + 0.075 + 0.066 \\
&= 0.191
\end{aligned}
$$

The Labour vote is composed of what remains:

$$
\begin{aligned}
\text{(23) Labour vote } (t_3) &= (0.50)(\text{AAB}) + (0.67)(\text{ABB}) + \\
&\quad (0.50)(\text{NNB}) + (0.67)(\text{NBB}) \\
&= (0.50)(0.09) + (0.67)(0.24) + \\
&\quad (0.50)(0.15) + (0.67)(0.20) \\
&= 0.045 + 0.161 + 0.075 + \\
&\quad 0.134 \\
&= 0.415
\end{aligned}
$$

At t_3, the division of loyalties for the new voters should have been 42% Labour, 39% Conservative, and 19% Liberal.

Even though the rate of growth of board schools slowed down by the time the generation at t_3 entered the electorate, the overall rate of political change accelerated. The Conservatives dropped more modestly at this stage, their support down from 48% to 39%. The Liberals shot down from 30% to just 19% of the new voters. Labour continued its meteoric rise, going from 27% at t_2 to 42% at t_3. It cannot be overstated that this change is predicated solely on discrete changes in educational practices, changes measured by trends in educational enrollment statistics.

As before, the effects of the new cohort on the overall vote will be mediated by the numerical preponderance of the two preceding cohorts. Assuming again that the new cohort displaces a third of the original electorate at t_1, we produce the transition matrix in Table 8.7. The appropriate calculations produce a total vote breakdown of 49% for the Conservatives, 30% for the Liberals, and the remaining 20% for Labour.

Must this process continue until Labour is the only party? The answer is no. At some point, the rate of Labour mobilization slowed down considerably. In the absence of sta-

TABLE 8.7. Transition Matrix for Electorate at t_3

Group		Degree of Support for		
		Conservative	Liberal	Labour
A	.198	1.00	0	0
N	.132	0	1.00	0
AA	.119	1.00	0	0
AB	.079	.50	0	.50
NN	.066	0	1.00	0
NB	.066	0	.50	.50
AAA	.089	1.00	0	0
AAB	.030	.50	0	.50
NNN	.017	0	1.00	0
NNB	.050	0	.50	.50
ABB	.790	.33	0	.67
NBB	.066	0	.33	.67

tistics on religious education after 1910, it is difficult to know just how this phenomenon occurred, but we can make some intelligent guesses. In the first place, the non-Anglican schools had been reduced virtually to a minimum by 1910. From then on, Labour would simply get increments of support from the already-converted. The same phenomenon must have occurred with the Ánglicans. More importantly, Labour would eventually begin to lose support from some of the already-converted. Politics crystallized firmly on class lines at the same time the social structure grew more complex and the middle class was enlarged. The Conservatives were able to offset early losses by attracting some of the board school students who had achieved middle class status. An equilibrium point was reached when Conservatives and Labour competed for the bulk of the votes, with the Liberals trailing far behind.

Although this simulation was meant principally to illustrate the process of electoral conversion, it can be judged against the historical record. The simulation suggested that each succeeding generation entering the electorate should have been somewhat less Conservative, significantly less Liberal, and manifestly more Labour. As these generations entered the electorate, party fortunes would fluctuate accordingly although there might be significant deviations caused by the issues associated with a particular election. To judge by the cohort data provided by Butler and Stokes, the scenario outlined in the simulation corresponded with experience.[57] Although their cohorts were defined by different cutting points, the trends in partisanship bore out the simulation. Each succeeding electoral generation became mildly less Conservative, significantly less Liberal, and much more Labour-inclined. The growth trend was such that change in aggregate partisan sentiment began slowly, speeded up between the second and third generation, and

[57] See Butler and Stokes, *Political Change*, p. 273. For a convenient summary of election results, see F.W.S. Craig, *British Electoral Facts, 1885– 1975* (London: Macmillan, 1976).

then slowed down to a point approximating equilibrium. The evidence supplied by Butler and Stokes shows that the electorate behaved as if the interpretation were correct.

Besides accuracy, this interpretation of party change has another virtue. It speaks to a problem which has long intrigued scholars, the role of Nonconformity in the development of the Labour party. Some observers have treated Labour as little more than an outgrowth of the Nonconformist conscience and have pointed to the key role played by certain Nonconformists in the party's early years.[58] Others have disagreed with this assessment, citing the conflict between Labour pioneers and the Nonconformist preachers and leaders who invariably supported the election of wealthy Nonconformist Liberals no matter what their political views.[59] The evidence is mixed. One cannot deny that many Labour pioneers had Nonconformist backgrounds nor can we overlook their almost universal tendency to speak of the movement in religious terms.[60] But these same leaders were almost at one in denouncing the institutional churches as too preoccupied with their wealthy parishioners.[61] Overt denominational appeals were frowned upon by Labour lead-

[58] C. B. Hawkins, *Norwich: A Social Study* (London: Phillip Lee Warner, 1910), pp. 287–288; Jack Lawson, *A Man's Life* (London: Hodder and Stoughton, 1932), p. 111; David A. Martin, *Pacifism* (New York: Schocken Books, 1965), p. 88; Stephen H. Mayor, "The Relations Between Organised Religion and English Working-Class Movements, 1850–1914" (Ph.D. thesis, University of Manchester, 1960), pp. 388–389; Stanley Pierson, "Socialism and Religion: A Study of Their Interaction in Great Britain, 1889–1911" (Ph.D. thesis, Harvard University, 1957), pp. i, 132; Philip Snowden, *An Autobiography* (London: Ivor, Nicholson and Watson, 1934), I, 63, 71; Robert Wearmouth, *Methodism and the Struggle of the Working Class, 1850–1900* (Leicester: E. Backus, 1954) and also his *The Social and Political Influence of Methodism in the Twentieth Century* (London: Epworth Press, 1957).

[59] Kenneth Brown, "Non-conformity and the British Labour Movement," *Journal of Social History* 1 (1975), 12–27; Thompson, "Tom Maguire," pp. 289, 291–292.

[60] Margaret McMillan, *The Life of Rachel McMillan* (London: J. M. Dent, 1927), pp. 84, 89; Lord Snell, *Men, Movements and Myself* (London: J. M. Dent, 1936), p. 99.

[61] Pierson, "Socialism," p. 250; Thompson, "Tom Maguire" p. 290.

ers.[62] And if the new movement was steeped in Nonconformity, why should it strive so conscientiously to establish
its own "Labour" churches?[63]

The ethos model suggests that both arguments are partially true. There was a carryover of quasi Nonconformists
into the ranks of Labour voters. The equations of Labour
support (13, 23) show that the children of Nonconformists
were disproportionately recruited into the new party. Because the Nonconformist schools declined so much more
quickly than the Anglican schools, proportionately more
Nonconformists than Anglicans were available to be mobilized. The rhetoric of Labour party leaders reflected a
kind of Puritanism, a belief that body and soul were unified,
not antithetical.[64]

Yet the persistence of institutional Nonconformity also
hindered the development of the class consciousness that
was necessary for the growth of Labour.[65] Nonconformist
schools did after all teach that social reform depended in
the last instance on the action of the individual in improving
himself once temptations to impiety were removed.[66] Man
may not have been irredeemable, but there was such a
phenomenon as human nature and it did set limits to what
any individual could achieve. The Labour pioneers, in contrast, put little credence in the notion of human obstacles
to progress. It was not enough to lessen the temptation, as
Philip Snowden, an inheritor of the Nonconformist teetotal
tradition, noted in 1908:

[62] *Eastern Daily Press* (Norwich), January 10, 1910, p. 4.

[63] K. S. Inglis, "The Labour Church Movement," *International Review of
Labour History* 8 (1958), 445–460; Henry Pelling, *Origins of the Labour Party*,
2nd ed. (Oxford: Oxford University Press, 1965), ch. 7; D. F. Summers,
"The Labour Church and Allied Movements of the Late 19th and Early
20th Centuries," 2 vols. (Ph.D. thesis, Edinburgh University, 1958).

[64] Pierson, "Socialism," pp. 297, 302–303; John Trevor, *My Quest for
God*, 2nd ed. (Horsted Keynes, Sussex: Postal Publishing Company, 1908),
p. 233.

[65] Robert Moore, *Pit-men*, p. 186.

[66] In the words of William Booth, the Methodist founder of the Salvation
Army, "Salvation means a revolution of man, Socialism of his environment"; see Pierson, "Socialism," p. 255.

When teetotalers talk about drink being the cause of poverty it is charitable to suppose that by poverty they mean a condition below that of ordinary respectable working class life. But if this be so, if their idea of the abolition of poverty is the raising of those who are below up to the standards of the thrifty artisans, then their ideas of poverty and those of the Socialists are widely different. But to attain even that state of working class affluence would require an improvement enormously vaster than the Temperance people imagine.[67]

The secular worker was not content that the environment should be purged of temptation; it had to be rebuilt further so that the unfettered capacity of every individual could be released. The graduate of the board school was inclined to demand more positive action than traditional Nonconformity could warrant.

The intent of this chapter has not been to challenge conventional wisdom so much as to note some problems with it, and to suggest the importance of factors which might profitably be incorporated into theories of electoral transformation. Necessarily tentative because of the extremely limited quality and quantity of supporting evidence, the arguments seem to possess some plausibility. Perhaps that justifies the hope that more attention will be paid to the political implications of changes in the agents of religious and political socialization.

[67] Philip Snowden, *Socialism and the Drink Question* (London: Independent Labour Party, 1908), p. 91.

CHAPTER 9

Conclusion

This study began with two goals—to describe and interpret the structure of voter alignments under the Third Reform Act and to account for the dramatic transformation of the party system after the First World War. The intent was to explain these developments in terms of general theories of political behavior rather than ad hoc historical circumstances and, in the process, to make some useful contribution to scholarly understanding of voting behavior.

The immediate goals were accomplished through an intensive multivariate analysis of electoral outcomes from 1885 through 1910 and by comparing the findings from the analysis with similar studies of the post-1918 electoral universe. The ecological analysis for the period before World War I demonstrated the primacy of religious forces. Class and regionalism had some impact but they were clearly secondary influences on the vote. This system changed fundamentally in the period between the general elections of 1910 and 1918. In the general election of 1918 and thereafter, class assumed primacy and religion joined region as a variable with limited and intermittent electoral power. The rise of Labour at the expense of Liberalism appears to have been part of a shift in electoral cleavage patterns and in the terms of political discourse. The restructuring of the electoral system by the Reform Act of 1918 facilitated the transformation.

The interpretation of these findings was of necessity less closely tied to the data. The religious division of the vote

250

before 1918 was interpreted as a reflection of divergent world-views held by the major religious groups in Britain, differences that resulted from conflicting interests and were promoted and reinforced both by patterns of communal interaction and political socialization. The religiously-based party system lost a crucial base of support when the mode of socialization changed upon the adoption of a system of state-supported, nonsectarian elementary education. The old partisan alignment, which had depended upon the transmission of distinctive religiopolitical outlooks in the denominational schools, gave way to a new alignment when the products of the new socialization practices first entered the electorate in large numbers. Though the traditional alignment did not disappear overnight, it assumed the level of a secondary cleavage, animating only a small and declining share of the electorate.

This interpretation does not purport to explain everything about politics in Britain, only to contribute to our understanding about a certain class of political activities in a particular time and place from a particular angle of vision. Even if the interpretation is essentially correct, it leaves room for many points of contention. For example, the interpretation suggests that certain social changes paved the way for a partisan realignment in which class, rather than religion, became the basis of political identity. Prior to 1870, it was argued, the electorate divided religiously because most of the voters were molded by religious institutions. The rise of board schools constituted a challenge to the religious institutions and reduced their importance as an agent of socialization. The worker, having been freed from a religious outlook, was able to choose a party on the basis of the most salient of his remaining social characteristics—his class. Many labor pioneers had been trying for some time to "awaken" the worker to his true interest as a worker; not until the board school reduced the importance of religion were such efforts likely to succeed. Class consciousness became important because the main obstacle preventing its emergence—the religious perspective—lost its agent of transmission.

Whether this shift in cleavage need have prompted the decay of one party and its effective replacement by another remains open to question. Could the Liberals have responded effectively to the new cleavage, as some scholars have argued, or was the party fatally impaired by the refusal of its constituency organizations to accept working-class representation? Were the Liberals doomed by irreconcilable splits within the leadership and by a series of bad decisions regarding strategy and tactics? The insights of the ethos interpretation do not speak directly to this kind of questioning, but the interpretation at least identifies the parameters within which the answers must fit.

The usefulness of the work to the study of voting must be evaluated by others. At the very least, the research has attempted to apply the conceptual models of social scientists in a historical context. Thus, the analysis of voting behavior was governed by an awareness of the various mechanisms that serve to translate social conflict into party competition. The review of changes in the electoral universe was informed by contemporary research on the role of conversion and mobilization as agents of political transformation.

Though it relied on the insights of existing theory, the study has attempted to enhance them by a new confrontation of data with hypotheses, a process akin to replication in the natural sciences. This was most apparent when it came time to utilize theories of partisan realignment in explaining the remaking of the Victorian party system. Theorists of "critical realignments" have tended in the main to focus upon dramatic events or sudden crises as the source of electoral change. A governing party with a stable majority is suddenly confronted with a major crisis, such as war or economic catastrophe. At that juncture, previous party loyalties seem to count for very little. If the entrenched party fails to deal satisfactorily with the problem, it may well lose the support of key groups who had previously been counted among its most loyal supporters. The disaffected voters turn to a minority party or new movement for some relief. If the new governing party succeeds where the previously established party failed, the voters may express their approval by transferring their votes and deep-seated loyalty, giving the old minority party a generation of hegemony. The process begins anew when the dominant party, after a generation of power, finds itself confronted with a major crisis beyond its capability.

The very suddenness of electoral change suggests the wisdom of focusing on traumas as a stimulus to realignment. Yet not all social traumas spark a party realignment because not all party configurations are equally susceptible to change. A party system becomes ripe for rapid transformation only when the traditional allegiances of voters to parties are weakened. A strong party system may absorb a shock, but when the bonds of loyalty between voter and party have been loosened by the process of secular decay, a catalyst of any kind may well inaugurate a realigning phase. Traumas are necessary but not sufficient for realignments of voters.

This insight makes theories of British party realignment more comprehensible. Most advocates of the traditional model argue that the old Victorian party system broke up under the shock of World War I and a split in the leadership. Why were these events sufficient to pry apart existing coalitions when other serious shocks had been absorbed in the past?[1] Our study suggests the wisdom of investigating long-term forces which undermined the party system.[2]

Why should party bonds grow loose over time? Partly, of course, time itself is a causal agent. With the passage of

[1] Ross McKibbin, *Evolution of the Labour Party, 1910–1924,* ch. 7.

[2] "What probably in the long run determines the shape of politics are the social movements, the groupings and regroupings in the mass of the community which are beyond the reach of politicians. . . ." G. Kitson Clark, *The Making of Victorian England* (New York: Atheneum, 1967), p. 240.

time, the voters who were molded politically during the last crisis begin to leave the electorate and are replaced by new voters who are more inclined to judge the dominant party on its capacity to solve today's problems. These new voters are ripe for realignment—but not totally so. Modern socialization studies highlight the success with which many parents transmit intense partisan loyalties to their children. So time alone may not account for the loosening of party ties.

The voters who do not pick up the party loyalties of earlier generations may have been socialized differently from their parents. In the British case, socialization patterns changed in quite unexpected ways when the passage of the Education Act in 1870 undermined the traditional agents of transmission. To fully understand new voters, then, one must appreciate how early life experiences make them different from preceding generations. That in turn requires that the scholar pay attention to changing social patterns, even those without any apparent political relevance.

Select Bibliography

The following list includes some of the major published works about or relevant to British electoral patterns under the Third Reform Act. For a much more extensive bibliography, readers are advised to consult pages 340–369 of the author's 1976 dissertation, "Patterns of English Voter Alignment Since 1885." (Copies are available from University Microfilms of Ann Arbor, Michigan.)

Alford, Robert R. *Party and Society*. Chicago: Rand McNally, 1963.

Allardt, Erik and Rokkan, Stein, eds. *Mass Politics*. New York: Free Press, 1970.

Bealey, Frank and Pelling, Henry. *Labour and Politics, 1900–1906*. London: Macmillan, 1958.

Birch, A. H. *Small–Town Politics: A Study of Political Life in Glossop*. London: Oxford University Press, 1959.

Blewett, Neal. "The Franchise in the United Kingdom, 1885–1918." *Past and Present* 32 (1965): 27–56.

———. *The Peers, the Parties and the People: The General Elections of 1910*. London: Macmillan, 1972.

Bochel, J. M. and Denver, D. T. "Religion and Voting: A Critical Review and a New Analysis." *Political Studies* 18 (1970): 205–219.

Bulmer, Martin, ed. *Working-Class Images of Society*. London: Routledge and Kegan Paul, 1975.

Butler, David E. *The Electoral System in Britain Since 1918*. 2nd ed. London: Oxford University Press, 1963.

——— and James Cornford. "United Kingdom." In *International Guide to Electoral Statistics*, edited by Stein Rokkan and Jean Meyriat, I: 330–351. The Hague: Mouton, 1969.

Butler, David E. and Donald Stokes, *Political Change in Britain.* New York: St. Martin's, 1969; 2nd ed., London: Macmillan, 1974.

Chamberlain, Chris. "The Growth of Support for the Labour Party in Britain." *British Journal of Sociology* 24 (1973): 474–489.

Clarke, P. F. "Electoral Sociology of Modern Britain." *History* 57 (1972): 31–55.

————. *Lancashire and the New Liberalism.* London: Cambridge University Press, 1971.

Clegg, H. A.; Fox, Alan; and Thompson, A. F. *A History of British Trade Unions Since 1889.* Vol. 1. London: Oxford University Press, 1964.

Converse, Philip E. "Some Priority Variables in Comparative Electoral Research." In *Electoral Behavior: A Comparative Handbook,* edited by Richard Rose, pp. 727–745. New York: Free Press, 1974.

Cornford, James. "Aggregate Election Data and British Party Alignments, 1885–1910." In *Mass Politics,* edited by Erik Allardt and Stein Rokkan, pp. 107–116. New York: Free Press, 1970.

————. "The Transformation of Conservatism in the Late Nineteenth Century." *Victorian Studies* 7 (1963): 35–66.

Craig, F.W.S. *British Parliamentary Election Results, 1885–1918.* London: Macmillan, 1974.

Dangerfield, George. *The Strange Death of Liberal England.* 1935. Reprint. London: MacGibbon and Kee, 1966.

Dogan, Mattei and Rokkan, Stein, eds. *Social Ecology.* Cambridge: M.I.T. Press, 1969.

Drake, M. "The Census, 1801–1891." In *Nineteenth Century Society,* edited by E. A. Wrigley, pp. 7–46. Cambridge: Cambridge University Press, 1972.

Ensor, R.C.K. *England, 1870–1914.* London: Oxford University Press, 1936.

Glaser, John. "English Nonconformity and the Decline of Liberalism." *American Historical Review* 63 (1958): 352–363.

Goodman, Gordon L. "Liberal Unionism: The Revolt of the Whigs." *Victorian Studies* 2 (1959): 173–189.

Gregory, Roy. *The Miners and British Politics.* London: Oxford University Press, 1968.

Gwyn, William B. *Democracy and the Cost of Politics in Britain.* London: Athlone Press, 1962.

Hammond, John L. *The Politics of Benevolence: Revival Religion and*

American Voting Behavior. Norword, New Jersey: Ablex Publishing Corporation, 1979.

Hanham, H. J. *Elections and Party Management*. 1959. Reprint. Brighton: Harvester Press, 1978.

―――. *The Reformed Electoral System in Great Britain, 1832–1914*. London: Historical Association, 1971.

Hechter, Michael. *Internal Colonialism: The Celtic Fringe in British National Development, 1536–1966*. Berkeley: University of California Press, 1975.

Heyck, T. W. "Home Rule, Radicalism and the Liberal Party, 1886–1895." *Journal of British Studies* 13 (1974): 66–91.

Hobson, J. A. "The General Election: A Sociological Interpretation." *Sociological Review* 3 (1910): 97–117.

Inman, Walter G. "The British Liberal Party, 1892–1939." Ph.D. thesis, Clark University, 1939.

King, Anthony. "Some Aspects of the History of the Liberal Party in Britain, 1906–1914." D.Phil. thesis, Oxford University, 1962.

Kinnear, Michael. *The British Voter*. London: B. T. Batsford, 1968.

Kleppner, Paul. *The Cross of Culture*. New York: Free Press, 1970.

Koss, Stephen. *Nonconformity in Modern British Politics*. Hamden, Conn.: Archon Books, 1975.

Krehbiel, Edward B. "Geographic Influences in British Elections." *Geographical Review* 1 (1916): 419–432.

Lawton, Richard, ed. *The Census and Social Structure*. London: Frank Cass, 1978.

Lijphart, Arend. *Class Voting and Religious Voting in the European Democracies*. Survey Research Centre Occasional Paper No. 8. Glasgow: University of Strathclyde, 1971.

―――. "Religious vs. Linguistic vs. Class Voting: The 'Crucial Experiment' of Comparing Belgium, Canada, South Africa and Switzerland." *American Political Science Review* 73 (1979): 442–458.

Lipset, Seymour Martin. *Political Man*. Garden City, New York: Doubleday-Anchor, 1960.

―――― and Rokkan, Stein, eds. *Party Systems and Voter Alignments*. New York: Free Press, 1967.

McCleod, Hugh. *Class and Religion in the Late Victorian City*. Hamden, Conn.: Archon Books, 1974.

McKibbin, Ross. *Evolution of the Labour Party, 1910–1924*. London: Oxford University Press, 1974.

Matthew, H.C.G.; McKibbin, R. I.; and Kay, J. A. "The Franchise Factor in the Rise of the Labour Party." *English Historical Review* 91 (1976): 723–751.

Mayor, Stephen H. "The Relations Between Organised Religion and English Working-Class Movements, 1850–1914." Ph.D. thesis, University of Manchester, 1960.

Miller, William L. *Electoral Dynamics in Britain Since 1918*. London: Macmillan, 1977.

———. "Social Class and Party Choice in England: A New Analysis." *British Journal of Political Science* 8 (1978): 257–284.

——— and Raab, Gillian. "The Religious Alignment at English Elections Between 1918 and 1970." *Political Studies* 25 (1977): 227–251.

———; Raab, Gillian; and Britto, R. "Voting Research and the Population Census, 1918–1971: Surrogate Data for Constituency Analysis." *Journal of the Royal Statistical Society*, ser. A, 137 (1974): 384–411.

Moore, Robert. *Pit-men, Preachers and Politics*. London: Cambridge University Press, 1974.

Nossiter, T. J. "Recent Work on English Elections, 1832–1935." *Political Studies* 18 (1970): 525–528.

O'Leary, Cornelius. *The Elimination of Corrupt Practices in British Elections, 1868–1911*. London: Oxford University Press, 1962.

Pelling, Henry. *Popular Politics and Society in Late Victorian Britain*. London: Macmillan, 1968; 2nd ed., 1979.

———. *Social Geography of British Elections, 1885–1910*. London: Macmillan, 1967.

Pierson, Stanley A. "Socialism and Religion: A Study of their Interaction in Great Britain, 1889–1911." Ph.D. thesis, Harvard University, 1957.

Price, Richard. *An Imperial War and the British Working Class*. London: Routledge and Kegan Paul, 1972.

Rasmussen, Jorgen. "The Impact of Constituency Structural Characteristics upon Political Preferences in Britain." *Comparative Politics* 6 (1973): 123–145.

Roberts, Robert. *The Classic Slum*. London: Penguin Books, 1971.

Rose, Richard. "Class and Party Divisions: Britain as a Test Case." *Sociology* 2 (1968): 129–162.

——— and Urwin, Derek. "Social Cohesion, Political Parties and Strains in Regimes." *Comparative Political Studies* 2 (1969): 3–67.

Stephens, Hugh W. "The Changing Context of British Politics in the 1880s: The Reform Acts and the Formation of the Liberal Unionist Party." *Social Science History* 1 (1977): 486–501.

────── and Brady, David W. "The Parliamentary Parties and the Electoral Reforms of 1884–1885 in Britain." *Legislative Studies Quarterly* 1 (1976): 491–510.

Thompson, E. P. "Homage to Tom Maguire." Rev. ed. In *Essays in Labour History*, edited by Asa Briggs and John Saville, pp. 276–316. London: Macmillan, 1967.

Thompson, J. A., ed. *The Collapse of the British Liberal Party*. Lexington, Mass.: D. C. Heath, 1969.

Thompson, Paul. *Socialists, Liberals, and Labour: The Struggle for London, 1885–1914*. London: Routledge and Kegan Paul, 1967.

Vincent, John. *The Formation of the British Liberal Party, 1857–1868*. Harmondsworth, Middlesex: Penguin Books, 1966.

────── and Stenton, M., eds. *McCalmont's Parliamentary Poll Book, British Election Results, 1832–1918*. 8th enl. ed. Brighton: Harvester Press, 1971.

Wald, Kenneth. "Rise of Class-Based Voting in London." *Comparative Politics* 9 (1977): 219-229.

──────. "Class and the Vote Before the First World War." *British Journal of Political Science* 8 (1978): 441–457.

──────. "Realignment Theory and British Party Development." *Political Studies* 30(1982): 207-220.

──────. "Stratification and Voting Behavior: Electoral Cleavage in Britain Under the Third Reform Act." *Comparative Political Studies* 15(1982): 57-83.

Walzer, Michael. *The Revolution of the Saints*. New York: Atheneum, 1970.

Wilson, Trevor. *The Decline of the Liberal Party, 1914–1935*. London: Collins, 1966.

Yeo, Stephen. "Religion in Society: A View from a Provincial Town in the Late-Nineteenth and Early-Twentieth Centuries." Ph.D. thesis, University of Sussex, 1971.

Index

Kenneth D. Wald is Associate Professor of Political Science
at Memphis State University.

Library of Congress Cataloging in Publication Data

Wald, Kenneth D.
Crosses on the ballot.

Bibliography: p.
Includes index.
    1. Elections—Great Britain—History. 2. Voting—Great Britain—His-
tory. 3. Religion and politics—Great Britain—History. 4. Social classes—
Great Britain—History. 5. Political parties—Great Britain—History.
I. Title.

JN955.W34   1983   324.941081   82-61392
ISBN 0-691-07652-9